LIKE WATER, LIKE FIRE

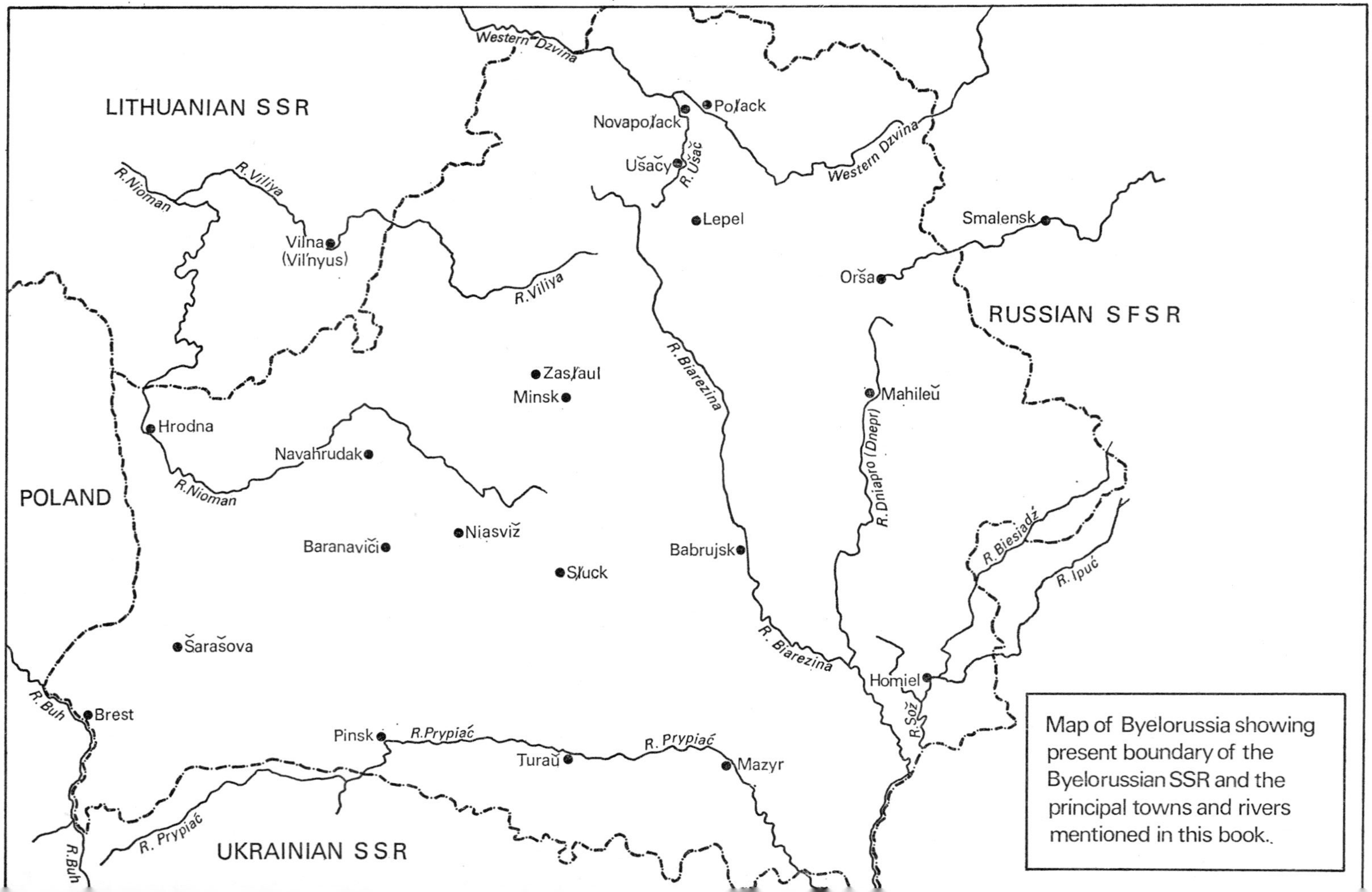

Map of Byelorussia showing present boundary of the Byelorussian SSR and the principal towns and rivers mentioned in this book.

LIKE WATER, LIKE FIRE

An anthology of Byelorussian poetry from 1828 to the present day

TRANSLATED BY
VERA RICH

London
GEORGE ALLEN & UNWIN LTD
RUSKIN HOUSE MUSEUM STREET

First published in 1971

ISBN 0 04 891041 4

UNESCO COLLECTION OF REPRESENTATIVE WORKS:
EUROPEAN SERIES

This work from the Byelorussian has been accepted in the series of translations jointly sponsored by the United Nations Educational, Scientific and Cultural Organization (UNESCO) and the National Commission for UNESCO of the Byelorussian Soviet Socialist Republic.

Printed in Great Britain
in 10 point Times Roman type
by Cox & Wyman Ltd, Fakenham

Once in days past, Lavon
Lived on earth, young and strong,
But freedom and fortune came never:
Heart and soul slept; he drowsed
In a tumble-down house,
When he walked, tears would strew his path ever. . . .

Straightaway rose Lavon,
Filled with forces unknown,
New-created, like water, like fire . . .

Janka Kupała: *In the night pasture*

ACKNOWLEDGEMENTS

In compiling and translating a work of this magnitude, comprising the poems of so many authors, each of whom has his or her own diverse interests, it is inevitable that a translator should need to thank those who have given help and advice on the many details arising. In particular, my thanks are due to the following libraries:

The British Museum Library;
The British Museum Newspaper Library;
The Bodleian Library, Oxford;
The Taylorian Institute, Oxford;
The School of Slavonic Studies Library, London;
The Byelorussian Library, London;
The Polish Library, London;
The National Reference Library of Science and Invention, London;
The Taras Shevchenko Memorial Library, London;
The University Library, Oslo;
The Arnamagnaean Institute, Copenhagen;
The English Folk Dance and Song Society Library, and
The County Library, Orkney;

and to the National Central Library loan service for their prompt tracing and supply of so many vital books.

In addition, I must thank the Royal Horticultural Gardens, Kew for checking so many details of the flora of Byelorussia, H.M. War Office, for advice on the management and control of tanks, and British Rail (in particular, Mr Frank Brooks), for details of the logistics of rolling stock.

I should also like to thank Mr K. J. Michalski, of the Oxford Law Library, for supplying details of the complicated background to the trial of Valancin Taułaj, Mrs G. A. Varley, who traced for me English folklore parallels to certain of these poems, and Olwen Way, who supplied some Welsh parallels, and also advised on certain matters connected with horse-rearing. Also Patricia Waller, for her technical knowledge and advice concerning the curing of pork both now and in the past.

Then, my Byelorussian friends, too many of them to list in full; I must, however, mention Bishop Česlaŭ Sipovič, for his valuable advice on all Church matters, Rev. Alaksandr Nadson, for supplying much of the biographical detail, my first tutor in Byelorussian Dominik Aniška, and his successor in the task, Rev. Archimandrite Leŭ Haroška, whom for so long I drove to distraction with my inability to master the pronunciation of the hard ‘ł’. My good friends, the ‘two Pauls’ – Navara and Asipovič – whom I burdened with so many inquiries during the course of this book – and their wives who stood the constant onslaught of inquiries so patiently! And to one I have never met, Jazep Siemiažon, in Minsk, for his suggested list of inclusions.

Finally, to those who have had a concern in the practical production of this book; to Dr Daniel L. Milton for his constant advice and concern (and, where necessary, the occasional 'prodding'), to Mr Peter Leek of Allen and Unwin, Ltd.), to the UNESCO Literary Committee for making this book possible, to Elizabeth Anne Harvey, for typing the bulk of the manuscript, to my friends and relations, who have had to 'live' with this book over eighteen years, and must by now have grown weary of my problems wherewith, and, last and most definitely not least (and in view of the title, most appropriately), to the Enfield Fire Service who salvaged the manuscript during a flood-cum-electrical-fire shortly before its completion.

To these and to all, my most grateful thanks.

VERA RICH

CONTENTS

Acknowledgements *page* 9
Introduction 13
A note on the pronunciation of Byelorussian 23
THE EARLY PERIOD (1828–1905) 25
Poems 27
Notes 40
THE *NAŠA NIVA* PERIOD (1906–1914) 41
Poems 43
Notes 86
THE YEARS OF ADJUSTMENT (1917–1939) 95
Poems 97
Notes 121
INTERLUDE – WESTERN BYELORUSSIA (1921–1939) 125
Poems 127
Notes 135
UNIFICATION AND WAR (1939–1945) 137
Poems 139
Notes 194
THE YEARS OF RECONSTRUCTION (1945–1953) 203
Poems 205
Notes 231
THE THAW – AND AFTER (1954–) 235
Poems 237
I 'I bid you welcome, life . . .' 237
II 'From fires of war . . .' 255
III 'Circling the world . . .' 276
IV 'The new dynasty' 286
V 'Pictures of my native country . . .' 292
VI 'In matters of love' 308
VII 'My singing, my native language' 317
Notes 324
Notes on authors 333
Author index of poems 342
Alphabetical index of poems 345

INTRODUCTION

I

The discovery of a new and 'different' poet is undoubtedly one of the most exciting events in the life of any poetry-lover. The discovery of a whole new literature of poetry is incomparably more so. Yet, with the increase of mass-communications and foreign travel, it would seem that the discovery of such new literatures must be left to the archaeologist in the hope that he may yet excavate scrolls or tablets in some hitherto undiscovered tongue (with for preference a convenient equivalent of the Rosetta Stone to aid the decoding), or to the anthropologist, that he may yet record some last traces of ballad and folksong before the steamroller of universal literacy crushes down these vestiges of oral tradition.

The concept of a new and undiscovered, and, furthermore, a written literature, right on our literary doorsteps so to speak, in Europe itself, seems to lie quite beyond the realms of fact – to belong, indeed, rather to the kingdom of Rupert of Hentzau and his fellows, or to stretch back into that saga past when Goth fought Hun in the Vistula forest and the unknown bournes of Reithgothaland lay 'somewhere between Poland and Russia'.

Yet such a land and such a literature exists, and if we do not know the land, it is because our geographical consciousness still tends to rule off Europe at the eastern frontier of Poland, and to leave the USSR (which we normally term 'Russia') stretching away eastward, undefined into near-infinity.

Yet such a view is out of date – fifty years out of date. It harks back to the era before the First World War, to the era and empire of the Tsars. For when, in 1917, that vast imperium began its catastrophic disintegration, there arose upon its ruins a number of new and nationally-conscious states. Just as farther west, when the Habsburg empire died there arose from its ashes 'new' nations, Czechs, Slovaks, Croats, Serbs, Slovenes – whose very existence had scarcely reached the ears of those abroad until their sudden emergence at Versailles – so, on the ruins of Romanov power, Georgians, Ukrainians, Lithuanians, Estonians and many others emerged from the shadows of minority existence and took the reins of statehood into their own hands.

Although, within a few years, the new Union of Soviet Socialist Republics had, to a large extent, consolidated itself within the old territorial limits of the Romanov empire, the legal status had irrevocably changed. Now it was a Union of Republics, and although the Russian Republic itself, both by its very size and what may be termed historical impetus, would remain the dominant force of this Union, and although the Russian language would remain the official language of the Union, nevertheless the Republics remained as legal entities – constituent Republics of the Union. Two in fact (in addition to the Russian Republic itself) became founder-members of the United

Nations, and it is with the more northerly of these – Byelorussia – and its literature, that we are here concerned.

II

In the middle of the last century, it might well have been said that the Byelorussian language, and indeed the Byelorussian nation itself, had a dim but glorious past, a putative future and an underground existence. Far away, down through the centuries, shone the memories of the Old Grand Duchy of 'Lithuania-Ruś' (Chaucer's *Lettow ond Ruse*) in which Byelorussians and Lithuanians (in the modern sense) had been equal partners in statehood, and in which, until the conversion of the Lithuanians to Latin Christianity in 1386, the Byelorussians had been the only literate member of the partnership. (The Byelorussians had been converted by missionaries of the Eastern Church in the tenth and eleventh centuries. Although there are traces of an indigenous system of writing before the coming of Christianity to the East Slavonic peoples, it was, as is usual, the conversion with its great need for hagiography, pastoral letters, monastery chronicles and the like that provided the first great impetus towards literary output.)

However, union with Poland and the gradual Polonization of the cultured classes, conquest by Russia with her ever-increasing desire for a unified, homogeneous and totally-Russian tradition from Kalisz to Vladivostok and 'from the Moldavian to the Finn', and ever-more-severe reprisal measures against any who dared raise the slightest voice against this policy, made the future outlook entirely uncertain. When, at the beginning of the nineteenth century, modern Byelorussian literature was born, it must have seemed, to the presiding spirits of literature, that here indeed was a star-crossed, indeed a near still-born infant.

III

Modern Byelorussian literature, by convention, dates from Vinkenti Roviński's *Travesty of the Aeneid*, written at the beginning of the nineteenth century, in imitation of a similar, Ukrainian work by Ivan Kotlyarevśkyy (published 1798). During the early years of the nineteenth century, a number of authors laid what may be called the foundations of the literature. To this period belongs the keen folklorist Jan Čačot, who made two important collections of folk poetry and ballads (*Piosnki wiesniacze znad Niemna i Dzwiny* – 'Songs from the Nioman and Dzvina' – 1839 and 1844) which he augmented in the second edition by didactic verses of his own on the virtues of diligent work and abstinence from 'hard' liquor. Another leading figure was Vincuk Dunin-Marcinkievič, the novelist and dramatist, who, in view of the conditions of the time, achieves a really remarkable detachment in his character-drawing. In his long narrative poem *Hapon*, for example, the villain of the piece, who is the cause of the hero's being sent away into the army, is not the Lady of the Manor, trying as a widow to hold her estates together, in constant terror of a peasant rising (who actually sends him into the army); nor is it the Bailiff (who tells the Lady that Hapon is a potential revolutionary), for he is motivated by unrequited love of Hapon's sweetheart Kaciaryna and believes that once his rival is removed, Kaciaryna will consent to marry him; nor is it the Innkeeper, who only carries out standing orders by reporting to the Bailiff that Hapon wants some drink on credit in order to celebrate his betrothal. Rather, the villain emerges as the system which makes the situation possible. Compared to many works written under comparable conditions in other countries, in which all landlords and their minions are painted in unrelieved black, the characters in *Hapon* emerge as real living people, with human motivation, rather than as the political lay-figures one encounters only too often.

Another important work of this period is the anonymous pseudo-epic *Taras on Parnassus*. The dating of this work presents a problem, but from internal evidence I personally would tend to place it some time between spring 1840 and summer 1844. The study of this work is further confused by the fact that the poem, as is common under censorship conditions, was circulated in manuscript form, so that a number of variant readings have found their way into the text. In this typically Byelorussian work, Taras, an honest and sober woodsman (of the type idealized by Čačot), stuns himself when surprised by a bear in the woods. When he recovers consciousness, he encounters

A small boy, somewhat round of visage,
All curly-headed like a ram,
And from his shoulder there, a quiver
Of arrows and a big bow hang.

This little Cupid directs him to Mount Parnassus, where he finds a great crowd of critics, writers and littérateurs fighting their way to the top. The crowd parts, making way for the élite:

Not one of them is not a toff! See,
'Tis Pushkin, Lermontov, Zhukovskii
And Gogol'; swiftly they do pass us,
Proceed like peacocks to Parnassus,

and in their wake, Taras makes his way to the top, where there is a house 'like a mansion, new and fair' and a well-stocked farmyard. The gods, it would seem, live in the style of Byelorussian peasants, but in unimaginable prosperity. Here is the apotheosis of peasant life – the lads playing stick-knife, cobblers sewing shoes for the goddesses, who

at their tubs are washing
Shirts for the gods, and pantaloons

Saturn (Father Time) who has walked 'much in the world' is mending his sandals, while Neptune and his children are repairing nets and fish-spears. Hercules and Mars are fighting, Zeus snoozing on a great Byelorussian stove, Venus powdering her face 'with something white', and Cupid flirting with the girls. Zeus calls for supper, which is served by Hebe:

First of all she gave them cabbage,
Then gravy served with crackling crisp,
Then, brimming with new milk, came porridge,
Just eat – as much as you can wish!
Jelly came next, with plums (served chilly),
And buckwheat swimming in its fat,
Then came fried goose, tasty and filling,
Enough for all the gods at that.
But when the sausages she brought them,
Brought, in the sieve, oat-pancakes fried,
Then Taras found his mouth was watering . . .

Drinking follows the food, dancing follows the drink, until, lured by the music, Taras himself dances, and Jupiter 'looks on and marvels'. Finally the god questions him

Where have you come from friend? And whyfore
Came you up to Parnassus, why?
What are you? You are not a writer?

Taras explains his presence there, is given 'groats and bread' to eat, and then is transported back home by the Zephyrs.

This lively tale is one of the landmarks of Byelorussian literature. Not only does it give fine scenes of Byelorussian life, all the more 'telling' since they are here magnified to divine proportions; it shows that the unknown author had mastered the traditions of classical literature so thoroughly that he could aptly and wittily adapt them for his own use. It shows, too, through the allegory, the sterility and pettiness of the 'approved' literature of the day, and, since the gods on Parnassus are shown as glorified Byelorussian peasants, the implication is that it is with the people of Byelorussia that the literature of Byelorussian should be concerned. As we shall see, this tenet was to become the guiding rule for many generations of poets to come.

IV

But, outside the pages of fantasy, life for the Byelorussian peasant was no heaven-on-earth. In 1828, when a liberalminded Catholic priest opened a parish school in his native village of Krošyn, he found to his surprise and delight that one of the serf-boys who attended it, the 15-year-old Paŭluk Bahrym, showed considerable talent as a poet. Within a very short time, as a result of serf riots in Krošyn, Bahrym was sent into the army for a term of twenty-five years (military service was frequently used in the Russian Empire for punitive purposes, as those familiar with the life of the Ukrainian poet Taras Shevčenko will recall). Although he lived until 1891, Bahrym is not heard of again as a poet after the brief flowering of his talent as a boy in Krošyn. One poem of his survives, the opening poem of this present collection – survives, because it was incorporated into a volume of memoirs, *Powieść z czasu mojego, czyli Przygody Litewskie* (My Times or Lithuanian Adventures) published in London in 1854. The author, the Polish Count Leon

Potocki, has incorporated into this work a description of an encounter with the priest-schoolmaster 'Fr Magnuszewski', and Bahrym himself appears under the pseudonym of 'Piatrok' (Peter) an 'easy' code for his own baptismal name of 'Paŭluk' (Paul).

Such a story may be taken as an archetype of the fate in store for those who attempted to write in the Byelorussian language, a language against which sterner and sterner measures were taken until its use for any literary purposes was finally forbidden completely, and Byelorussia became merely the 'North-western Region' of the Tsar's empire.

V

Yet the story was not over. The Byelorussian land with its poor and often marshy soil had bred in its people the twin virtues of determination and perseverance, and, however harsh the reprisal measures against it, Byelorussian literature, and in particular, Byelorussian poetry still survived. Literary works were smuggled abroad for publication – and the finished books (signed, of course, with a pseudonym) were smuggled back again for illegal distribution. Thus the 'father of modern Byelorussian literature', Francišak Bahuševič, who wrote under the pseudonyms of 'Maciej Buračok' and 'Symon Reŭka spad Barysava', had his first collection of poems *Dudka bielaruskaja* (Byelorussian Pipe) produced in Cracow in 1891 and his second collection, *Smyk bielaruski* (Byelorussian Bow) in 1894, produced in Poznań (which cities were then under Austro-Hungarian and Prussian rule, respectively).

But in 1905 there came a dramatic change. A spirit of revolution was abroad within the Russian empire, and, although its immediate aims were frustrated, the first cracks began to appear in the monolith of absolute power. In St Petersburg the newly formed *Duma* began to take its first tottering steps in the direction of constitutional government. And throughout the empire, ethnic minorities were at last free to publish in their mother-tongues, and although such publications would still not be free of government control, this step was undoubtedly one of most historic significance.

In Minsk, the Byelorussian capital, was founded the newspaper *Naša Dola* (Our Will). This enterprise soon fell a victim to its editors' over-zealous liberalism; it was closed down by the authorities in 1906. Its successor, *Naša Niva,* was more moderate in tone, and survived through the dark days of anti-Revolutionary reaction under Premier Stolypin, which were seen by the poet Janka Kupała as the 'kingdom of the night' where

> The aspens creak with wood half-rotten,
> Wild beasts on gravemounds howling, whining;
> On highway, on a path beset with
> Thorns, in yokes like cattle fettered,
> The living corpses go, undying . . .

through years of more or less stringent control, until the outbreak of the First World War.

Naša Niva means 'Our Field', more properly, our ploughland; and, indeed, it was the fertile field in which literature of the time could take root and grow. Indeed, throughout the nine years of its existence, it could be said to embody the Byelorussian literature renaissance, and indeed, it gave its name to the chief literary movement of the time: *Našaniŭstva*, – in other words, *Naša Niva*-ism.

VI

'And the good Lord, looking down from the height of heaven, had pity for the land of Bielaruś, and said: Let there be Byelorussian literature! And, behold, there was Naša Niva!'

Like all its kind, the epigram quoted above has its measure of truth, in addition to the usual measure of cynical exaggeration. Byelorussian literature does, indeed, appear to have been created overnight, by and through *Naša Niva*. The group of earnest young writers (formal studio photographs of them exist, complete, if memory serves me correctly, with potted palms) did, in the course of a very few years, create between them the basic requirements of a literature: poetry, drama, essays, short stories, novels. Each used several pseudonyms, partly to confuse the authorities, partly to give the impression that their numbers were greater than in fact they were, thus hoping to attract still more aspiring writers to what was obviously a flourishing project. But although *Naša Niva* and its adjunct, the Byelorussian Publishing House in St Petersburg (whose name translates picturesquely as the Sun-will-look-in-at-our-little-window-too Press) could create literature in the sense of spilling upon the public consciousness so many thousand words per week/month/year, the establishment of a newspaper and of a publishing house (however quaintly named) cannot of themselves create more than an output of verbiage. The picture gained from what one may call the 'folklore' or 'legend' of *Naša Niva* is of a group of dedicated young men and women, sitting at their desks, conscientiously and by schedule 'writing literature' – Mr A. a novel, Mr B. an epic, Mr C. a drama and Miss D. a lyric, according to a pre-assigned plan of what a 'literature' should contain.

Yet nothing could be more remote from the truth. Among the *Naša Niva* group we find the names of the novelist Ciška Hartny, the literary critic Anton Novina, the poets Janka Kupała, Jakub Kołas, Źmitrok Biadula, and Maksim Bahdanovič, that *enfant terrible* who insisted on publishing his works under his own name (and not, as was the *Naša Niva* rule, under a pseudonym) and who introduced into Byelorussian poetry the 'classical' verse-forms of Europe. We find, in fact, the names of the great masters of Byelorussian prose and poetry, so that *Naša Niva* begins to appear more the spontaneous literary group found in all countries and literary traditions rather than the earnest committee of legend.

VII

What then was the essence of '*Naša Niva*-ism', the concepts and ideals which bound its writers together? In one word – Byelorussia; an awareness of their country, her lands, her people, her folklore, her history, her future. There is surely no aspect of Byelorussian life that cannot be found in their pages. 'A peasant, a dull peasant I', sings Kupała, and this identification is far more than the literary device of first-person monologue; it is a deep and personal identification. 'I love our land', sings Kanstancyja Bujła, and it is the voice of them all. 'Pictures beloved of my native country' are 'gladness' and 'pain' not only to Jakub Kołas, but to each and every one of this group. The harsh, yet lovely whiteness of winter, the sudden bursting of spring,

> . . . the harvest, day-long mowing,
> Fires in the summer-pasture nights,
> The flocks of birds migrating, going,
> Storks, geese and cranes in southward flights;

these are the very essence of *Našaniŭstva.* The folklore is there too; wood-elves, *rusalki* and – in the works of Biadula, even the old pagan gods – people the woods and forests with mystery. The past is also there – the historic past of the old monastery chronicler and the girls in the Radziwiłł girdle factory, together with that other 'past' which exists only in folk-memory – the 'past' of strange heroes and dark, near-nameless deeds, done in the mists of antiquity 'a century or more' ago. Here too is a people 'many million strong', whose 'spirit' is 'atremble', on the march, demanding the right 'to be called human'!

And, in this poetry, implicit, yet to the discerning eye, self-evident, emerge those symbolic patterns by which government controls might be deceived, and which were to colour Byelorussian poetry for ever with potent and evocative overtones from the days of its birth. Thus night or winter symbolized the forces of reaction and oppression, the young bride awaiting her bridegroom is Byelorussia awaiting independence. (In Biadula's lovely *A winter tale,* these two motifs are beautifully integrated into the lovely picture of the Sleeping Beauty in her palace of ice, while the bridegroom who is to awaken her is now no fairy-tale prince, nor even some symbolic peasant-figure; it is the reader himself who must 'call her by name' and bring spring, i.e. liberation, to the frozen world.) Wild geese migrating (as in Irish literature) symbolize exiles, whether those who fled specifically for political reasons, or those who were forced abroad for the economic necessity of living (which in itself must be a reflection upon the 'situation' and 'system' that produces such a necessity); those who

> 'would not have left our dear country
> If there had been bread for our feeding.'

and (again as in Irish), Easter is inextricably linked with the idea of national resurgence. As a result, the poetry of the *Naša Niva* period exists on several levels of interpretation, and although it would be untrue, and highly misleading, to state that every Byelorussian poem ever written about a girl on her wedding-eve is 'really' about Byelorussia (any more than it would be true to say that every Kathleen praised in song is 'really' Ireland, or every rose is 'really' England) nevertheless, the symbolism of *Naša Niva* has bequeathed to the Byelorussian language, and in particular to its poetry an aura of connotation that, in its economy, can be compared perhaps only to Chinese.

VIII

As has already been stated, *Naša Niva* was an early casualty of the First World War (its editor, Janka Kupała, passing *his* wartime in an army roadmaking squad, a circumstance doubtless attributable not so much to Tsarist incompetence but to the time-honoured military principle of a job for every man, and every man in the wrong job). War passed into Revolution, and the forces of Revolution signed its separate peace with the Central Powers. Unlike her southern neighbour, Ukraine, Byelorussia had not yet made her bid for self-determination, and so was not represented by a separate signature on this treaty, but by March 1918 the independence movement was in full flood, and on March 25th (traditionally, in Byelorussia, the first day of spring), the Byelorussian National Republic was proclaimed in Minsk.

The following winter (January 1, 1919) the Byelorussian Soviet Socialist Republic was officially proclaimed in Smalensk. From that date onwards, the Revolutionary Wars give the next few years a confused picture of conquest and reconquest, invasion and counter-thrust best left to the military and not the literary historians.

When the smoke of war clears, we see the Byelorussian lands partitioned, with the western territories under Polish rule, many of the Byelorussian intelligentsia now living beyond her new frontiers, and a literary scene of currents and cross-currents, of literary group at logger-heads with literary group, as poets, playwrights and novelists sought, each in his own way and through his own talent to adjust himself to the new post-Revolutionary situation, to come to terms with the unpalatable fact (as had the English Romantics before them) that no Revolution can produce the millennium overnight, and to set about the new problems of the creation of a culture 'socialist in content and national in form' – a phrase adopted by Stalin in his report to the Sixteenth Party Congress in 1930, but actually coined some years earlier by the 'Excelsior' group of writers in Minsk.

Even to read the names of these groups gives an immediate picture of the busy activity of Byelorussian literature in this period: *Excelsior*, *Revival*, *Vitaism* to name but a few; and among this great upsurge we find the poets, not only the survivors from *Naša Niva* days, but poets of the new generation, poets like Michas Čarot, Kandrat Krapiva and, perhaps greatest of all, Ŭładzimir Duboŭka.

But this period of activity was followed by one of quiescence; the years of plenty by years of dearth. The 'Stalinization' of culture throughout the Soviet Union proved inimicable to poetry. Many writers turned entirely to prose, notably Biadula, who produced in these years his lively and spirited autobiography. Some disappeared from the literary scene altogether, until their works, and they themselves if still living, made a sudden reappearance in the 'thaw' of the mid-fifties. Even the great Janka Kupała, since 1924 'People's Poet of Byelorussia', sank into virtual inactivity. His one major work of this period was the long narrative *The Fate of Taras*, written in 1939 to commemorate the sesquicentenary of the birth of the Ukrainian national poet, Taras Shevčenko, the author, incidentally, whose life and works have undoubtedly had more effect on Byelorussian poetry than any one other non-Byelorussian.

IX

The Second World War produced, at first, no great changes in the Byelorussian poetic scene. True, under the terms of the Molotov–Ribbentrop pact, Western Byelorussia was detached from what had been Poland and incorporated into the Byelorussian SSR, bringing with it a number of writers who had developed their talents under Polish rule – notably among them Maksim Tank, a number of writers – Kupała and Biadula in particular, perished during these years, while others borne westward as a result of the Nazi occupation of Byelorussia, with its insatiable demands for slave labour, settled, after the end of the war, outside their homeland. (Of these Natalla Arsieńnieva, now married and living in New York, is perhaps the most notable example.)

Yet, apart from the usual crop of highly-emotional patriotic verse which any war evokes (and which normally raises a blush of embarrassment under peacetime conditions), the war introduced no perceptible change in the overall sterility of the scene.

The famous 'thaw' of the mid-fifties, however, could not but produce an effect in Byelorussia. Literary journals were founded or refurbished, new poets took up their pens, old names suddenly appeared in print again. As death claimed the last of the *Naša Niva* poets, others were waiting to take up the torch. Varied in theme and outlook, from satiric humour to the traditional bitter-sweet of melancholy, from the fields of Byelorussia to the planets and back again, each issue of *Polymia* and *Maladość* promise and bring something new, something different. Byelorussian poetry, born in adversity, nourished in hardship, has grown to fruition and can well take its stand as a new, but worthy member of the poetries of Europe.

X

In Janka Kupała's poetic drama *In the Night Pasture*, the mysterious prophet-like figure of the Stranger sings the Lay of Lavon, long-slumbering, but suddenly aroused

> by forces unknown,
> New-created, like water, like fire!

These are the forces of Byelorussian poetry, the water of life, the physical waters of Byelorussia with its marshes, lakes and great rivers, and the symbolic waters of birth and of death; the midsummer fires of the night-pastures, the glow of winter cottage windows – and that overwhelming spiritual fire of patriotic love and fervour for the land of one's birth.

But it is the task of the translator to channel that water, and to carry the torch of that fire into another language and another idiom. How can this be done or attempted? More specifically, how in this case *has* it been done or attempted?

Writing now as translator, let me say that, a poet myself, I would feel a betrayal of my task in producing any version that did not reproduce the poetic form of the original. If a poet expresses his thoughts in a poem, the form, as much as the content, gives shape and meaning to those thoughts. A sonnet, for example, 'says' something by the very arrangement of its rhymes that fourteen lines of unrhymed verse cannot hope to convey. The rhymes of the original are preserved therefore – if not always as 'perfect' rhymes, at least in the form of an assonance, dissonance, half-rhyme or eye-rhyme. Moreover, in almost every case, the difference between 'masculine' (monosyllabic) and 'feminine' (disyllabic) rhymes has been preserved. Further, since Byelorussian poetry is stress-based (and not like French or Polish poetry which operates by counting syllables) the same rhythmic patterns fall naturally into an English context, whether the formal iambs and anapaests of the older tradition or the free forms of the moderns. The extra stylistic 'flourishes' of alliteration, internal rhyme, etc., also common to both Byelorussian and English poetry have been preserved here. Yet throughout, I have aimed at a translation that is line-for-line with the original, adding as little as may be, losing as little as possible.

But enough of this apologia! The task of the translator is to translate, not to explain and justify the finished translation. Byelorussian is perhaps the least known of the Slavonic languages – indeed, there exist no textbooks for the learning of it apart from those actually used by Byelorussian schoolchildren – and under such circumstances, translations must be judged and appraised largely by a readership that will have no knowledge of the original. Whereas, in the case of a work translated, say, from French or German, a large proportion of one's readers will have at least some knowledge of the original, and will (one hopes) praise the work for the merits of the rendering – an elegant phrase here, a pun neatly turned there, a precise rendition of such-and-such a difficult passage – here it is not so.

Here, truly, the translator's art goes largely unpraised, and is only observable where an awkwardness or infelicity of phrasing indicates that here some hazard has been met and only imperfectly overcome. Yet since *ars est celare artem*, perhaps it is better so. The translator is no verbal acrobat, displaying his talents with a 'look-how-clever-I-am' air; his skill must and should go unremarked. To change the metaphor, he is no maker of stained glass windows, colouring the light to his own fancy and according to his own design, he is the glazier who must strive that if we see, in translations, through a glass darkly, that as little as possible of the radiance is obscured. Thus far my aim; to the poets of Byelorussia, true authors of this work, to the Byelorussian people, and to all those who through these pages shall find something of the beauty and richness of Byelorussian poetry, I dedicate this book.

VERA RICH

London, March 25, 1968.

A NOTE ON THE PRONUNCIATION OF BYELORUSSIAN

Although, now, the Byelorussian language is normally written in the Cyrillic (Slavonic) script, the historical links of Byelorussia with Poland have resulted in the use of the Latin script as an alternate method of writing the language. Latin-script spelling of Byelorussian was codified by the *Naša Niva* group (*Naša Niva* itself was published in two versions, one in each script), and follows, in general the normal 'continental' sound-values for each letter. The following features should, however, be noted:

c = **ts** (as in **b**its).

ch as in lo**ch**, **Bach** etc.

č = **ch** as in **ch**air, **church**, etc.

g does not exist in Byelorussian, except in a few loan-words from foreign languages. Where a **g** might be expected (by analogy to other Slavonic languages, or in proper names), an **h** is regularly found. Thus Siarhiej (proper-name), is equivalent to Russian Sergei.

i is the normal long vowel denoted by this letter. But in the group **ia**, **ie**, **io**, **iu** it is equivalent to English **y** (as in **yak**, **yet**, **yo-yo**, **you**th).

j = **y** as in boy. In the groups **-ja-**,**-je-**,**-jo-**,**-ju-** it is equivalent to English **y** (as in **yak**, **yet**, **yo-yo**, **you**th). In these groups, the **-i-** form is used after a consonant and the **-j-** form after a vowel or initially.

ł = the 'hard' back **l** as in tab**l**e, or as in the Cockney pronunciation of such words as 'milk'. It is pronounced far back in the throat, and is very close, phonetically, to a **w**. (In Polish, this letter is now pronounced like the English **w**.)

l = the normal 'soft' front **l** as in **l**eaf.

s = the normal **s**-sound as in **s**ee.

š = **sh** as in **sh**e.

u = the long **u**-sound as in b**oo**t.

ŭ = the semi-vowel **w** as in bo**w**.

y = the short **i** sound as in b**i**t, but pronounced with the tongue somewhat farther back than in English.

z = the normal **z**-sound as in **z**oo.

ž = the sound of **s** in measure, pleasure.

NOTE

1. An acute accent is written over **c**, **n**, **s**, **z** when they occur finally in certain words, or when they occur before another consonant which is itself followed by a 'palatal' vowel (i.e. followed by the groups **-ia-**,**-ie-**, **-io-**,**-iu-**, or by **i**). This denotes that the consonant is to be given a 'soft' or 'palatalized' pronunciation. For those to whom this book is their first introduction into the sphere of Slavonic literature, the translator would recommend that such

'soft' pronunciations are a refinement best left to the expert. The significance of these accents is noted here only for the sake of completeness.

2. From time to time in the course of this book, certain Byelorussian words, having no exact equivalents in English, will be used. These terms, normally italicized, will be explained in the notes at the end of each section.

3. For elucidation of points arising in specific poems, the reader is likewise referred to these notes.

4. Biographies of the individual poets, and indices of the poems, by author and by title, will be found at the end of the book.

5. From time to time throughout the course of this book, reference will be made to certain Russian and Ukrainian proper names. For these, the regular 'English' system of transliteration will be used, to preserve, as far as possible the forms to which the reader is accustomed, Pushkin, rather than Puškin. The '**ch**' sound as in Chekhov, will, however be written as **č** throughout, to avoid confusion with the Byelorussian gutteral '**ch**'. This will entail a slight inconsistency (notably in the name of the Ukrainian poet Shevčenko), but no real loss of clarity.

THE EARLY PERIOD

1828–1905

These are the poems of the era of oppression, when the Byelorussian language was subjected to severer and severer reprisal measures. The tragic lyric of Bahrym, the singing melodies and biting satire of Bahuševič, the patriotism of Łučyna, far from his home, working as a railway engineer in the Caucasus, writing in a language that had legally ceased to exist, yet lived on in his pathos so near akin to comedy and comedy so near to pathos – these are truly notes of the pipe that shall cease 'only when blood is failing'. These are the pioneers of Byelorussian literature, and this selection ends, appropriately, with the first published poem of Janka Kupała, and an affirmation of the future, written by Ciotka on the very eve of the foundation of *Naša Dola*, the first Byelorussian newspaper.

Pauluk Bahrym

PLAY THEN, PLAY

Play then, play then, lad so little,
On thy cymbalom and fiddle,
But the bagpipes I must play, for
I in Krošyn cannot stay more.

A lord in Krošyn rages harshly,
And with clubs they slew my father,
Mother grieving, sister keening;
Whither, hapless one, art fleeing?

Whither do I flee? God bless us!
To the wide world, trackless deserts;
Into werwolf I'll be turning,
Looking back at you with yearning.

Fare thee well, my dearest mother!
If thou hadst not borne me ever,
If thou hadst not fed me, tended,
Happier thy life had wended!

If a kite's lot I'd been given,
Free from lords I would be living,
To serf-labour they'd not bend me,
Nor for a recruit intend me,
Nor to Moscow's army send me.

I shall live no more a shepherd,
And a soldier's life is heavy,
And I fear to grow, most surely,
Where I shall live ever poorly.

Flittermouse, O flittermouse,
Why didst thou not settle thus
O'er me, that my height remain
As the wheel of father's wain?

Francišak Bahuševič

MY PIPE

I a pipe shall fashion,
Play on it so clearly,
That through the wide world scattered
Everyone shall hear me.
Ah, I'll play so sweetly,
Like a joyous greeting,
Like a wedding, truly –
But not long enduring.
I'll cease playing quickly,
Ere the pipe start splitting,
Ere the folk are deafened,
Breast grown parched and heavy,
And all strength decaying
From the joyful playing,
And tears fall and spill so
On the arid willows . . .
In mist will soul flow out, like
Rolling smoke, all cloud-like,
In haze on the river,
Fall where dewdrops quiver,
Bedew the grain with lustre,
That ripe ears thickly cluster.
But men shall eat that harvest,
And tears once more be smarting.
Well then, pipe, play clearly,
So that all may hear ye,
So that ears be aching,
Such a music making
That the earth start quaking!
Play so glad that round ye
One and all come bounding,
With their arms akimbo,
Start to dance so nimbly,
Like a whirlwind wheeling,
Till pain sets them squealing,
Till they rock with laughter,
And again dance after . . .
That the very hills go
Dance like ocean billows,
As lords at a ball dance,
So let one and all dance!

Set the dust-smoke wheeling,
Till the world starts heeling,
And all stagger, reeling!
(Our brother's home doth spin so,
For he loves the inn so!)

Why do ye not play, then?
Know ye not the way, then?
Have ye learned not, ever?
Like fish from the river,
On the ice a-flapping,
Just so I, it happened,
Forty years flapped, yearning,
Yet knew no returning,
Nor found, when I sought, a
Single drop of water,
Water that springs, mounting
Up in such a fountain,
That if your thirst you slake ye,
A free man 'twill make ye.
Play then, gladly play!
Otherwise, make way!
....
Uselessly complaining,
Sense there's none remaining!
With *this* pipe I'll not bother,
I shall make another.
Now a pipe I'll fashion
From grief and bitter passion,
Yes, I'll make another,
With woe brimming over.
It shall play with moaning,
Till the earth start groaning,
It shall play so doleful,
That the tears come rolling,
Awesome play, and fearful,
This my pipe all tearful! . . .
'Tis made, as I did say it,
Now to try and play it!
    Play then, play so clearly,
Recalling all so nearly . . .
Day and night-time ever,
Like my eyes, weep over
The ill-fate of our people,
Ever, ever weeping,
To the end weep ever,
Wailing like a mother

Who her babes must bury;
One day, two, three carry
Still your lays of anguish
For folk who, dying, languish!
May you play so clearly
That sharp pangs press nearly.
When the tears cease falling,
Pipe shall cease its calling –
But look around you, mounting
From the blood's own fountain
Tears will rise and flow then,
All things shall you know then,
Only when blood is failing
Pipe shall cease its wailing.

HOW THEY SEARCH FOR TRUTH...

Since from this world simple truth perished, unfriended,
They set out to seek her with candle-flame lighted,
They lure her with gold, gather people, invite them,
Take oaths on the cross – vain the toil thus expended!
Like a stone dropped in water, for aye truth has vanished!
Then created they Law-courts, the Boroughs established,
Arbitrator and Synod, Officials in legions,
Senate, Councils and High-Courts, Departments and Regions,
Justices most of all, Constables and Assizes,
Like stones in the field or like stars swarmed these prizes!
And thus life became hard, to be called without reason
As a witness, to drag round the whole summer season
From court unto court, and so easy this happens,
You don't have to seek it – just wait, and they'll trap you!
Once I was off on a visit to Vilna
To my son; by the roadside there stood a mare grazing,
Some fellow was standing right by the mill there,
Beyond the mill was a bitch howling and baying,
And somewhere 'Help! Help!' cried a woman's voice, pleading,
And over the bridge a fine carriage came speeding.
But what was all this, then? It seems (if you'd asked me)
There's howling, there's driving, there's maybe some laughing
(For the miller stood by the gate, roaring with laughter;
Why was he laughing? I did not ask after!)
The mill's left behind; through the wood I now clatter,
'Neath the hedge by the roadside some fellow lies, surely,
Without cap, without footgear, and dressed very poorly;
But I'm on a journey, about my own matters,

And I've no time to stop. On I travel intently;
Besides, lying around there are people a-plenty.
I look round; someone after me hot-foot comes flying;
'For the love of God, stop for a moment!' he's crying.
I stop and I wait. Then he questions me, wryly:
Who am I? Where from? Who can identify me?
And he says I must come to the mill with all swiftness,
The Constable needs me forthwith as a witness.
I return; I look round: the coach lies in the river,
The miller no longer is laughing, however,
The horse to a post the Gaffer is leading,
The barber a dripping-wet noble is bleeding,
There's a hole in the bridge like a house in size, truly,
Two urchins are chasing the snapping bitch, duly,
A woman is standing there, skirt torn to ribbons,
On forearm and ankle the red blood is dribbling,
And they bring up a waggon, gruesomely loaded
With the corpse I'd seen lying back there by the roadside.
The constable asks me to testify, deeming
Did the miller incite the dog? Was the dame screaming?
Did the bitch bite? Or men beat her? I'd spotted
Whether the bridge-planks were broken or rotted?
Had I seen how the miller stood rocking with laughter?
How the lord, coach and coachman plunged into the water?
How the coachman was drowned and the lord was saved after?
How the thief round the mill sought for horses or ponies?
How he stole the mare? Fled with her off to Rykoni?
Did I know the full name of the murdered man over
There? Or who killed him? And I must uncover
Had I carried him there and abandoned the corpse?
Had he money? And had I purloined it, perhaps?
(And I was struck dumb; not a word would come out!
I was ruined! God sent me a hard cross, no doubt!)
Why had I no wish the coachman to save?
Why didn't I catch by the mill that sharp knave?
Why didn't I chase the fierce bitch from the dame?
Why try to escape ere the Constable came?
The whole day he worried at me – and for naught!
May the fiend take you off! Then I gave him a rouble!
To pocket it sleekly would give him no trouble!
Off I drove! Eight weeks later, the Constables sought
Me and served Writs upon me, – of them a long tale:
First to witness: the miller incited the dog;
And second to witness: the bridge had no rail;
Third to witness: that someone ran off with the nags;
Fourth to witness: the lord tumbled into the water
And came up, but the coachman was never seen after;

Fifth to witness: the corpse by the roadside abandoned
Was murdered, and from it two people went rushing,
And that I was pursuing these twain in my waggon,
But they made their escape, and hid in the brushwood;
But with the sixth Writ, the charge fell on me,
That I proffered no aid when the Coach tumbled over;
I started these writs to obey carefully
At Christmas, and finished . . . the First of October.
I sowed not, made hay not, nor went out a-reaping,
I mortgaged the hay-field, no chance for to keep it,
Was forced to sell up all I owned, not a doubt,
Lost my all in the Courts, as if six times burned out,
Sat six weeks in the jail, paid the fine for Contempt
(Non-appearance) thrice over, perhaps, yet, you see,
Truth still remained hidden, and in the attempt
To find her, this rigmarole happened to me.

MY HOME

Poor, indeed, my cottage, on the village limit,
Set midst sands and rocks, right over by the spinney,
Right beside the forest, right beside the wood there,
None could reach it, even though he sought some good there.
There are no strong waters, there is not a crumb there,
So, then, who would seek it, who would need to come there?!
But though there is no bread, I'll not beg from a neighbour,
I shall yet survive, with toiling and with labour.

Bad, indeed, my house, with its foundations rotted,
Smoky, too, and dark, and yet I love this cottage;
And I would not change it, even for a palace, –
Dearer is my door-peg than any stranger's latches.
A birch grows on the thatch (the thatch with moss grown over)
– My cottage is more dear than the whole village of another.

Friends advised me gain a fine new house by marriage,
With fertile ploughlands and a wealthy bride; then in a carriage
And pair, they said, I'd drive like His Worship the Assessor,
I'd live like a lord, they said, a great possessor;
But dearer far to me this corner, half decaying,
The stone beside the road, the sand around the gravemound,
Than well-builded mansion, than broad fields of a stranger!
For a fine coat this my ragged smock I'll not be changing.

Neighbours have invited me and still invite me.
I'll not go, there is no need, because, 'tis said, unsightly
Ulcers from a stranger's bread the lips will cover,
He will lose his own who hankers for another's.
I'll not leave my cottage, even though you press me,
I'll not come to you, except that you arrest me.

And although by main force from my house you thrust me,
One day I'd return, like bear into the brushwood.
Though the house be tumbledown, the fields o'er-grown there,
Yet, though barefoot and in tatters, I would surely go there.

I would saw fresh logs, would root the moss out wholly,
I would build my house anew, somehow and slowly.
I would build a larder, forge a quern, all newly,
All the bread I ate, though black, would be mine, truly!
Why then do ye call me, wherefore do I need ye?
Nor to take your food, nor to toil to feed ye.

DO NOT SHUN ME . . .

Do not shun me, my lord, nor recoil,
Because callouses all my hands cover;
For such is the badge of hard toil,
And will not defile you, no, never.
'Tis the medal of suffering and working,
And no plague-spot will meet thy inspection;
Then give me thy hand, without shirking,
Since mine is not stained by infection.
Ah, uncover thy head with more zeal,
When I bow to the ground thus responding,
Thy head I'll not pluck off, nor steal,
And with mine, Sir, thou'lt not be absconding.
From my garb do not flee in such hurry,
I am not ashamed of my smock!
But thy frock-coat – I'd never have courage
To put on that devilish frock!
Thou dost look, eyes askance, coldly peeking
At my shirt, made at home by the women;
It is soaked with my sweat; for a week now
I've not had a change of clean linen.
But *thine*? 'Tis like paper, like snow!
But who sweated, who bleached it and wove it,
Who sewed it, who span it? . . . And lo!
All this sweat on thyself thou hast loaded.

In such a shirt, shame would soon bite me,
That I'd earned it not with toil and thrift.
I grudge it thee not, though 'tis whiter,
I'd not take it from thee as a gift!
But cast thine eye now on my cottage,
It leaks and it rots, it leans skewly,
Inside rotten, and standing on rottage,
How it stands yet perplexes me truly.
Do not wonder, my lord, how I live;
Nobody helped me to build it,
Though a sluggard I'm named, I can give
The world food, and with breath I can fill it.
Thou hast learned what the books say is true,
And much olden-time wisdom lies there;
All things by the book canst thou do;
But the book for the peasant is – where?
Whence are we such Wisdom to know?
We know but the plough and the clod,
And we live but to plough and to mow,
But we live in the fear of our God.
If I only could guide a pen right
I'd have written a book like a field.
How we plough and we sow, I would write,
How we mow and reap God's blessed yield.
Maybe thou mightest read that scrawl too,
Find a yearning to work, as 'twere pleasant,
Pay the peasant callouses their due,
And shun not the poor lot of the peasant.
To me, a blind man, thou wouldst offer
Thy hand, on the road thou wouldst set me,
So that I'd not be roaming here, longer,
Where brushwood and thorns sore beset me.
My feet and my heart they rend sorely,
In the heart breeding evil and hating,
Maintaining a constant wrath for thee,
To ill-deeds lead, from truth deviating.
Forgive the blind man who walks skewly,
Forgive him who sees not, though weeping,
The blind grope – no wonder 'tis, truly;
But a sighted man in the pit leaping?

Janka Łučyna

TO OUR NATIVE LAND

Thou art spread widely with forests and marshes,
With sand-dune expanses that grant but poor living,
My mother, my country, and thou in thy harvests
No undue bounty of bread to us givest.
And thy son wears but a smock, poor and ragged,
Shod but in sandals from bast-fibre woven,
His coach is a pony-trap or horse-and-waggon,
And the nag draws it onward as though soundly dozing.
Everything in thee is poor; oft the peasant
Ploughman will weep, for his ill-fortune grieving,
Labouring, toiling. He dreams not, however,
That some day, far distant, he might ever leave thee.
And the unlovely cottage, its goods poor and shabby,
The niggardly field, common-land without grazing –
But we, having once clad ourselves in old jackets,
Love and treasure these things, for 'ours' we may name them.
May God grant the sandy soil nourished and healthy,
Made so by the ploughman with blood and sweat straining,
A full belly is good, though we may not be wealthy,
And on festival days there's a dram for the draining.
And the sun of true wisdom, through clouds' murky hollow,
Will glance brightly down on the soil of our country,
And our children shall live, in the ages to follow,
With a good fortune, a fortune of bounty.

WHAT JANKA THOUGHT CARTING WOOD TO THE TOWN

Now 'tis Christmas, Yule rejoicing,
On the frost the sledges rollick,
All the world is glad and joyful,
Everywhere is song and frolic;
Lads and girls are dancing gaily,
Are they drinking just a drappie?
In a word – 'tis holidaying!

Well, old nag, why are you stopping?
Why are you . . . ? The going's heavy?
And you're hungry? Stop your whining!

Is it easy for me? Ever
Seen this smock, old, torn, the lining
Nothing but fresh air? Now boldly
At the frost; no time for flopping,
Let's get home, for stars are shining.

Well, old nag, why are you stopping?
Townsfolk are in need of firewood,
And for it they will pay plenty;
I'll sell the wood, and buy some rye then.
I've piled the load up big and lofty,
Since 'needs-must' still keeps me hopping,
Though it's wicked out, and frosty.

Well, old nag, why are you stopping?
In the inn 'tis warm and jolly;
Just one for the road . . . That's out now,
For I owe too much to Solly!
I'd get it in the neck, no doubt now!
What a season! O misfortune,
Must you strike me neck and crop now! . . .
Gee-up nag, the hill's before us!
May you drop dead if you stop now!

THE MUSICIAN

I would have played much, but now all my strength goes,
And string after lyre-string is breaking,
Although valiant song is not yet in its death-throes
And thought after thought is awaking.
I would have played much, but death says 'Hold!' to me,
For the grave it would bid me make ready.
Ah, strings, ye may break then, what harm can it do me?
In the grave we shall lie down together!
Maybe from this lyre there will grow a green willow,
And from the snapped strings snowy flowers,
Maybe in its shadow will come to play children,
Joyfully through the spring hours.
And, maybe, then, one of those children will whittle
A flute, grandchild to the lost lyre,
And will play on it so the whole earth hears its ditty
And knows it my echo sincere.
And the strings of the grandfather, untimely broken,
Shall chime out like bell-notes resounding,
And the songs that its lifespan had left half-unspoken
In its scion yield harvest abounding,
And, on All Souls' Night, below the dark willow
Will the living word echo forth truly,
And the song with a thousandfold strength shall peal, thrilling,
And my lyre shall live again newly.

THE FAITH OF A BYELORUSSIAN

I believe we shall be people,
Soon our dreaming will be o'er;
We'll scan the world more widely, deeply,
And the age shall write our law.
Not with ink on paper, treasure
Hidden in some archives' store, –
It will take of sweat a measure
And upon the ploughland pour,
Watering the earth which gives us
Sap to swell the grain for bread.
We eat, and through the folk 'tis whispered:
'Rise up, O ye in blindness bred!'

I believe in strength within us,
In our free-will, tempered hard,
Fire I feel, not coldness, in us,
Friends, we are not made from card,
Not of plaster, but stone burnished,
Made of iron, made of steel,
They have forged us in the furnace
So we stronger be in zeal.
Now, friends, we are granite mighty,
And our spirit dynamite is,
Mailed fist, breast in armour shining,
Time to rend our bonds confining.

Janka Kupała

THE PEASANT

I am a peasant, all men know it;
Where-e'er the world's broad acres lie
Men mock, and take good care to show it –
  A peasant, a dull peasant I.

To read and write – 'tis past my knowing,
Smoothly my tongue I cannot ply,
I am but ever ploughing, sowing –
  A peasant, a dull peasant I.

From toil I win my bread but sparely,
Cursing endure, and wrathful cry,
And time for rest I know but rarely –
  A peasant, a dull peasant I.

Oft-times no bread for my babes' feeding,
My wife's boots torn to shreds, well-nigh;
No money to relieve my needing –
  A peasant, a dull peasant I.

In youth and age at endless toiling,
Till bitter sweat-drops blear the eye,
Like a plough oxen, ever moiling,
  A peasant, a dull peasant I.

When sick and poor, I must endeavour
To cure myself. A wondrous try!
Without a doctor I am better! –
  A peasant, a dull peasant I.

In tatters I am doomed to perish
Like mushrooms that in woodlands lie,
Like a cur from this world to vanish –
  A peasant, a dull peasant I.

But while I live on earth, however,
Though long my tale of days rolls by,
Brothers, I'll not forget, no never,
  A man, although a peasant, I.

And whosoe'er comes asking for me
Will hear from me this simple cry,
That, though men scorn me and ignore me,
  I'll live, I am a peasant, I.

NOTES

p. 27: *Play then, play . . .*
The story behind this poem is told in the Introduction. It was first published in Count Leon Potocki's *Powiesc z Czasu mojego, czyli Litewskie przygody* (My Times, or Lithuanian Adventures) together with a Polish translation and a somewhat fictionized account of Bahrym. The first edition of *My Times* appeared in London in 1854.

lines 2–3. In his notes, Potocki points out that the cymbalum and fiddle are traditionally the instruments of rejoicing, but the bagpipe the instrument of mourning.

lines 22–25. This refers to the folk-belief that if a bat should alight on the head of a child or young person not done with growing, that they will remain stunted from that day forward.

p. 30: *How they search for truth*
lines 6–8. Except to experts in jurisprudence, the particular functions of these officials and spheres of jurisdiction is hardly relevant to the understanding of the poem. The impression gained from the original is of an enormous conglomeration of officialdom, the exact function of any part of which is irrelevant.

line 55. Rykoni. Apparently a local pronunciation, for the small settlement of Rukoni (now Rukainai), some 25 km. south-west of Vilna, which is now within the Lithuanian SSR.

line 83. The First of October. Literally, on the Feast of the Patronage of Our Lady. This feast-day, kept by the Eastern Church on October 1st, is the traditional first day of the indoor winter season.

p. 32: *My home*
line 15 ff. In Byelorussia, in the old days, it was normally the custom for the bridegroom to take the bride to his (or his parents' home). Occasionally, however, a young man would seek to relieve his poverty by marrying and going to live at his wife's home. Such an arrangement theoretically had its merits, if, for example, a farmer had many daughters but no sons – a strong young son-in-law or two could help him work the farm and ultimately inherit it. In practice, of course, the brides in question were liable to be of the 'elderly, ugly' type described by Gilbert. At the best of times, the position of the bridegroom in the household was anomalous, and the situation was as fruitful of jokes and anecdotes as the 'mother-in-law' situation in English humour.

At the symbolic level, the author indicates the temptation to rise to the level of the gentry by assimilation into Polish or Russian culture, like 'His Worship the Assessor' (who goes, in the original, by the Polish title of *Pan*).

p. 35: *What Janka thought . . .*
line 26. 'Solly' – i.e. Šlomka – diminutive of Solomon. In Byelorussia, innkeepers were normally Jewish.

THE *NAŠA NIVA* PERIOD
1906–1914

In this era, the pent-up forces of Byelorussian literature found their first, abundant outlet. At first in halting measures, but with greater and greater confidence, the poets emerged in the new, vital, creative milieu that arose in and around the newspaper, *Naša Niva* itself. At first concerned almost entirely with their country and her problems, the poets gradually expand their range of subjects, on the one hand to the personal – romantic love, its joys and sadness – and on the other to the verse-forms and patterns of western Europe, so that by the end of the *Naša Niva* period, we have a full and rich poetic literature, diverse and varied in both theme and structure. Here we find the early works of Kupała and Kołas, as well as the later works of poets of the older generation, such as Ciotka; here, too, is contained the whole brief span of creative activity of Bahdanovič, whose premature death from tuberculosis robbed Byelorussia of more poetic treasures than can be estimated. And here, too, is Buiła's *I love our land . . .* that has, long since, become a folk-song, sung by thousands who have, perhaps, hardly heard of its author, as well as by those who rightly acclaim it as the essence of that movement of love for, and concern over, the land and people of Byelorussia that is the essence of *Naša Niva.*

Janka Kupała

MY PRAYER

I'll make my prayer with my heart and my thoughts, and
Pray with my soul filled with song brimming o'er,
That with its tumult of snowstorm, black fortune
Over our land will ride raging no more.

I'll make my prayer to the bright sunshine, praying
In winter it may hapless orphans make warm,
Pleasantly over the harvest-fields playing
It may glance down more often upon our dark homes.

I'll make my prayer to the clouds with their thunder,
Which often play wildly high over our heads,
That they may pity the poor and the suffering
And will not their lightning and hail on them shed.

I'll make my prayer to the stars, tell my grieving
That they far too often to nothingness burn,
For I heard that whenever a star falls from heaven
Someone leaves this life for the slumber eterne.

I'll make my prayer, might and main, to the tillage,
That it grant for the toil more abundant a yield,
Giving wealth to the tumbledown homes of the village,
That our people see hopes, long-forgotten, revealed.

I'll make my prayer with my heart and my thoughts, and
Pray with my soul filled with song brimming o'er,
That with its tumult of snowstorm, black fortune
Will not howl o'er our land, over me, evermore.

PRELUDE TO STORM

What do I see? All quiet? 'Neath defamation
Everything sleeps. Is it true? Has the foe
Conquered? Are all who once fought for the nation,
By tyrants o'erthrown, in the grave lying low?

Is it true the whole people has fallen so lowly,
To the despot has yielded and said not a word?
Is the spirit of freedom, the spirit of holy
Revolt dead, and can by no effort be stirred?

Too few the misfortunes, the oceans of weeping?
Are the fetters too few, and the torment and grief?
O no! For the heart something other is speaking;
In this silence I place not, I place not belief.

It is only like this before storms in the summer,
When the bird dies away and the sun glances shy,
While clouds in the heavens flock one on another,
Till the thunder rolls, shattering earth and the sky.

TO THE ENEMIES OF THINGS BYELORUSSIAN

What is it, lords, that you are seeking?
And what compels you to the need
To sound the tocsin at the speaking
A Byelorussian voice has freed?

What terrifies you in his speaking?
Believe me, he steals not from you.
Only his own words is he seeking,
Those with which he was born and grew.

And now to 'guard' us you are coming,
As if sprung from the earth, unseen;
And what, till now, have you accomplished?
And where, until now, have you been?

Your brother is benighted, needy;
His house outwears the ages' span;
For years he knew no thoughts of freedom,
The own true brother robbed by – man.

Do our sad songs hold terrors yawning
For you, dull grief holds terror stark?
You dread the sun at spring's first dawning?
Do you prefer the cold and dark?

The Byelorussian – he affrights you
Because he dares to say, to do?
Ah, much the learning that awaits you
To pay your brother honour due!

Come, cease to feed upon injustice, –
Each nation to itself is lord;
The Byelorussian too may muster
In the Slav family's countless horde!

Why crust the breast with harsh callouses,
– Abuse and onslaught combative?
The brilliant truth – you will not dowse it:
The Byelorussian lives, will live!

These 'boorish' natures still have borne more
Burden than this their necks now bear!
The gloomy whistle of informers,
Believe me, will not fright nor scare!

To freedom, equal recognition
We are now hewing out the way!
Posterity shall hold dominion
Where the grandsire weeps today!

NOT FOR YOU

Not for you am I, lords, O no,
In my free time composing poems –
That which deep in the heart slept low –
I rouse, and to men's judgement show it!
Not for you am I, lords, O no!

Not for you am I, lords, O no,
At times myself of quietness ridding,
When in the eyes bright teardrops grow,
Arising at thoughts' anguished bidding –
Not for you, am I, lords, O no!

Not for you, am I, lords, O no,
Wasting my better days in sadness –
In war against eternal woe
I live, and feel no touch of gladness –
Not for you am I, lords, O no!

Not for you am I, lords, O no,
Straining to turn the word's new furrow
In wasted land where dense weeds grow,
In Biełaruś, our own dear country;
Not for you am I, lords, O no!

Not for you am I, lords, O no,
Weeping the fate of my own nation,
In the mud you would grind me low,
With baseness of unwelcome strangers . . .
    Not for you am I, lords, O no!

Not for you am I, lords, O no,
Singing. You comprehend not anguish,
Your heart will never leap in woe
At cries of friends who, suffering, languish,
    O never will it, lords, O no!

Not for you am I, lords, O no!
Life is but pleasure to delight you,
Replete, wine-filled, you torpid grow,
The word of truth cannot excite you,
    O never can it rouse you, no!

Not for you am I, lords, O no,
But for the poor and the downtrodden,
I suffer with them, throe for throe,
With the same fetters am I laden . . .
    Not for you am I, lords, O no!

Not for you am I, lords, O no!
But for the fortuneless, benighted,
And from them echoes to me flow,
Through leafy woods and cornfields flying,
    But never to you, lords, O no!

FROM THE SONGS OF MY COUNTRY

A land in misfortune's keeping
    Is our Biełaruś,
Janka and Symon her people,
    Her birds lark and goose.

Her fields are but rocks and hillocks, –
    All is drenched with sweat –
A mass of knotted roots her tillage,
    With sand and humps beset.

Sparse from the field the crops are wrested,
 – Though you toil your most –
Barley smut-plagued, rye infested,
 Charlock chokes the oats.

Wealthless villages that nurtured
 Orchards do not know,
Only here and there do birch-trees,
 Like thin landmarks, grow.

And in the villages live poorly
 Folk, bent with woe and lack,
Feet in bast sandals rotting sorely,
 Rough linen chafes their back.

Dark this nation, dark benighted,
 Hard 'tis to relate,
Tattered they in rags unsightly,
 And illiterate.

Everyone would mock and spurn them,
 Call them 'fool' in scorn . . .
A folk so poor . . . one feels a yearning
 With them, too, to mourn.

Like a grave, it seems, unlovely,
 Something forth doth flow
From Biełaruś, my own dear country,
 Yet I love her so.

I, when from her separated,
 Might and main do weep . . .
Ah, indeed, the wolf his native
 Brushwood doth find sweet!

Though at home I oft know hunger, –
 I'll live on water, bread . . .
Worse, by far, in a strange country,
 There more tears are shed.

There you'll find no heart of brother,
 None there is your own,
You'll live in conflict with others,
 All alone, alone,

And should you sing a native ditty,
 Who, O who will hear?
Vow, then, to love your native country,
 Than your life more dear.

AND, SAY, WHO GOES THERE?

And, say, who goes there? And, say, who goes there?
In such a mighty throng assembled, O declare?
Byelorussians!

And what do those lean shoulders bear as load,
Those hands stained dark with blood, those feet bast-sandal shod?
All their grievance!

And to what place do they this grievance bear,
And whither do they take it to declare?
To the whole world!

And who schooled them thus, many million strong,
Bear their grievance forth, roused them from slumbers long?
Want and suffering!

And what is it, then, for which so long they pined,
Scorned throughout the years, they, the deaf, the blind?
To be called human!

TO THE REAPERS

Where are you, brothers glad, where are you, mower-lads?
How long must we wait for you, still?
Time to whet the scythe, go forth to reap and to mow!
Time to show forth your strength with a will.

While dewdrops still gleam, let the scythe be made keen,
Let the hay in its swathes duly fall,
Let an end be at hand of rye-plague and rough sand,
Let the people behold, one and all!

Like a fire the sun glows, in streams the sweat flows,
But for you this is nothing anew,
Hardly grown to a man, you your hard toil began,
And no one had pity for you!

In streams the sweat flows, with a sleeve wipe your brows,
Swing the scythe with a cheerier gait,
And from downcast breast, bring forth your song of tears, sing
The native song of your own fate.

Sing and reap, might and main, while the bright days remain,
While there are no clouds in the height,
For earth, scythe and plough is beauty enow,
This is our only delight.

THE SPRING WILL YET DAWN . . .

Do not fear though clouds, treacherous, cover
The welkin from bourne unto bourne,
Though the darkness has cast its spells over,
Though the raven above the field hovers;
The spring will yet dawn.

Do not fear, although leaves, yellow-withered,
Fall in forests from bourne unto bourne,
Though no song-bird the whole day has twittered,
And alone now the shy hare darts swiftly;
The spring will yet dawn.

Do not fear, though poor tillage lies useless
And barren from bourne unto bourne,
That by peasant hands reaped, luckless, brutish,
The harvest is gathered in, fruitless;
The spring will yet dawn.

Do not fear though free forces in fetters
Are drowsing from bourne unto bourne,
Right is stifled by night unrelenting,
And death digs new graves, thickly sets them;
The spring will yet dawn . . .
The spring will yet . . .

WHEN WOODLANDS GLEAMED

When woodlands gleamed with guelder-rose and
Lime with blossom laden,
Golden dreams we dreamed in those days,
Thou and I, dear maiden.

The free birch-trees sang to greet us,
Lullabying, hushing,
And there murmured, rustling sweetly,
Osiers and rushes.

*

When the ears of rye swayed, graceful,
With a full crop laden,
Then we used to meet, embracing,
Thou and I, dear maiden.

Brightly glittered, brightly glinted,
Scythes among the grain then,
And the flowers and wild herbs wilted,
And the dews all waned then.

*

When the rowan-berries ripened,
Red and heavy-laden,
Then we glanced about us shyly,
Thou and I, dear maiden.

Under dead leaves dreamed the heather,
The green pines bent, sighing,
Somewhere in the dark wood ever
Cranes and geese were crying.

THE GRAVEMOUND

I

Deep in Biełaruś, set amid wasteland and marsh,
Where a river flows, noisily swirling,
A memorial of days fled and vanished long-past
Dreams, a gravemound, grass-grown, sempiternal.

Deeply rooted, the oak high above spreads its boughs,
On its breast is parched herbiage clinging,
And above it, dull breathing, the wind moans and soughs
A dirge for past years sadly singing.

At Midsummer a bird perches on it and sings,
In Advent a wolf howls upon it,
By day the sun spreads forth its rays in bright strings,
By night the gold stars gaze down on it.

Clouds have spread the wide sky, O a thousand of tim
From far and wide thunders crashed o'er it,
It stands there, a monument man-made, a sign . . .
But this, legend says, is its story.

II

Near the river bank, on a steep hill towering tall,
    A century or more back in history,
A castle rose (proof 'gainst all foes was its wall)
    Dread and brooding it gazed to the distance.

At its feet, the broad lands spread away, far around,
    Lofty fir-trees, black swathes of the tillage,
Houses, moss-grown like ghosts, homes of families serf-bound,
    Lay there, many a slumbering village.

In the castle a prince dwelt, renowned the world through,
    Dread, remote as the castle his dwelling,
All before him must bow willy-nilly, he knew
    No mercy to thoughts of rebellion.

He oppressed and tormented at home and abroad,
    He and his bold warrior retainers,
Till from out of men's hearts prayers arose heavenwards,
    And in secret a curse arose baneful.

III

Then one day the prince held a feast rich and fine,
    Marriage feast of the princess his daughter,
At the tables flowed rivers of overseas wine,
    For miles echoed the music and laughter.

To the wedding the noble guests came from at least
    Half the world, to the feasting and pleasure,
None could recall such a notable feast,
    Such robes and such jewels and such treasure.

One day and two the feast rang through the land,
    The music and goblets chimed gaily,
All the guests wished for was theirs to command,
    They invented new revelries daily.

But then, on the third day, the prince planned for all
    His warband this gratification:
For an old harper he ordered them call,
    A minstrel far-famed through the nation.

IV

The folk of those parts knew his harp-music well,
    His lays seized the heart and would hold it;
But those lays and those songs, notes of flute, notes of bell,
    Strange, indeed, was the tale as men told it.

They said he had only to go forth and play,
    Strike the strings, sing his song never-waning,
And sleep fled from the eyelids, all sighs died away,
    Not a murmur from cherry or plane-tree,

The deep woods hushed, no squirrel nor elk would dart forth,
    The nightingale ceased its deep quiver,
The alder-fringed stream left its everyday roar,
    And the roach hid its fins in the river.

Wood-sprite and rusałka to mosses would cling,
    Peewit ceased its 'peet-peet' a brief hour,
At the bell-notes he struck from the harp's living strings,
    Lucky bracken for all men did flower.

V

Forth from his ploughland village, the servitors brought
    The bard to that castle so stately,
Set him there, between maples and limes, on the porch,
    On the threshold of brick tessellated.

The smock on his back was but simple attire,
    His beard seemed as if white snow fell there,
In his thought-laden eyes there gleamed forth a strange fire,
    On his knees lay the harp-storyteller.

He passed his thin fingers across the steel strings,
    The song-music preparing and tuning,
The notes strike the cold walls, and echoing, ring,
    And in depths of the hall they die, booming.

The strings were made ready, the notes were in tune,
    Not one glance at the feast or its grandness,
The white-haired old man sat there, sunken in gloom,
    Awaiting the prince's commandments.

VI

'Bard of ploughlands and woods, why art silent so long?
    To my serfs thou art nightingale famous!
Play for us today, give to us of thy song,
    A prince gives no commonplace payment!

If thou singst to our taste, if thou pleasest our guests,
    I shall pile thy lute with ducats hoarded,
But if one of us find thy song lacking in zest –
    With the rope thou shall be well rewarded!

Thou knowest my fame, of my might thou dost know,
    I know much of thee, hearing men tell so;
And just as thou singest, I'll sing to thee so!
    'Tis time to begin now, good fellow!'

The bard heard and gave ear to the prince's command,
    In the grey eyes, sparks brightly were leaping,
He touched the strings once, touched them twice with skilled hand
    And the living harp-strings began weeping.

VII

'O thou prince, thou prince famous the whole wide world through,
    Thou thinkest in no thoughtful fashion!
No minstrel is quickened by gold's brilliant hue,
    Nor by drunken din of marble mansions!

My soul would be crushed by the ducats' great mound,
    No laws, Prince, bind the harp nor confine it,
To heaven alone heart and thought must account,
    To eagles, to sun and stars shining.

Look thou, Prince, on thy ploughlands, meads, woods, widely-spread,
    My harp and I know *them* our betters,
Thou has power, Prince, to torture, hast power to behead,
    But free thought into chains canst not fetter.

Dread and famous thou art, and this castle of thine,
    From the walls blows, it seems, winter chilling,
And a heart has thou like this brick threshold so fine,
    And a soul like its vaults, deeply builded.

VIII

Look then, thou famous lord, on thy fields, far and wide,
See the trace of the plough as it roams there;
But hearst thou what the songs of the ploughman betide,
Where and how live the men who find homes there.

Look into thy vaults, O Prince, deep underground,
Beneath thy great hall builded under,
Brothers writhe there by thee thrust in mud deep, profound,
And alive the worms eat them and plunder.

With gold thou wouldst darken, with gold thou wouldst lure,
But didst thou see, Prince in thy palace,
That human blood shines on that gold evermore,
Blood unquenchable by thy power's malice.

Thou coverest velvets and silk with fine jewels,
From fetters they are the steel filings,
They are frayed rope from a gallows, a noose,
Such, Prince, is thy noble attiring.

IX

Thy board is well-victualled; beneath lie bones spread,
Bones of peasants in poverty dwining,
Thou takest thy pleasure in white wine and red,
– The tears of an orphan's sad pining.

Thou hast builded thy palace, so dear to thine eye,
With bricks and stone polished to beauty;
These are tombstones from graves, dug out of due time,
Flames of hearts, these, into stone transmuted.

Thou takest thy pleasure in music and song,
You, O body-guard, quaff deep your revels,
But has thou heard how in that music there throng
Groans, cursing thee and thy kin ever.

Thou art pale, thou dost tremble, O prince, mighty lord,
Thy guests glower, thy servants stand dumbly . . .
It is time now, O Prince, to grant me my reward,
Excuse my song, an it were clumsy!'

X

The prince stands, silent stands, blazing vengeance he looks,
    The hall hushed, naught of jesting nor laughter. . . .
The prince thought, he took thought, and his sabre he shook,
    And tinkling the echo ran after.

'Equal thou to the sun! Bard, I summoned thee here
    To sing meetly my princess' wedding,
Thou dotard and fool. Whoe'er did thee rear,
    Thou degenerate scion of base breeding!

Thou hast dared stand against me in thy blind despite,
    With a song made the universe tremble,
I have much wherewith such upstarts to requite,
    Who against me would boldness dissemble.

I pay all, I love all as befits princely worth,
    Thou desirest no gold – let it pass, then!
Sink the dotard alive with his harp in the earth!
    I or heaven? Show him which is master!'

XI

They seized the old minstrel, they bore off the man,
    And with him his harp clear and tuneful,
To the steep bank, where sounding the wild river ran,
    They led the bard forth to his dooming.

They chose them a place and they digged them a grave,
    Three fathoms 'twas wide, and three deeply,
They buried him there and an aspen stake drove,
    Raised a mound of three fathoms there, steeply.

There came there no joiners a coffin to make,
    No neighbourly eyes were there weeping,
The harp then was silent and he – and grief's ache
    And silence, as if night came creeping.

But the palace resounded and loud the noise rang,
    Folly, music, together with laughter,
Many wine kegs the prince drained, then many began,
    Thus the wedding feast passed of his daughter.

XII

And year after year passed by, passed and flowed,
    And over the bard's gravel mound there,
Wormwood sprouted, a young oak commenced there to grow,
    And with speaking mysterious resounded.

And time passed away, hundred years or more,
    And among the folk flowered these rumours:
Once a year, at night, the old man, as of yore,
    Rises from the mound, white as snow looming.

And he strikes on the harp, and the strings echo clear,
    To the nerveless hands over them straying,
And he sings, but the living ken not what they hear,
    At the moon he stares, white as he, playing.

And they say, should a man ever fathom that song,
    He will never know sorrow nor weeping . . .
Maybe this is true – hark with your soul, hearken long . . .
    Gravemounds will tell much in their speaking.

SONG TO THE SUN

With the free sound by tall fir-trees whispered,
    With the mists that on sleepy dales fall,
With a tale of long years, near and distant,
    We cry to thee, sun, one and all.

Unbind the gold rays of thy tresses,
    Kindle warmth where fields lie in chill span,
Fill with flowers where meadow-swathes rustle,
    Sow new budding shoots on the land.

Take the harsh, humble earth, a spouse cherished,
    In a marriage eternal, and then
Flow forth in a mirror-like freshet,
    Among valleys and mountains and men.

Over villages and the tilled plain, sow
    A glittering, life-giving dew,
Bathe thyself in the flowering rainbow,
    Bless the heart, grant the soul peace anew.

As on Solstice-day, sun, in thy plenty
    Thy glance of life thou dost renew,
O rekindle the fame of our country,
    Rekindle our nation anew.

Let the sycamores rustle and murmur
    To us thoughts and fables eterne,
And let those sounds fly, further, further,
    To the wide world, O let their flight turn.

Where the Kryvian lowlands lie misty,
    From thy high free house let thy glance fall,
With a tale of the years, near and distant,
    We cry to thee, sun, one and all.

COME FORTH

Arise thou, my country, my mother undying,
Enough now of winter's servile slumbering!
Enough, now, for thee, of tear-laden sighing!
Come forth to the field, to the ploughland come hieing!
Come forth to welcome the Spring!

Away with the rags thou hast spun through long ages
From fragments of awns, from grief's bitter sting!
Come forth from under the wild winter's aegis
That over thy head raised up its outrages!
Come forth to welcome the Spring!

The chillness with whirlwind and snowstorm dug deeply,
Many a grave for thee oft hollowing,
The snowdrifts for thee a night lodging were keeping . . .
But see, snows are melting, rivers are leaping!
Come forth to welcome the Spring!

From the North came the storm winds to toss thee and batter,
Like a branch stripped of its leaves, buffeting,
From the West beasts came swarming, to tear thee and tatter
Thy breast . . . and yet still thou dost live on, unshattered –
Come forth to welcome the Spring!

They have blinded thy babes with injustice, tormented,
And into the coffin untimely did fling,
Taught them fables that thou in thy grave sleepest ever . . .
But one spark of sunlight that treason has severed;
Come forth to welcome the Spring!

Radiant, festal, bright beauty to gown thee
As a free bird, to the height soar and wing,
Join with the sun, shine with starlight around thee,
Sing forth thy songs, in thy glory abounding,
Come forth to welcome the Spring!

A crown of sharp thorns thou dost wear on thy brows now,
Thy mansion the sky and the fields' beautying,
Thy kingdom on all four sides stretches forth, drowsing,
Thy servants a million hands, worn with callouses . . .
Come forth . . . for thee waits the Spring.

MY SONG

My song did not send forth its shoots among blossoms,
Blossoms of the ever-flowering noon,
In a sad midnight a field-plot forgotten
Brought it to birth there where cockle was strewn.

Primaeval forest and night, nurture bringing,
Nursed it with fairytales of a dumb fate.
Rain and the dewdrops bathed it in the springtime,
Snowstorms wrapped it in a winter embrace.

My song has no velvets to clothe and endue it,
Will not fly to the wide world with thoughts swift and lithe;
It knows well enough Biełaruś and her beauty,
To rustle with forest, to sing with the scythe.

To wander in thought through a land conquered, wasted,
Believing in better dawn, trusting it true,
For when the old lamp's final flame is exhausted,
The nation will kindle tomorrow's anew.

My song has no need of a great hall, bright-glowing,
To listen to music in princely abodes,
It pulses and beats like a freshet free-flowing,
And sun and the stars and vast space are its lodes.

It has no need of the spur of the mighty,
Lackeyish services it does not know,
Living freedom its pledge, eternally binding,
One service – to freedom immortal – it owes.

My song does not seek for welcome or greeting,
Favours from hearts long turned to a tomb,
The free wind that blows from the far world will meet it,
Go with it and in its music commune.

The skies and the fields to friendship it beckons,
It hears the primaeval grief of the pines,
In stormy meanders it catches the echoes,
It seeks in the stars the future to find.

My song will not catch today in its embracing
Of thought every settlement and every home,
But houses in ruin and people in slavery,
Where seeds sprout not in the furrows unsown.

Time, like a waterspring, flows, unstagnating,
The old day no more will guide life, there will come
A new day to us and new folk, renovating,
Renewing the thoughts of old times begun.

My song does not seek for golden *čyrvoncy*,
The future will find within it no flaw,
It only would live in its native country,
To sing in the hearts of good folk evermore.

To sing, and with time, and at the due season,
Echoes in the villages' slumbering incite,
And all Biełaruś, immense as the seas are,
To gaze upon in a sun-brilliant light.

YOUNG BIEŁARUŚ

The free wind has sung free songs to thy name,
    Green woods caught them with friendly voices,
The sun called with its flame to a seed-time far-famed,
    The stars poured faith into broken forces.

And in time of storms, troubles and mighty desires,
    Thou hast budded and bloomed, long-awaited,
In a life-freshet, over the land of thy sires,
    Thou hast flooded and poured, unabated.

Thou has flooded and poured, in a bright tale of life,
    Through field, woodland, hill and vale streaming . . .
From thy native flower-copses thy crown is made bright,
    Like a swan's plumage, brilliant gleaming.

Thou dost quiver and echo with songs of the bards,
Long-past years thou dost raise up and nurture,
Today's forward leap thou wouldst never retard,
Boldly facing mysterious futures.

In the sun thou goest bold, lovely flower of fire,
Gently sowing forth dreams, gold-adornéd;
Thou fearest no neighbour, though great be his ire,
Thou fearest no path briared and thorny.

From end unto end, frontier mound unto mound,
On the breezes renewal is borne now,
And, embracing the soul, without limit or bound,
Mother-joy for the better day born now.

Now there are no axes among forests green,
Felling young pine-trees in frosty winter,
Now there are no reapers from dawn to dark seen
In summer with scythes ringing, glinting.

Strength is known in the hands, without tears songs are blithe,
Desirous of glory, breasts quiver,
In their books a new law, with pens of sun-scythes,
New people are writing for ever.

Blossom them, and raise, soaring upon eagle's wing,
Souls, hearts and thoughts slumbering dully,
Awaken and forth into great spaces, bring
Strength by the witch-noose unsullied.

Send messengers forth, send unto the world's bound,
As falcon from falcon-nest winging,
Let them fly, fly away unto warriors sound,
Set the thunder of good news far-ringing.

Enough, dearest country, in field, wood and brake,
Hapless orphan, thou spendst night's long glowering,
Enough of thy heart's-blood wrong drank as a snake,
And cold winds blew, through thy bare bones scouring.

Arise from the depths, thou of falcon-born race,
O'er sires crosses, their woes, degradations,
O young Biełaruś, come thou forth, take thy place
Of honour and fame among nations.

Jakub Kołas

OUR NATIVE LAND

Native land, our poor land stricken,
In forests, swamps and sandhills lost,
Hardly a fair meadow beckons . . .
Only heather, scrub and moss.

And mists like a shroud are winding
Over forest, over grove!
O thou country, poor, benighted!
Land forgotten by God's love.

Our field brings forth naught but trouble,
There the folk can live but poor.
In the mud they live, they stumble,
And they work – their sweat they pour.

Sadly here and there a village,
You look – the heart with pain must sigh,
In the courtyard, firewood, kindling,
Rubbish-heaps and middens lie.

A roadside cross stands, rotted nearly,
A cluster of dry poplars loom . . .
All like a prison, hushed and dreary,
Or as if upon some tomb.

And when, perchance, a song is sung there
How that song goes drearily,
You would like to flee, to run – where?
You do not know where to flee.

Native land, our poor field stricken,
Orphan-like thou dost appear,
Sad, and like to our fate reckoned,
Thou art like our darkness drear.

DO NOT FRET

Do not fret that sun hangs lowly
And the dreary days draw nigh,
Nor that autumn soon comes wholly,
And on the lowlands shadows lie,

Do not fret that cold snows lying
Shall conceal the earth from sight,
Our land shall not perish, dying
In the darkness of that night.

Comes the hour: the snows will melt then,
Spring will come to us again,
From the sky the sun glance gently,
All the earth recover then.

Do not fret that in hard usage
We live, benighted evermore,
That fate eternally pursues us,
That we shall be forever poor.

Do not fret that clouds hang o'er us,
That the sun ne'er greets our eyes;
Do not fret that fires come pouring
In the night-time through the skies –

Evil shall pass like smoke dissolving,
All that chokes us and confines;
Friend, believe – you shall behold then
Golden life in our land shines.

NATIVE PICTURES

Pictures beloved of my native country,
You are my gladness, my pain,
What can it be lures my heart to your bounty?
What binds me so with its chain

To you, my low hills, set among native tillage,
Rivers and forests and mounds?
Sorrow pervades you, misfortuned grief fills you,
Sorrowful beauty abounds.

Whenever I lay myself down, close my eyelids,
I see you there, clear to my gaze,
Softly, like living forms, you come, beguiling,
With a fair beauty ablaze.

I hear the ripe harvest in glad conversation,
The quiet complaint of the leas,
The happy drone of tall woods' murmuration,
The song of the mighty oak-trees.

Pictures beloved, O pictures of yearning,
Tillage and folk, own and dear,
Songs slowly languid, songs deep with mourning! . . .
I see you and hearken you here.

STAND BACK, MOVE ASIDE

All my life goes vainly,
Things turn out awried,
Everywhere they hail me:
'Stand back, move aside!'

Dear God, how I've struggled,
Crafty as serpent tried,
Everywhere I've ventured –
'Stand back, move aside!'

I wed: though the matchmaker
Was firmly on my side,
Her people poked their nose in:
'Stand back, move aside!'

And Kandrat, my neighbour,
(Though I'd a worthy bride)
Struck out his foot and tripped me –
'Stand back, move aside!'

I once went to the city,
A big parade I spied,
I wanted to press forward –
'Stand back, move aside!'

The grain bin was empty,
In hail the rye-crop died.
'Give me, good sir, assistance!'
'Stand back, move aside!'

All my funds had vanished,
To seek work I tried.
Is there no employment?
'Stand back, move aside!'

All in rags and tatters,
Shirt falling from my hide;
'Pray good people, help me!'
'Stand back, move aside!'

Ihnat would launch into the
World his son, his pride:
'This is my son, your honours!'
'Stand back, move aside!'

They brought bread to the village,
A swarm of hungry tried
To push through with their knapsacks -
'Stand back, move aside!'

I've a head. To be a
Deputy I tried.
'You are no elector,
Stand back, move aside!'

Yet, I've had my moment,
The truth I will not flout,
Twice in my whole life I
To the front came out.

I roused up the village,
A hard year, and no doubt!
Down came the militia:
'Come here, you, step out!

He roused up the village.
Sergeant, you see the lout?
Constables, be ready!
Take him, march him out!'

THE PEASANT

A peasant I, poor wretch bent wanly;
The peasant all men spurn and scorn,
They draw the very life-blood from him,
Burdens beyond his strength pile on him;
His hands are all calloused and worn.

A peasant, son of hardship's grieving,
Reared upon chaff from early youth;
My belly from boiled potherds heaving,
My feet in sandals of bast weaving,
Tattered and poor my clothes in truth.

A peasant, son of want's despoiling,
Of food and sleep I've no full share,
Bent by the burden of my toiling,
All day for just two *zloty* moiling,
And all abuses I must bear.

Peasant – no bell to me is reaching;
But, like a worm, doubt gnaws me so:
Does the priest lie, from pulpit preaching,
God gave the Tsar his crown? Such teaching
Surely is not the truth, O no!

Peasant – yet honour is remaining,
I bend, until the due hour comes,
Silent, still silent, uncomplaining . . .
But soon I shall shout forth, proclaiming:
'Ready, my lads, take up your guns!'

O SPRING . . .

O spring, O long-
Awaited one!
You will return,
Come back again!

The joyful singing,
Welcoming,
Of water-brooks
Be heard again,

The grove will waken,
And with song
In green leaf clothe
Itself again,

The woods resound
With whistling birds,
The meadow wear
New grass again,

And from the south
With levin-light
The stormcloud press
Its way again.

And the first thunder,
Music-like,
Mysterious
Roll forth again,

And all the earth
Will shake again,
With rain will wash
Itself again,

In nature all
Be born again,
And youth to it
Return again,

But thou wilt not
Return again,
Return again
To me, sweet youth!

O spring, O long-
Awaited one,
You will return,
Return again!

THREE WISHES

Land and bread we are seeking,
Hard is a beggar's task,
Heaven grants not our needing,
No words for more to ask.

Sun and light we are seeking,
Hard 'tis to stumble blind,
Hard to live without greeting,
Like some accurséd-kind.

We seek life, freedom cherished,
Hard 'tis the yoke to bear –
And it will never perish,
Perish away nowhere.

Extracts from *THE NEW LAND*

I

THE FOREST-WARDEN'S HOMESTEAD

My native nook, dear land that bred me! . . .
I have no power to forget thee!
Often when, from the roadway weary,
From my life's springtime, poor and dreary,
To thee on wings of thought I hasten,
And my poor soul finds rest and grace then.
O how I long, from the beginning
To tread again my road of living,
Step by step the whole path trace over,
And from the road those stones to gather,
On which young force and strength were wasted –
Back to that spring I'd wend my paces.

O Spring, O Spring, thou art not for me,
I shall not go, with thee to warm me,
To greet thy coming, joyful, merry,
Thou, Spring, I must forever bury.
For that wave will return here never
Which rolled away on the swift river,
But, into vapour oft transmuted,
Cloudward it soars on sunshine plumage,
Then, back as rain, falls to the river,
(For no one can escape, no, never,
The laws which life for him writes valid)
Or lies as mist on dale and valley;
But who is it that thinks to show where
Lies it as water or as snow there?
And thou, like wave upon the river,
Young spring, wilt come back to me never . . .

And now, again, before me rises
That nook in all its lovelinesses,
The curving stream-bed of the freshet,
The spruce tree and the pine that ever
Above the stream embrace together,
Like young folk in their love's devotion,
The last eve before separation.
I see the woods around the homestead,
Where once girls gaily, in the gloaming,
Sang their songs in a lovely chorus,
Late from work passing by the forest.

Notes of their fluent songs, far-trilling,
Once again by the woods were mirrored,
And with them all the hills resounded,
Forth in free billows, gladness bounded,
And firs and spruces sempiternal,
Beneath those song-notes, young and vernal,
Stood silent in some meditation,
And in their quiet murmuration
Were born the prayers of evening whispered,
Aloft, high into holy distance.

About the forest-warden's steading,
Like a lovely horse-shoe spreading,
Old and high, a forest briared,
There the round-leafed aspens' spires,
With firs and oak-trees interlacing,
Spruces their cloudy crosses tracing
High in the heavens clear, mysterious
Words to the pine-trees softly whispered,
And, like widows, ever sadly,
They in loneliness would stand there,
And so mournful was the gazing
Of their heads, aye meditating!
Now retreating, now advancing,
The woods the green meadow parted,
Here and there curves lovely wandered,
Round the homestead in fair meanders,
That one must stand there and admire them . . .

....

By the orchard, in the farmyard,
There a lean-to and a barn stood,
Under the lean-to were gathered
Tools and harness, cart and waggon,
Wheels and axles, old sledge-runners,
Skeps for bees – quite few in number –
Still unfinished, sundry vessels,
Old tubs, a half-bushel measure,
And all kinds of trash and lumber,
Sheltered from the rain and sun there –
For, of course, it *could* be needed.
The barn, thatched with straw, had faded
Into grey with long years passing,
Tufts of straw where winds had tossed them
Dangled from it, wild, dishevelled;
Somewhat, too, by boys bedevilled,

On the thatched roof climbing, crawling,
(That, they found, a game enthralling!)
And 'neath the gable, in a cobweb,
An orphan ear of grain was bobbing,
In the stillness, very quietly –
Truly, only God almighty
Knew how long it had kept hold there.
Another building, even older,
With roof warped and rotted dire,
Stood across the yard – a byre,
Hardly in one piece, as it were
On fence-post propped to dry, a pitcher,
Cracked by the poker. Old, worm-eaten,
By the winds battered into leaning,
It seemed like some old soul grown senile,
From beggar's fortune bent and leaning.
To one side, in the field, quite handy,
Was a wretched cold-house standing,
Like grief-bitter orphan bending,
With roof into the earth descending.
Within the courtyard, the house loomed there,
Looking smart and nicely groomed there
Beside the rest, ramshackle, faded,
Like a yeoman-peasant maiden,
On feast-days, by the Catholic chapel,
Holding her skirts up a little,
With her umbrella walking grandly,
Trailing a tail of skirts, the sandy
Dust from the path behind her sweeping,
And in the lads' eyes coyly peeping.

Beyond the house, the home-field started,
Where graceful swaying rye was planted,
Oats, barley, buckwheat and the rest there . . .
It was a very cosy nest there . . .

II

SUNDAY MORNING

A holy day! From early dawning,
Pancakes for breakfast baked that morning,
Already by the stove, with oven-
Prong in her hand, there stood the mother . . .
Round her the children scampered, peering,
Laughing and singing, interfering.

In its place stood the working table,
With kneading-trough and dough; the ladle
Was there at work, rapidly going
Into the kneading-trough and throwing
The dough out quickly on the griddle.
The batter gave a rapid sizzle,
Noisily flowed the griddle over,
Then into the hell-heat of the oven;
And, in the twinkle of an eye-lid,
Out from it, ready, baked like tiles, came
Pancakes, underneath all waffled,
And rising up with splendid puffing,
And, straight away, from mother's hand came
Tossed on the work-bench, these fine pancakes.
And long the children watched them, vying
To catch the pancakes in their flying,
And spread them keenly with good dripping.
The chopped meat stood there in its kitchen
Bowl, and the things to give a savour
Of sauce – 'twas no exotic flavour –
Onion, pepper and bayleaf, taken
With a few slices of good bacon,
Flour and *kvass*, nothing more, but never-
The-less, breakfast excites one ever.
For children, the best feast-day party
Is when they can eat well and hearty,
The griddle on the stove-ledge chinking,
So near, so dear to them this clinking,
With such a joyful humour ringing,
It sang to them its holy singing,
Their hearts and ears sweetly caressing,
Filled souls with joy beyond expressing.
So pleasantly, so sweetly sounding,
Unique in pleasantness abounding,
Filled all their bodies to the limit,
Fetched them from bed in half-a-minute.
Not in vain then was Uncle's habit;
When he must rouse them, swift and rapid,
To drive the cows out, he was given
To chink the griddle in the oven.
Now, having stuffed themselves with eating,
They turned to childhood's games, repletely.
One with a stick went chasing quickly
Around the house, scaring the chickens.
Sisters, like little piglets rolling,
Romped in the sand. Aleś went strolling
Beside the spring, that here came flowing,

Out of the forest, its curve going
About the homestead; whistling merry
To charm the birds, and picking berries
Into a jug. Each went off easy
His own way, at his own task busy.
Michał to the wood went early, in it
To make his rounds, his usual custom;
Antoś was unused to lengthy slumber,
And when he could find a spare minute,
Some free time on a holiday he,
At least once weekly, went off gaily,
To plumb the Nioman's depths his wish – he,
Our Anton was an avid fisher,
He was an expert, a real craftsman.
Ŭładzik took out the cows to pasture,
(Poaching the meadows of another);
And at home, with the children, mother
About her housewife's labours fussing,
About eternal labours bustled,
Now in the field, now at the stove, a
Toil, you would say, that's never over.
This, done, on *that* she is beginning,
Never a moment comes that in it
She's time to fold her hands a minute –
That is the life, alas, of women!
So now, at last, she closed the oven,
But now the household work was over,
Off to the garden, beets she's needing,
The pigs require another feeding.
And Juzik, too, the little fellow,
Still small and silly, tried to follow,
Always beneath your feet you'll find him,
Or, dragging like a tail behind you,
Ever distracts you with his needing,
And sets the heart within you bleeding.

Maksim Bahdanovič

*   *   *

Look, and see a world eternal
Marvellous and many-hued.
A. Fet

Greeting to thee, life in freedom,
Oaks' canopy above the head,
With sky and hills and fields all gleaming
    Through the leaves' net.

Rags of shadows in the clearings
Lie concealing the bright gold,
Whose layers from below appearing
    Gleam through torn holes.

And the sun, towards the night-time
Flirts its red fan in the sky,
And the wind, by it excited,
    Far away flies.

When the twilight palely glimmers
And the waters turn to dark,
Then in silver needles shimmer
    Assembled stars.

And equal dear and fair become the
Brilliant gleaming and the shade,
The day whose birth awaits its coming,
    The day which fades.

SOFT WARM EVENING . . .

Soft warm evening, quiet breeze, new rick of hay,
You have laid me down upon the earth to sleep,
No bright dust along the roads like smoke-cloud plays,
In the heavens, the moon's pale horn glimmers, strays,
In the heavens, quiet the stars' first blossoms peep.

A shooting star falls in a burning tear,
Plumage softly sighing, a white owl glides past;
And, my soul at one with nature, I see clear
The stars tremble in the wind above me here,
In the quiet, I hear the growing of the grass.

IN WINTER

Hail, frosty evening, ringing, calling,
Hail, crunching crisp, soft spread of snow,
No snowstorm blows, the wind has fallen,
And freely the light sledges go.

Like phantoms, birches whitely hover,
Under night-time's dark-blue quilt,
In the heavens, the stars shiver,
Frozen utterly, frost-chilled.

The moist moon from on high is shedding
A shaft, transparent and aglow,
And with silver cloaks is spreading
The blueing acres of the snow.

With sledges cleave the snow, good horses!
Gay copper bells, ring out with zest!
Forests and fields fly in swift courses,
The blood is boiling in the breast.

ROMANCE

Quand luira cette étoile un jour,
La plus belle et la plus lointaine,
Dites-lui qu'elle eut mon amour
O derniers de la race humaine
Sully Prudhomme.

Venus has risen above the broad skyline,
Brought in her wake shining memories of love,
Do you recall, when we met for the first time
Venus had risen above?

From that time forth, evermore I'd go gazing
Upon the night sky, seeking long for that star,
Within me a deep silent love for you blazing
From that time forth, evermore.

But the time of our parting draws near, ever nearer,
Thus does our fate, does our fortune appear;
Deeply, profoundly I loved you, my dear one,
But the time of our parting draws near.

In that far country, my love buried under
My heart, dull and dreary, each night, high above,
I shall gaze on that planet, my heart filled with wonder,
In that far country, my love.

Gaze upon Venus once more, when far distant
One from another, there mingling we'll pour
Our glance – let love flower if but for an instant,
Gaze upon Venus once more.

THE CHRONICLER

His soul grown weary-tired in life's stern tempests fending,
Within cloister walls his days he now is ending.
Here is silence, here is calm – no hubbub and no noise.
Copying a chronicle four years he has employed.
Copying the whole from an ancient parchment,
From first word to the last, of Mahileŭ and what passed there.
And here are deeds of good and ill-deeds equally
Set in the record. Just so the industrious bee
Even from bitter flowers can fill its combs with honey.
Then of events he saw he adds true testimony.
Here are the things which came to pass in former ages,
What men thought then, and of what disputed sagely,
Why they fought, and how the true faith they defended –
By this paper all made known to their descendants!
All is long-forgotten, dead, on waters drifting –
But now it will arise, once more in memory living,
When they find his simple, unadorned narration,
Telling of that life, its hopes, its expectation.
Just so the blue sea carries to the shore
To us a little flask where resin once was poured,
Covered with small mussel shells and mud. Long, truly,
It lay in the water, much it did endure there;
Some fishermen may find the bottle, stave it in,
And, so it happens, they may find there is, within,
A letter. By the custom of the sea, some message
Sent by shipwrecked sailors. Somewhere they have perished
In the ocean; maybe centuries rolled on
Since that time, maybe the nation now is gone,
And, all is changed, and even memory is drowsing!
But, letters, you once more will waken and arouse men,
And then about their forebears they will learn, and read
About their woes and joys, about their noted deeds,
To whom they made their prayer, what for they were seeking,
Where on the deep sea floor the waves forever keep them.

THE WEAVER-WOMEN OF SŁUCK

From native home, from native tillage
To the lord's court, for beauty's sake,
Luckless girls taken from their village,
Girdles of gold to weave and make.
Long hours of toiling they endeavour,
Forgetful of their girlish dreams,
Labour at the broad weaving ever,
Where the Persian pattern gleams.
Outside the walls, the smiling tillage,
The blue sky gleams beyond the pane,
And thoughts go wandering, willy-nilly,
There where the spring's in flower again,
There by the rye, in the bright distance,
The cornflowers shine with azure still,
And waves of chilly silver glisten
Where rivers gush between the hills;
Edge of an oak-wood, dark in verdure . . .
And hands, forgetful at the loom,
Neglecting the designs of Persia,
Weave in the native cornflower bloom.

SNOWSTORM

Wind beats on the rooftop drums,
Thunders on them, rings and hums,
Music ever louder poured
From the ball of the Storm-Lord,
Wind beats on the rooftop drums,
Thunders on them, rings and hums,
Now there seethes a wine of snow,
Gushing in white foaming flow,
Wind beats on the rooftop drums,
Thunders on them, rings and hums,
In the streets, drunk wildness blows,
Booming, drunken snowstorm goes,
Wind beats on the rooftop drums,
Thunders on them, rings and hums.

MY NATIVE COUNTRY . . .

My native country, how God's ban doth blast thee,
How thou dost bear sorrow and ills!
Stormclouds and marshes . . . Over poor harvests
The wind may roam at its will.

To ruins thy native villages topple
With grief the breast stifles and chokes; –
Behold these poor homesteads, birch-trees and poplars,
Everywhere gloom-stricken folk . . .

How much upon strong backs they have borne there,
How worked with those toil-blackened hands;
How many times were they forced to bear torture
From forests and dales and broad lands.

Do you but turn your eyes on this people –
The heart chokes within you for grief,
How many woes see you, how much of weeping,
How many needs, sans relief.

A song sings of how, fordone by his loving,
Janka, the widow's son, dies,
There, where a sad birch is drooping above it,
The grave of a poor lad now lies.

Rumours and tales of accord, fortune's favour –
The heart hears of them not a word,
Woe chokes and stifles the nation's breath ever,
Woe everywhere is the lord.

In a wide wave it has spread like an ocean,
Drowning our native land quite . . .
Friends, can we vanquish this woe of our nation?
Friends, do we yet have the might?

SWIFTER, BROTHERS . . .

Swifter, brothers, advance to the fray
With life, leaving all terror aside,
Fearful folk's cries cause us no dismay,
Though the battle be spread far and wide . . .

Against water-flow as it pours
Only that which is living can ride,
And the wave of the stream ever-more
Bears away what has ceased, what has died.

TO A SINGER . . .

Now, then, my young friend, that the heart in man's breast,
As if stone-hewn, is hard, unresponsive,
Always upon it weak verse will be smashed,
Without kindling in it holy conscience.

From steel one must forge, temper flexible verse,
Patiently working and plying,
Then, when you strike, like a bell 'twill resound,
And from cold stone the sparks will come flying.

SONNET

Un sonnet sans defaut vaut seul un long poème.
Boileau.

Where the Egyptian sands spread far around,
Close where the waves of azure Nile are flowing,
A tomb stood many thousand years: men going
Within, some seeds hid in a jar were found.
Although the grains were parched and dried, still sound
Their vital force awoke, and, new life knowing,
Flourished abundantly, young ears were growing,
In spring the crop stood high above the ground.

Forgotten land of mine, this is your symbol;
At last thy people's spirit is atremble,
I believe it lies not in sterile sleep,
But that it will surge upward like a fountain,
Which, rushing in a mighty, sounding leap,
Pierces the soil, into free spaces mounting.

FROM THE SONGS OF A BYELORUSSIAN PEASANT

I bend and I toil until, stretched to breaking,
My life like a rotten thread gives,
And did I but know how much sweat would be taken
And poured from me, I could not live.

My feet tramped out viersts by the hundred on hundred,
Bridges and roadways I built.
I poured out my sweat when in pieces I sundered
Dry soil with my plough as I tilled.

I toiled over sandhills and quagmire, I suffered
No little of torment and pain,
And I'll not be ashamed when I sleep, the earth under,
Of hands by toil blackened, engrained.

Now the hour comes to die; sweat and tears are gnawing
My life away, like mouse's teeth;
Anguish bends me, like snowstorm on willow out-pouring,
Ne'er in my life could I breathe.

Fortune gives but a glance, then flies off, far far distant,
I could only know it in dreams;
So let, let my life then be sundered this instant,
Like the rotten thread that it seems.

II

I sought from the wealthy and prayed them for bread,
They gave me but stones and no more,
And between them and me these stones were firm-set,
Like a wall built by giants they soar.

And the wall grows, ever higher and higher,
And many men greatly do fear;
What will come to pass when it shakes and falls dire,
Whom will it bury under it here?

EMIGRANTS' SONG

There are in this world such far-rovers
Who believe not in God nor in devil,
Who delight in bright banners high over
The ships that in ocean ports revel.

They have none here to leave whom they cherish,
For they have neither kin nor belongings,
They care not if they live or they perish,
On one sole aim are fixed all their longings:

To visit lands, so far unsought-for,
To taste there of fortune and grieving,
And to perish among the salt waters
Of blue seas where white foam is heaving.

But we do not seek such a bounty,
It is not far lands we are needing,
We would not have left our dear country
If there had been bread for our feeding.

And in clatter and noise of streets roaming,
Where the crowd, ever-restless, whirls streaming,
We dream of the village, the Nioman,
And Libava with harbour lights gleaming.

*   *   *

When Basil died, far on the march,
He dreamed of his land at the last.
'Farewell, ah, farewell, ploughland strips,
Farewell, too, to you, unploughed fallow,
I shall never plough you again,
Nor at dawn so a rich crop of grain,
Dark meadow, I'll not gaze on thee more,
Thou clean, broad field stretching boundlessly!
Nevermore to walk across thee shall I go,
Nevermore the green grass shall I mow.
I am leaving thee, pinewood sincere,
Dark and dreaming, forest primaeval!
No longer shall I hear thee rustle so,
No more lay thy lofty pines low.

Ah, farewell to you, family dear,
Ah farewell to you, my dearest friends!
No more to press you close to my heart,
Sit with you, in jokes and talk take my part.
Ah, a reverent farewell, Biełaruś,
Thou my country all fortuneless.
Thy son does not forget his mother,
For thee he'll lie here, earth his cover . . .'
When Basil died, far on the march,
He dreamed of his land at the last.

LAVONICHA

O Lavonicha, Lavonicha my dear,
I remember you in loving words sincere,
I remember your curved brows' black downy haze,
I recall your bright eyes and your merry gaze,
I recall your lively form, and, more than this –
I remember well that you knew how to kiss!

O Lavonicha, Lavonicha my dear,
You sang louder than the nightingale to hear,
In the dance you always took the foremost place,
'Snowstorm', 'Jurca', 'Bull-calf jig' – you set the pace,
And at harvest time, so boldly reaped you on,
That it quite astonished your no-good Lavon!

O Lavonicha, Lavonicha my dear,
Half the village are your gossips; it is clear
You know how to welcome guests – a hostess gay –
You've learned always just the proper things to say,
How to cheer, and how to make dull grief depart,
And, in season, how to press friends to your heart.

O Lavonicha, Lavonicha my dear,
May God grant your life be long and never drear,
May you live in joy among this world so sad,
As you once brought gladness, so may you be glad,
May my memories of you ne'er disappear,
O Lavonicha, Lavonicha my dear!

From *THE MADONNAS*

Lumen coeli, sancta rosa.
Aleksander Pushkin.

I
IN THE VILLAGE

Beauty of young maidens sets the heart a-dancing,
And the souls of mothers have power to entrance us;
Higher beauty when they merge in living grace!
Artists, painters ever bow before its face,
Striving always through their canvas to discover
In a maiden's face the devotion of a mother.
Thou, O Virgin-Mother, art that beauty's sign –
From beneath the brush Thy holy features shine.
And I gaze on them in mystic trepidation,
My heart striving for the land of my own nation.
And I recollect all my long-past years!
Among my past life's images, dark and drear,
As I, eager, seek, with soul perturbed and stormy,
One event of long-ago appears before me.

Once upon a working day in summer-time
I passed through a village. In a dreary line
On both sides of the winding narrow lane, the houses
Stood there, grey, decayed, like old rags, dull and frowsty;
In the walls their windows staring blindly back,
And even the thatch itself was rotted black.
All was ruins, grown old; here death had come crawling.
Only here and there was something still adorning
The village dreariness. The poppy still unfurled
Bright flowers like butterflies, where many colours swirled,
Beside the path, and with them made the soul grow carefree.
Then, too, one might notice here and there a pear-tree,
Crooked, gnarled with age . . . and that, indeed, was all –
But no one to be seen, no people, none at all –
All in the fields. No trace of bright skirt for a moment,
No new bride passed with pails to bear the water homeward,
No white caps of peasants to be seen, nowhere,
No sounds of colts' neighing echoes in the air,
No sad song was heard, floating, ringing, flying . . .
Then, how strange! There came the sound of infant crying.
Hearing this, I started and looked round. Alas!
I'd scared a little boy; he crawled upon the grass

Beside the path, on hands and knees, poor little baby,
Towards his nursemaid – she a girl of eight years, maybe –
And now he'd reached her, and into her lap straightway
He hid his little head, voice fearful with dismay,
And, as the tip of a small birch nods in the breezes,
The girl bent to the little boy to calm and ease him,
And wiped his tears, and started murmuring to him,
Exactly, as a mother would. And thus, within
One living form, the two mingled and merged together,
The stature of a girl, the manner of a mother.
At that moment she, childlike in form, and thin,
Seemed sudden to appear filled to the very brim
With some far-spreading native loveliness within her,
And, I recall, by soul grew finer for an instant,
But maybe in the girl it was not loveliness –
In that thin, grubby, puny little girl expressed –
But something higher which great Rafael endeavoured
To show through the features of Our Lord's own Mother.

. . . . . .

A better page thou art in my life's diary!
I read you once again quiet and joyfully.
Let many of these years be borne off by the freshet,
Let in the dark abyss the lovely features perish
Of this sweet little girl, lost from my memory,
Yet I believe in hardship's hour they'll gaze on me.

* * *

Biełaruś, thy folk long have been yearning
For a golden and brilliant day,
See, the eastern sky kindled and burning,
Count the fires that in flying clouds play . . .

Kanstancyja Bujła

I LOVE

I love our land, that dearest country,
Where I was born, where I did grow,
Where first I learned of joy, good-fortune,
Where first I shed a tear of woe.

I love our Byelorussian nation,
Cottages where green orchards throng,
The ploughlands, gleaming gold with harvest,
Our woods and groves, their murmured song,

The river that pours forth its waters
Far into distances unseen,
The yellow brilliance of its sandbanks,
Its limpid waves with crystal gleam.

I love the spring, adorning gladly
The earth with flowers and green anew,
The storks a-chatter at their nesting,
The song of skylarks love I too.

The hot tranquillity of summer,
And summer tempests with their rain,
How thunder rumbles, how black storm-clouds
Flicker with darting lightning flame.

And I love, too, the mournful autumn,
The scythes' and sickles' early chime,
As men go forth to reap the harvest,
The mowers at haymaking time.

I love the winter, cold and frosty,
Its patterns on the window-glass,
And the white snow that cloaks the ploughlands,
Sparkling with gleams of brilliant stars.

I love, in fine warm nights of summer,
Late in the courtyard oft to laze,
To watch the bright stars as they glitter,
Upon the golden moon to gaze.

And I love, too, our native music,
The songs sung in the fields by girls,
When the clear melody, far-flowing
Across the ploughland ripples, swirls.

Because I love my native country,
All things within this land are dear,
Where with first joy I grew acquainted,
Where first in sorrow shed a tear.

Źmitrok Biadula

* * *

On the soul's anvil a first verse I forged,
And sorrow served me for a hammer;
That song's midnight cry in my heart deep I lodged.
And the heart told its woe in loud clamour.

On the soul's strings a first verse played I loud,
The echoes raced far to the distance;
And with them the ploughman his strip deeply ploughed,
And with teardrops the eyes were all misted.

A WINTER TALE

A snowy night hangs, a savage night hangs,
A grey pelt above forests' wild tresses.
In white plumage of snow, in a white silk of snow,
Valleys, hills under rich snowy dresses.

In the wild of the woods, the age-slumbering woods,
Dwell a people, ill-natured, unspeaking.
In a palace of glass, on a bed all of glass
Lies a maiden with sun-bright hair, sleeping.

Go you, call here by name; go you, wake her again –
Then tall fir-trees will utter harsh creaking.
Then the tempest will moan, then the tempest will groan,
White-eyed winter complain with loud speaking.

Winter then, in alarm, winter then, fearing harm,
In a frenzy of frost will spin, swirling;
Like a horse without rein, like a grey-and-white flame,
The blind snowstorm will rush, rearing, whirling.

And the maid will sigh deep, stir in heavy-dreamed sleep,
With her fingers brush brows clear of hoar-frost,
She will gaze all around, unrestrained, all around,
Sad the grey wolves will howl in the forest.

Go you, rouse her again – and the spring comes again,
Over ploughland larks revel unstinting,
On the river, ice cracks, and away the floes break,
And the playful floods wash out the winter.

NOTES

p. 43: *Prelude to storm*
An earlier version of this translation was published in *Manifold*, No. 3, 1962.

p. 44: *To the enemies of things Byelorussian*
stanza 7 is strongly influenced by pan-Slavist ideas. In general the Byelorussian attitude to pan-Slavism is ambivalent: in the theory of its pioneers, notably the Slovak Kollár and the Czech Hanka, pan-Slavism was envisaged as an equal brotherhood of free and independent nations, united by common ethnic and cultural traditions for their mutual benefit. In Russian Imperial theory, however, pan-Slavism became a concept by which 'big brother' Russia would 'protect' (i.e. dominate and absorb) the 'lesser' Slav nations. Here Kupała is thinking of pan-Slavism in its pure form, as proposed by Kollár. Earlier in the poem (*stanza 3, line 1*) he seems to be referring to Russian Imperial interpretations of the same idea.

p. 46: *From the songs of my country*
stanza 3, line 2. 'rye infested', i.e. plagued with the parasitic *Rhinanthus*, which by drawing nutriment from the root of the plant, results in the production of 'ears' that are mere empty husks, with only a small, dry seed inside. The only English name I have been able to locate for this condition of rye is 'rattle-box'. I have ventured therefore to slur, in this case, the precision of this translation, since *Rhinanthus* sounds out of place in a 'peasant' poem of this kind, and 'rattle-box' *nimis difficile fuit in versus inserere!* – without appearing somewhat ludicrous.

stanza 4, properly speaking, refers to northern Byelorussia only. Farther south, well-tended orchards and cottage gardens are a typical feature of the landscape.

stanza 5, line 3. 'bast sandals' – these are the famous Byelorussian *łapci*, woven of interlaced strips of lime-bast. Although very comfortable to wear when dry, *łapci* when wet, if not changed or dried (as would be the case when worn by a peasant working long hours in wet fields) can give rise to a condition similar to that known in the First World War as 'trench feet'.

p. 48: *To the reapers*
stanza 2, line 1. Owing to the difference in climatic conditions, and also in traditions, hay, in Byelorussia, is cut when still wet with dew. As students of English folk-songs will recall, this conflicts with the English traditional practice, e.g.

The golden sun is shining bright,
The dew is off the field,
For us it is our main delight
The fork and rake to wield.

stanza 2, line 3. *Rhinanthus* again!

p. 50: *The gravemound*
This poem, undoubtedly, presents a problem from the point of view of subject-matter. Generally, when Kupała writes of a 'prince' he is writing of the idealized picture, presented by *Naša Niva* theory, of the old Grand Duchy of Lithuania, according to which theory the prince was protector and father of his people, acting

not arbitrarily, but only after due consideration and deliberation with his moot (*vieča*):

> The prince on his throne (round him free liegemen clustered)
> Gave forth his law to the free folk of old;
> They heeded the prince, yet the prince was not master,
> – *He* heeded the word the moot-bell to him told.
>
> (Janka Kupała: *On the Nioman, stanza 6*)

It need hardly be said that this picture presents an ideal rather than any accurate portrayal of historic fact. 'By reviving past centuries of national consciousness and comparing and contrasting them with the wretched present conditions, the poet wished to awaken the national conscience of the nation, to compel it, while drawing strength from past centuries, to shake off serfdom.' (S. Stankevič: 'Kupała in Fact and fiction', *Byelorussian Review*, No. 3, 1956.) Neither need it be said that the prince in *The Gravemound* does not conform to this ideal picture. Who and what, then, is he? He does not appear to be a Russian – the vague dating of 'a century or more back in history' seems to take one before the three partitions of Poland, which brought Byelorussia under Russian rule. Nor, however, does he appear to be a Pole – Kupała would probably have referred to a specifically Polish ruler as *Pan* (Lord) rather than *Kniaz* (Prince). After much deliberation, I have come to the tentative conclusion that this poem may best be understood as a late-flowering of the 'Gothic revival', in the East Slav variant developed by the Ukrainain Taras Shevčenko, by which the plots are those of Gothic horror, but the setting and protagonists are native and national. Kupała's Prince is thus, as it were first cousin to Shevčenko's Prince (who, in his poem *The Princess*, rapes his own daughter), belonging to the class of villains, *per se*, from whom, *ex hypothesi*, any dastardly deed may be expected. Against such a background, Kupała's interpretation and use of the theme as a vehicle for a nationalistic message becomes clear and reasonable.

Archaeologically speaking, the gravemounds of Byelorussia date from prehistoric times, although barrows appear to have been raised over notable heroes right up until the end of the pagan period (*c.* AD 1000). In the popular imagination, however, as in all countries, such mounds and barrows tended to become identified with any convenient local myth or legend.

The planting of trees on gravemounds is an ancient Slav practice, which persisted well into historical times (see, for example, Taras Shevčenko: 'Bewitched', in *Song Out of Darkness*, London, 1961). In popular thought and legend, these trees are seen to embody in some manner, the spirits of the dead persons buried beneath, and, like Polydorus in the *Aeneid*, can tell the story of their life and death to the sensitive listener. Incidentally, in his discussion of the associated variant of the Binnorie ballad (*The Two Sisters; Folklore Fellows Communications*, No. 147, Helsinki, 1953), Paul Brewster identifies the 'speaking tree' motif as being of Slavonic origin, but raises the logical objection that it would take a considerable number of years for a small sapling thus planted to grow to the size needed to convey the news (either by rustling its branches, or, as in the 'Binnorie' variant, by the use of its wood to make a harp). This however, is not cogent, as an experiment carried out by myself and two Byelorussian friends will testify. Using a rowan tree (traditionally planted on the grave of a young married woman), and the site of a demolished air-raid shelter as the nearest convenient equivalent to a gravemound, we set in position and implanted a tree of some twenty feet in height. It rooted well, needed no attention after twelve days from planting, and within six weeks from transplantation its foliage had recovered from the initial drooping. and rustled excellently in the wind. Although the oak-tree in *The Gravemound* has had, of course 'a century or more' to become established, and, in any case, is a natural seeding, and not a specially-planted memorial tree, nevertheless, the picture of the gravemound with its guardian tree, with which the poem opens and closes, is so significant in Byelorussian folk tradition, that a proper explanation of the practical details seems to be in order.

section IV, stanza 4. Rusałka is the name given in many Slavonic languages to a legendary being, a kind of fresh-water mermaid, whose attributes, however, differ slightly from country to country. In Byelorussian, the rusałka is envisaged as a more-or-less adult, although irresponsible, being (in contrast to the rusałka-children of Ukrainian folklore); she normally has a fish-tail, but can, in the summer, come up on land, grow legs, and haunt the standing corn. (She is a useful threat to warn children from attempting to run into the cornfields and thus damage the crops!)

'Lucky bracken'. In Slavonic folklore, it is said that on Midsummer Eve, at midnight, the bracken will blossom with beautiful white flowers. He who witnesses this marvel, and, more particularly, he who can pluck one of the magic flowers, will receive the usual fairy-tale benefits – three wishes, treasure, a beautiful bride, etc., according to the locality in which the story is told. (One of the most compelling uses of this motif is that of Gogol' in his tale St John's Eve (from the cycle *Evenings on a Farm near Dikanka*), an anonymous English translation of which appears in *Great Short Stories of the World*, chosen by Barrett H. Clark and Maxim Lieber, London, 1926.)

p. 56: *Song to the sun*

It may be noted that throughout his poems, Janka Kupała is greatly fascinated by the idea and symbol of the sun. It is not unmeaningful that the second element of the poet's name is that of the old pagan Byelorussian sun-god Kupała, whose feast day, at Midsummer, being replaced by that of St John the Baptist, gave to the Saint the agnomen of 'Kupała'. The name 'Kupała' appears to be of Finnish origin (cf. such gods as Jumala in the pantheon of the *Kalevala*) but is associated in Byelorussian folk-etymology with the past tense of the verb *kupać* – to bathe (masc. kupaŭ; fem. kupała; neut. kupała, pl. kupali, deriving from an older kupał, kupała, kupało, kupali). It may further be noted in this regard that the poet who adopted the pseudonym of Janka Kupała was born on the day following Midsummer Day.

stanza 2, line 1. An expansion of the idea implicit in the Byelorussian *Raspusci załacistyja kosy* – unbind (thy) golden '*kosy*'. The word *kasa* (pl. *kosy*) means both a 'beam of light' and a 'plait' or 'braid' of hair, thus making possible at this point a compactness of expression that requires expansion in English into a full-scale metaphor. (The third meaning of *kasa* – 'a scythe' does not seem significant to this passage.) We may note that the sun is here personified as a young girl, combing her hair; later, in *stanza 3*, the sun is seen as a bridegroom about to enter into marriage with the (undoubtedly-feminine) earth. The word *sonca* – 'sun' being grammatically neuter in Byelorussian, this ambivalent personification is possible.

stanza 5, line 1. 'on Solstice-day.' Literally 'On the feast of Kupała'. Presumably here it is the old pagan festival of the summer solstice (June 21st) that is meant, rather than Midsummer Day (June 24th) the feast of St John the Baptist, which is intended here, although the latter interpretation would be the more normal one.

stanza 7. 'Kryvian' – of or pertaining to the *Kryvičy*, a tribe originally inhabiting the Smalensk area, but whose name has been extended to become a synonym for the whole Byelorussian nation. Jan Čačot, for example (see preface), spoke of his poems as being in the Slavonic-Kryvian language (*w mowie Sławiano-krewickiéj* as he has it in his Polonized spelling). Symbolically, and in poetry, the name of *Kryvičy*, becomes one to conjure with – having the same overtones, for example, as the expression 'enfants de la patrie' in the *Marseillaise*.

p. 57: *Come forth . . .*
stanza 2, line 1. 'awns' are the small airborne particles set free during the process of preparing flax for its manufacture into linen. A family circle comprising several girls and women can, in an evening's work set up a considerable cloud of flying awns – so much so, indeed, that October, the month in which the women begin to process the flax-crop of the previous summer, is called in the Byelorussian calendar *Kastryčnik* – the month of awns.

stanza 4. 'From the North', i.e. from Russia. Although much of Russia lies in the same latitudes, or even to the south of Byelorussia, Kupała here seems to visualize the might of Russia as being concentrated at the then capital, St Petersburg. (But there may also be an echo of Jeremiah, 1: 13–14.) From the West . . . from Poland.

p. 58: *My song*
This poem shows a strong influence, in style, from the poetry of the Polish Impressionists, notably Przybyszewski.

stanza 11. Čyrvoncy. The Russian Červonets (Čyrvonec in Byelorussian) was a gold coin (later replaced by a paper note) equal to 10 rubles 'Guinea' or 'sovereign' would have the same kind of flavour in English.

p. 59 ff: *Young Biełaruś*
stanzas 7 and 8. 'Kasa' again. Here the text presents a crux. The new laws are to be written with *piorami z kos* – with pens made from 'kosy'. Are they pens of sunlight, or are they pens of scythes? (Clearly, they are not pens of tresses!) Kupała's preoccupation with the sun-symbol could well suggest the former; on the other hand, the use of the reaper symbolism (in poems such as *To the reapers*, and, indeed, the contrast with *stanza 7* of this very poem, might well suggest the 'scythe' motif. It is probable that Kupała did not intend the ambiguity to be resolved – hence I have ventured to combine both motifs into the compound 'sun-scythes' – an image well in tune with the atmosphere of this poem.

p. 63: *Stand back, move aside!*
The title (and refrain) *Asadzi nazad!* corresponds to the Russian *Osadii nazad!*, the formula used by the Tsarist police for 'moving on' or 'moving along' a potential trouble-maker.

stanza 11. 'Deputy', i.e. to the Duma, the embryonic parliament established in St Petersburg after the 1905 risings (see introduction).

p. 64: *The peasant*
stanza 3. Złoty. Although the Russian *zolotoi* (in Byelorussian, złoty) was originally a gold coin, the word was used colloquially in nineteenth-century Byelorussian as the equivalent of 20 kopeks, so that 'florin' would have the correct flavour in English, or a 'quarter' in the USA.

p. 65: *O spring . . .*
This translation was first published in *Manifold*, No. 6, 1963. The poem itself has been set to music and is a popular Byelorussian song.

p. 67. Like the other great narrative of Kołas, *Symon the Musician*, *The New Land* was written (and published seriatim) over the course of a number of years, the latter portions differing considerably in style and complexity from the beginning. The first eight chapters of *The New Land* were composed while Kołas was in prison for Nationalist activities in 1908 – hence the keynote of exiled longing in the opening sections. It may be noted that *The New Land* is largely autobiographical in content.

part I, paragraph 5. 'on fence-post propped to dry, a pitcher'. A typical Byelorussian phenomenon. Earthenware pots, jugs and similar vessels after scouring were inverted over the 'head' of a fence-post to dry and sweeten. (The fence being of the post-and-arras-rail type.)

'a yeoman-peasant maiden'. The yeoman-peasants (*šlachcicy-zascianko vcy*), literally, noble-peasants were the descendants of those peasants in the earlier days of feudalism, who, living on crown lands, held in fee simple directly from the ruler, being free of all feudal service save military service in time of war. Following the emancipation act of 1861, there remained no legal difference in status between yeomen-peasants and the ordinary variety (the former serfs) – nevertheless, the yeoman-peasant villages tended to hold themselves aloof from the bulk of the population, to whom their often-pathetic attempts to live according to a style which they could no longer afford were a regular source of humour.

The Catholic Chapel. kaściol (from Polish *kościół*) when used in Byelorussian means specifically a Roman Catholic church (the normal Byelorussian word for church, which would be used regularly for an Orthodox church or generally a church of unspecified denomination, being *cerkva*) although in Polish *kościół* does not have any specifically denominational implication and may be used (in combination with a suitable adjective) to denote a church of a non-Catholic denomination (e.g. *kościół Anglikański* – Church of England). The yeoman-peasants, in fact, were not exclusively Catholic – nevertheless, there was a somewhat higher proportion of Catholics among them than among the population as a whole. Here, by using *kaściol*, Kołas adds to the overall impression that the girl is trying to ape the manners and airs of a Polish gentlewoman (with umbrella and sweeping train of skirts). Like the 'epic' similes of Homer and Virgil, this picture has only a vague relevance to the subject to which it alludes (the house), and is intended to be enjoyed as ornament for its own sake.

part II. The culinary descriptions in this section will be clarified if it is remembered that Byelorussian 'pancakes' are baked in the oven, not fried in a pan. (The resultant confection has a certain affinity with Yorkshire pudding, although still retaining the basic pancake taste and texture.)

kvass (occasionally spelt in English *quas*, as per Arthur Bryant *The Years of Endurance*, Ch. 12) is a kind of small beer fermented from bread-rusks soaked in water. It can be (and is) used as a souring/pickling agent in a manner similar to weak solution of vinegar.

Aleś – diminutive from Aleksandar.

Antoś – diminutive from Anton.

Ŭladzik – diminutive from Ŭladzimier (Vladimir).

Juzik – diminutive from Jazep (Joseph).

p. 72: *Greeting to thee*

The epigraph. Afanasii Afanasievič Fet, 1820–92, a Russian lyric poet, is often catalogued under the name of Stenshin (the name of his natural father) which he adopted by law in 1876. For a discussion of Fet's work, and certain translations (not, alas, including the poem quoted here) see: Oliver Elton: *Sheaf of Papers*, 1922, pp. 114–19.

The passage quoted here is from Fet's lyric commencing *My s toboi ne prosim čuda* (see A. A. Fet: *Polnoe Sobranie Stikhotvorenii*, St Petersburg, 1901, Vol. II, Appendix, p. 536). It is noteworthy that in Bahdanovič's own personal copy of Vianok (his one published collection of poems) in which this work first appeared, that stanza 2 and the epigraph are crossed out.

p. 73: *In winter*

This translation was first published in *The Muse*, Vol. 8, No. 2, 1964.

p. 73: *Romance*

This translation was first published in Vera Rich, *Portents and Images*, London, 1963.

The epigraph raises some interesting problems. It is taken from an early poem of Sully Prudhomme (from *Stances et Poëmes*, Paris, 1865, p. 32) and repays reprinting here in full:

L'IDÉAL (a Paul Sédille)
La lune est grande, le ciel clair
Et plein d'astres, la terre est blême,
Et l'âme du monde est dans l'air,
Je rêve à l'étoile suprême.

A celle qu'on n'aperçoit pas,
Mais dont la lumière voyage
Et dont venir jusqu'ici bas
Enchanter les yeux d'un autre âge.

Quand luira cette étoile un jour,
La plus belle et la plus lointaine,
Dites-lui qu'elle eut mon amour,
O derniers de la race humaine!

It is clear from the entire poem that 'elle' refers to 'cette étoile' and not to the poet's beloved, although Bahdanovič seems to take it to refer to the latter. In my article: 'Maksim Bahdahovič in Byelorussian Literature', *Journal of Byelorussian Studies* (*JBS*), Vol. 1, No. 1, 1965, it was tentatively suggested, on the basis of somewhat different evidence, that Bahdanovič may have drawn some of his foreign-language epigraphs, not from the cited works themselves, but from some 'handbook of famous sayings', since most of the quotations used as epigraphs seem to be of the rather 'obvious' type, found in calendars, birthday books, and the like. The fact that this passage from Sully Prudhomme, taken out of context, is given a change of interpretation by Bahdanovič does not necessarily imply that he did not know the original in its entirety (it is not uncommon to find, when comparing an isolated 'quote' with its original context, that the sense has been somewhat strained in transition from its integral place in the original text to its solitary state as epigraph), however, it should be borne in mind that this poem appears in *Stances et Poëmes*, a volume unlikely to be given wide circulation within the Tsarist empire, since on pp. 136–41 of this same collection we find the two poems *Choeur Polonais* and *Le Gue* written in honour of the Polish-Byelorussian rising of 1863 (see below, p. 198, note on Kalinoŭski).

stanza 1, line 4. Byelorussian, having the usual Slavonic verbal structure, with 'aspects' predominating over 'tenses', has no true pluperfect – the past-perfective aspect doing duty for both perfect and pluperfect. It is grammatically impossible, therefore, in English, to keep the identical repetition of the verb in this stanza.

stanza 2. This stanza is cancelled in Bahdanovič's personal copy of *Vianok* (see note to *Greeting to thee*).

p. 74: *The Chronicler*
This poem, and that which follows, are from the cycle *Staraja Biełaruś*. Other titles in this cycle include *The Scribe* (*Pierapisčyk*), *The Book* (*Kniha*) – actually a psalter – *Hopelessness* (*Bieznadziejnašć*), dealing with Skaryna, the first Byelorussian printer (see the relevant notes on pp. 195, 199), and *Quiet Evening* (*Cichi viečar*) which describes the practice of folk-medicine, in order to free a girl from the pangs of hopeless love. This translation is discussed in *Maksim Bahdanovic in Byelorussian Literature*, q.v.

line 6. 'Mahileŭ' (Russian: Mogilev) is a Byelorussian city on the river Dniapro. First mentioned in history as a fortress in 1267 and as a town in 1526, Mahileŭ contains four churches which have survived from the sixteenth and seventeenth centuries. Acquired by the Russian Empire under the First Partition of Poland, in 1772, Mahileŭ lapsed into relative insignificance, although still remaining the administrative seat of the *gubernia* (province). Its old importance was only restored with the coming of the railway in 1904.

p. 75: *The weaver-women of Sluck*
This translation is quoted in full in *JBS*, loc. cit. The famous Słuck girdles, elaborately woven, with gold and silver thread worked into the brocade-type design, were made at the factory of the Radziwiłł princes in Słuck. This factory was closed in 1844, due to the decline in popularity (both on account of Russian pressure, and the influence of Western fashion) of the old Polish noble dress of which these girdles formed an important part. Bahdanovič, writing his poem more than sixty years after the closing of the factory, has, in fact made some errors of fact; the 'Persian' design, mentioned here was not, in fact, produced at Słuck, but was the speciality of the other Radziwiłł factory, some miles away, at Niasviž (see *Encyklopedia Staropolska*, Warsaw, 1958, p. 328). Further, Bahdanovič seems to envisage the looms as being operated by women only, whereas Mickiewicz (in whose time the factories were still operating) describes the looms as being worked each by a man and a girl:

> Jak paca mistrzów w Słucku lity pas wyrabia,
> Dziewica siedząc w dole krośny ujedwabia,
> I tło ręka wygładza, tymczasem tkacz z góry
> Zrzuca jej nitki srebr, złota i purpury
> Tworząc barwi i kwiatky: tak dziś ziemię całą
> Wiatr tumanami osnuł, a słonce dzierzgało.
> (Pan Tadeusz, Bk. 6, 576–80)

(Just as in Słuck two artists weave a massive girdle:
Sitting below, the girl plies the loom's silken burden,
Smoothing the ground-work, while the weaver from above her
To her throws down the threads, gold, silver, purple colour,
Creating tints and flowers: so today the wind was weaving
The earth with wisps of fog that the sun embroidered, gleaming.)

Here, *tkacz* (weaver) is clearly masculine – the feminine would be *tkaczka* – also the fact that *mistrzów* is masculine genitive plural would indicate that one at least of the pair was masculine. While it would be normally invidious to quote a literary work in language to contradict information implied in a work in another language (particularly in so fraught a context as that of Eastern Europe), nevertheless, it does seem that Mickiewicz was more likely to have been correct in this case, on historical grounds alone.

line 20. During the *Naša Niva* period, the cornflower was adopted as the national flower of Byelorussia. This motif is particularly strong in Bahdanovič, and occurs in several other works notably in his prose-poem *The Apocrypha* (see *Manifold* 27, 1968), in which it is equated with the 'songs' which give meaning and significance to the wearisome lives of the people, and hence, by implication, to all that poetry and song meant to the national resurgence inspired by *Naša Niva.*

p. 75: *Snowstorm*
This translation is quoted in full in *JBS*, loc. cit.

p. 76: *My native country*
stanza 5. It does not seem possible, at this date, to identify the particular song Bahdanovič had in mind. It is noteworthy, however, that in Byelorussian folklore (and in Slavonic folklore generally) widow's sons are traditionally lucky and make good against fearful odds. The unhappy fate, therefore, of this 'widow's son' comes as a kind of reversal of the natural order of things, which intensifies the atmosphere of the poem considerably. A somewhat similar 'inversion' of a folklore motif occurs at the end of Janka Kupała's play *Paŭlinka.* In the latter, the heroine Paŭlinka loves Jakim, but is betrothed by her parents to Adolf. After a series of misunderstandings, the parents are brought to believe that Adolf's designs on their daughter are not, after all, honourable – and the discomfited suitor is dismissed. 'Aha' think the audience, 'the problems are over, and now for Jakim and the happy ending!' But no – a neighbour enters with the news: Jakim has been arrested for nationalist activities! Paŭlinka shrieks and faints, and the final curtain falls on a scene of confusion. On the stage, coming as it does after a 'traditional' plot of parent-crossed lovers, the effect is horrifying – as if, say, the Sleeping Beauty failed to waken or the glass slipper fitted an Ugly Sister! This 'inversion' concept, fully developed in Paŭlinka is only implicit in Bahdanovič's poem, but the basic intent is the same – the subconscious suggestion that the regime of oppression is not only harsh and cruel, but is contrary to the natural order of the world.

p. 77: *To a singer*
This translation is quoted in full in *JBS*, loc. cit.

p. 77: *Sonnet*
The epigraph is from N. Boileau, *L'Art Poetique, chant II, line 94.*

The 'legend' of the germinating wheat is refuted in John Percival: *The Wheat Plant*, 1921, pp. 32–4. This does not, of course, invalidate the poetic 'truth' of the concept, any more than, say modern genetic theory invalidates the debate of Apollo and the Furies in *The Eumenides*.

p. 79: *Emigrants' song*
This translation is quoted in full in *JBS*, loc. cit.
line 20. Libava, now Lepaya (Latvia), the 'outport' for Byelorussia.

p. 79: *When Basil died . . .*
The metre of this poem is somewhat strange – each line seems to scan as a unit, but in little relationship to the adjacent lines. Either Bahdanovič has been influenced here by Polish syllabic metres, or the broken jerky effect is intended to indicate the disjointed thoughts of the dying man. The alternation of rhymed and unrhymed couplets, adding greatly to the poignancy of this poem's 'atmosphere' inclines me to think that the latter is the correct explanation.

p. 80: *Lavonicha*
The jest of this poem is that the lady's given name is *not* Lavonicha! *Lavonicha* means simply 'wife of Lavon'; her own name, Hanna or Viera or whatever it may be is never mentioned. The nearest effect in British literature would have been if Dylan Thomas had put into some character's mouth a love-song to 'Mrs Dai Jones' – it being assumed at the same time that Dai Jones himself was very much alive.

stanza 3. 'gossips' in the etymological sense of Old English *godsibb*. The Slavonic relationship expressed by *kum* (fem. *kuma*) includes several relationships by baptism: here, Lavonicha will be *kuma* ('gossip') to (a) the parents of her god-children; (b) the godfathers of her god-children, and by extension to the wives of the godfathers of her god-children; (c) the godparents of her own children (supposing, of course, that she and 'no-good' Lavon have been blessed with issue!); (d) by extension, all those persons to whom 'no-good' Lavon is *kum*. Even allowing that group (d) will be small and group (c) possibly non-existent, for so popular a lady as Lavonicha, 'half the village' may well be no exaggeration!

p. 81: The 'cycle', *The Madonnas*, consists of two poems, the first of which, *In the Village*, is given here in full. This translation is quoted, *in extenso*, in *JBS*, loc. cit. The epigraph is from Pushkin's *Scenes from the times of knighthood* (*Stseny iz rhytsarskikh vremen*), see *Polnoe sobranie sochinenii A. S. Pushkina*, Moscow–Leningrad, 1949, Vol. 5, p. 482. To date, no English translation of *Scenes from the times of knighthood* exists.

p. 83: *I love . . .*
This poem has been set to music, to a traditional tune, and has become a most popular Byelorussian song, even being sung by boys' and male-voice choirs (in whose mouths the feminine verbal endings of the past-perfective in the first and last stanzas can sound a little incongruous).

THE YEARS OF ADJUSTMENT

1917–1939

As we have said, *Naša Niva* itself failed to survive the outbreak of the First World War; the *Naša Niva* movement, however, continued for a time, unchecked by the increasing difficulty of war conditions. Indeed, in some sense, the *Naša Niva* movement never came to an end; only gradually, as national resurgence was followed by the Revolutionary Wars, and the Revolutionary Wars by the Peace of Riga and partition was there a gradual change and adaptation, the years of turmoil producing in the writers a greater deepening of intensity, a richness and exuberance of language, a growing certainty of touch as, faced by conflict and confusion on all sides, the poets explored deeper and deeper into the inner world of their art.

The literary history of Byelorussian in the 1920s has yet to be written, being clouded and confused by the era that followed, when Stalin's purges plucked from the literary scene of Byelorussia not only many fine writers themselves, but also the whole body of their so-far-published work. Only in the last decade or so editions of poets like Pušča or Dudar begin to restore this loss, often from personal memories of texts once feared gone for ever. Yet enough of this exciting era of poetry remains for us to enjoy its exuberant life-force, its prosodic variety, its vigorous compounding of adjectives, the biting wit of Krapiva (the 'nettle') at the expense of the new bureaucracy, the *pietas telluris* of Kołas, ever-greater in impact as his genius comes to its fullest flowering. And, with the passing of the old, as the traditional village gives way to the mechanized commune, Kupała, witnessing the sweeping away of the strip tillage, the 'dumb fields and the hay-filled meadows', the 'ploughland village', the 'rustic tradition, plain and grand' which were the roots and heart of *Naša Niva*, he yet wishes for his people 'new fate' and 'new glory', and in the rhythms of folksong praises now, not the 'maiden at the raw flax spinning', but her successor, the young girl-pilot, who, he foresees, will 'fly to the sun on a bird's plumage soaring'.

Jakub Kołas

TO WORK

Brothers! A mighty road before us
Awaits us and our native land!
Harvest has come, much toiling for us –
Sow learning's seed on every hand.

Bear forth the light – in darkness dreaming
Lies this our nook, our country dear.
Let our land rise anew, let gleaming
Light shine forth on our people here.

Let this conflict reach fair cessation,
No tsarist lash nor lord's hired brute,
Lord of its home, the sovereign nation
Bring order out of all dispute.

SYMON THE MUSICIAN

INTRODUCTION TO BOOK III

O my land, my land so lovely,
Well-loved corner of my race!
What in God's world is more beloved
Than these banks, with brightness graced,
Where the rivers glitter silver,
Where the woods hum murmuring song,
Where buckwheat breathes honey, quivering
Cornfields murmur on and on;
Than the monuments unending
Of the marshes, of thy pools,
Where wide space its thoughts is blending
Under freshets gushing cool,
Where the osiers weep in autumn,
Where in spring bright meadows blow,
Where birch-trees in a path long-trodden
Like a lovely highway grow?

Ah, you gravemounds, old past counting,
Witness of ages deaf and still,
Who has raised you here, abounding?
By what hand and by whose will,

As guardians of old-time causes,
Were ye scattered on the plain?
What the centuries have taught ye,
You will not reveal again!
In uneven paths you sally
Forth where distances invite,
On towards the wondrous Vialla,
And where Dźvina shimmers bright.

My native land! In earth's abundance
Where another to be found,
Where beside such waste and rubbish
Beauty rises to confound?
Where, among poverty, there blossom
Wondrous riches, bright and clear,
Where are human fate and fortune
Met with laughter as but here?

Janka Kupała

HERITAGE

From forebears' ages, long since gone,
A heritage has come to me,
Among strange folk, among my own,
Me it caresses, motherly.

Of it to me dream-fables sing
Of first thaw-patches, vernally,
The woods' September murmuring,
An oak-tree lone, half burned away.

Memories of it, like storks aclack
Upon the line have woken me,
Of a mossed fence, old, gone to wrack,
Fallen near the village, brokenly;

The dreary bleat of lambs that pours
Out in the pasture, endlessly,
The caw of the assembled crows,
On the graves in the cemetery.

And through black night and through white day
I keep, my watch unceasingly,
Lest this my treasure goes astray,
Lest by drones it should eaten be.

I bear it in my living soul
Like torch-flame ever bright for me,
That through deaf darkness to my goal,
Midst vandals it may lighten me.

With it lives my thought-family.
Bringing dreams of sincerity . . .
And its name, all-in-all must be
My native land, my heritage.

Jakub Kołas

RESONANCE

Whether scythes chime in the time of the harvest,
    Or a young girl sings a song,
Or the sky flashes with lightning fires darting,
    Or the wind blows, raging-strong.

Or thunder, loud-roaring, rolls forth in cloud-masses,
    Or thunderbolt rumbles o'er woods,
All find an echo in broad free expanses,
    All touches their strings in accord.

And you, when you meet with the grieving of someone,
    Or you hear weeping and tears,
Or somewhere injustice holds fiercest dominion,
    You will re-echo it clear.

And you feel joy, and your hopes will fly, soaring,
    That good news yet will befall,
Let then your strings smile, let their notes, louder-pouring,
    In songs, filled with happiness, call!

From *THE NEW LAND*

XVI

EVENINGS (extract)

Native pictures, scenes that call me,
How dear you are, how you enthrall me,
How often, in well-loved succession
You rise before me in procession!
And so attractively come smiling,
With living porphyry beguiling
Across the woods, with sheaves gold-gleaming
Of arrow-rays on ploughland streaming,
And with diamantine dewdrops
When, its burning ray far-strewing,
Through the foliage net-window,
Quietly on it the sun glints so,
And caresses it and loves it,
Spreading rainbows bright above it.

I see level lands, far over
Nioman water, and their clothing,
Oats in strips and rye in bands there,
That like sea of gold expands there,
Buckwheat tablecloths whitely gleaming,
And two wings of forest, seeming
Like moustaches, the dark gulley
Pierced with water, harsh and stubborn,
Terraced junipers grisaille, where
White moss and poor lichen frailly
Spread above the yellow dunes there
Where the timid hares find refuge.
I hear the multi-chorused singing
Of woods and meadows with scythes ringing,
In harmonious haymaking.
I hear tempest thunders shaking,
The dull noise of abundant rain,
The chiming song of fields of grain,
And, by a graveside, quiet weeping.
Long now that voice is silence keeping,
Long now these all have gone for ever,
With only memory as their cover.

Yet still invisible threads viewless
Strongly-strongly bind me to you,
Pictures of my dear country, ever!
Ah, pathways, you are all grown over,
That once to my dear nook were leading,
Whence the yellow sands are keening,
Under the summer sun the blinding
Heatwave and, the sad gilding shining
Over the silver-flooded Nioman,
So near the heart, so much one's own there.
Not with wormwood are you beset so,
Not with aloes, not with nettles,
Not with rushes, nor with weeds grown –
With Byelorussian grief and need grown.
But, while heart beats with life's pulsation,
It knows no reconciliation,
With violence or woe that plunders
And tramples down our native country.

Dear land of torments sempiternal,
May lips and hands be cursed eternal,
Hands that have forged thy chains, exulting,
Lips that spat in thy face, insulting.

Let fire and heat with anguish flaming,
Burn out for age this insult shaming
That from past years holds lordship over
Those who their native treasure honour,
And who with heart and soul are straining
To be their own true self remaining.
Live on, my land, let hopeful longing
Burn in thy heart forever stronger,
If not we, our sons' generation,
Shall see thee stand, entire, a nation.

XXX

THE DEATH OF MICHAŁ

The end . . . A word so simple-seeming,
Yet ever new and multi-meaninged!
How often, 'neath the cross of torture,
In the soul's pangs, we raise imploring
Hands and eyes filled with strange burning,
For liberation's instant yearning!
A happy instant – gone are fetters.
The end – and some closed circle shatters
Into non-being, goes for ever
Yielding its place unto another,
Time, and the faith in that end fated
Destroy decay's sepulchral sating.

The end . . . how much of meditation,
And how much sad deliberation
Lies in this word, simple and doomful,
In divers forms and aspects looming,
When, a last boundary, is seen to
Stand the end, firmset between you
And all that you know dearest, sweetest,
That fired your spirit and set beating
The heart with power uncanny, magic,
Like a hymn on the lips of rapids,
That, in the turbulent water's voices,
Where the sun with itself rejoices,
Murmurs full-vigoured, murmurs freely,
Bell-like chiming, white-foam-seething.

And you too, my dear narration,
Mirror of life and meditation,
A simple fate, traced firm for ever,
Where echoes of truth and freedom quiver
Eternal, you see twilight yonder

Already, the lute's timid chiming
Grows quiet, your day's silent declining
Draws near, your last steps now you wander.
And I am grieved: I lived together
With you, with one thought, one soul ever,
I carried you in a mother's fashion,
Who carries the child's unclear impression.
And you, it seems, have not been born in
A happy time to this world's storming,
For still the spring is far far distant,
Behind a wall well-builded hidden,
Captive in a dread prison pining,
While over us the siege of night-time
Hangs in a darkness thick, oppressing,
And with a heavy heel is pressing,
Like an attack (and none can fight it)
On all that gave to life new brightness.
And while the night was passing slowly,
And, all-in-all, life rotted wholly,
And then the road, the road before us,
Parting with homeland, fears hang o'er us,
And then the wandering, forced upon us,
And the weary struggle onwards
For interest of life still yearning,
And then, the foeman's heel returning.

How often lived we, my narration,
Through fleeting hour of separation
From native land, an hour of grieving,
Joy's instant, inspiration giving!
The soul burned then with holy fire,
With concord, harmony suspired,
Blending mysterious music secret,
And then was heard the grain-ears' speaking,
In native furrows, distant ringing,
And bright-eyed reaping-maidens' singing,
The sight of hills, steep-sided clinging,
Of groves and shaggy-headed pine-trees,
All so gentle, all so kindly,
Like a good-hearted old grandmother,
They warmed the heart and drew it thither,
Before the eyes they stood, as living,
The speaking strings were all aquiver,
They played in harmony united,
Upon unseen tablets writing
Three words that never flowered to life;
Runes of the ages they inscribed . . .

And so the farewell hour is coming,
And the last step of your long roaming!
....
Alone Michał kept warm the striving,
The cause to due completion driving,
But, unbeknownst and all unnoticed,
Ill-luck prepared, its nets were woven
To throw upon Michał, to snare him,
Heeding naught and for naught caring,
Like an enchantment maleficient,
Then, by chance, Michał grew suspicious:
Saw thick smears of red blood coming!
'Eh, brother, here's a sorry omen!
The end for Michał and no error!'
He thought it a strange kind of terror.
Even the heart was failing in him.
What was it, truly, had come on him?
Was this death truly, come untimely?
No, no! Too soon to think of dying!
Michał was dread-struck. Melancholy
And the dark scroll of illness wholly
Wraps him round in all his being.
He feels alone in this world, seeing
Hostile fates and their power, staring
Into his eyes, unlovely glaring,
And rising in dread battlementing,
'Twixt life and him, Michał, preventing.
Now, for the first time, he felt the anguish
Of that dread moment, past withstanding,
That lies for all in ambush waiting;
Death is an evil past escaping.
'And must I die, and shall this body
Rot in the earth, a scar unlovely
Upon the earth's fair body laid?'
And there pressed terrifying shades
Upon the heart, upon the spirit.
And then, as clear as in a mirror,
He saw the seals of death before him,
And all its phantoms, clearly forming;
He felt he was a dust-mote only,
And human life a single moment.
....
For some time now, since winter's coming,
In the strong grip of illness struggled
Michał, an illness evil, heavy,
Undesired and unexpected.
Worse still: this sickness had been coming

For a long time, not just since summer,
And from this fact its might was growing,
That it came stealthily, unnoticed,
For several years it came on, creeping,
And in the grog-shops found good feeding,
Till it had spread its fill, then mighty
It struck Michał down swiftly smiting.
At first Michał tried to resist it,
Would not surrender to this sickness,
Then to a course of cures he hurried,
(Most from a home apothecary!)
He drank tisanes and herbal potions;
They did no good to his condition.
And, far too late for such a case,
They took to the doctors poor Michaś.
....
Michał struggles in fear, and utters
A cry, the curtain slightly flutters,
His eyes he opens with an effort –
Against his hand a hand is pressing,
And someone's eyes, all filled with pain there,
To his own blurring eyes seem chained there.
No strength is left to struggle longer,
With deep regret, with trembling horror,
He calls to those around to save him,
Brother, children, wife to aid him.
But heaven waits, deafly, severely,
Will not incline an ear to hear you,
No matter how you beg and plead,
– Tear your breast, pluck the heart from in it,
You will not melt its harshness, win it,
No matter how you intercede –.
It is far off; dumb and unmoving,
Silent it is, and empty proving.
'Michaś, my dearest, do you know me?'
He lifts his eyes, painfully, slowly;
He sees his wife there. 'Hanna . . . Mother . . .
Give me your help now! . . . O my brother!
Help me! Help me, my children dearest!'
And, bitter as gall or wormwood, tears are
There, from the eyes deep-sunken flowing . . .
Michał sighs – his voice lower, lower . . .
'Quick, the blest candle! Quick, he's going!'
Face marked with lines that anguish wreaked there;
His hands upon his breast fell weakly,
And Michał once more shuddered, shaking,
And once more his eyes fluttered open,

It seems there's something must be spoken,
Deeply he sighs, his breath is failing,
Then suddenly, he sees it plainly:
'Antoś! . . . I'm dying . . . Brother dearest! . . .
I've burned out . . . I am disappearing . . .
You are in charge . . . the only one . . .
My brother best . . . like my own son.
God did not grant that I know freedom,
In my own furrow cast the seed in . . .
The land . . . the land . . . there, brother . . . forward,
Build on it . . . give it proper order . . .
Live a new way . . . secure . . . and steady . . .
Don't leave them! Ah-ah – I . . . am . . . ready! . . .'
No living words, the heart-beat vanished,
Antoś the cooling hand in anguish
Kisses with bitter sobbing, groaning,
Falling upon the body, moaning.

In the field, in the field,
By the path drooping,
There leans a cross,
O'er a grave stooping.

The pathways run far,
To the wide world tending,
They lead back home,
To this dear grave wending . . .

O, you pathways of human kind, you
Narrow tracks, you pathways winding!
You stumble on your way unsurely,
Wandering as if dense woods hung o'er you,
The highway with broad stream allures you,
The rosy-blue horizon draws you,
Where sunlight pleasantly is gleaming,
Where thought upon its loom is weaving,
Thus to weave a new world of life,
To give the heart peace, rest from strife,
And banish its deep cares forever! . . .
O spacious highway, when, O when,
Will you bloom in the world of men,
Drawing our every road together.

Janka Kupałà

TO THE EAGLETS

I

Ah, rise up on wingspread soaring,
Eaglets, strongly, fiercely, boldly,
On the grave of days of yore, and
Over slumbers in tomb folded.

In the rumbled roar of thunder,
With the blast of flashing lightning,
Bring forth, for new years unnumbered
A so-far-unheard-of brightness.

Scythes and sickles for your grasping,
Broadswords forged from steel, bestowing
Whirlwinds gave to you, storms blasting,
That howled here with raging blowing.

The shadow of past days accurséd,
Where the lash and whip once revelled,
Eaglets, sweep away, disperse it,
With new vigour, with new fable.

And the hour has struck already
For the mighty consummation;
Go forth, from ruts foul and muddy
To the Byelorussian nation.

In the magic of a round-dance,
In a freedom all unbounded,
Without chains, in free space twirling,
See, our fate already whirling.

II

To you the Hammer and the Sickle
    Fate gave to warn, to show you,
That each of you, a giant mickle,
    Would not droop shoulders lowly.

That your new-won liberation
    You know and honour rightly,
And in ponderous consummation
    Your waves rise, dread and mighty.

May re-echo and may thunder,
Like whirlwind eternal,
That softly-bedded will not slumber
Free-will's fireflower vernal.

* * *

An ancestral bequest befell you,
– Wooden plough and harrow,
That in due time, after the deluge,
You come forth to the furrow.

That you might plough this your own ploughland,
Broadly, deeply, surely,
That in good fortune you may sow land,
Like a clear gaze, purely.

That this seed then may sprout and raise its
Shoots in joyful shining,
Together with your youth, in praises
Falconlike entwining.

* * *

Your grandsires left you a bequest, their
Tempered scythes bestowing,
That in the sun's wake you might quest and
Bear them to the mowing.

That you might hew down all the foison
Of weeds and rank grasses
Pouring forth venom that with poison's
Fire through the life-blood courses.

That your scythes may ring out o'er a
Land wrapped deep in slumber,
So that from night to dew of morning
Their chime be aye remembered.

* * *

To you at birth there was bequeathed a
Treasury of singing,
To be for you a thing of sweetness
In life's dawn of springtime.

That you might sing, grow silent never
In joy, in grief's emotion,
Sing, like a wave resounding ever
In a stormy ocean.

That the unceasing notes flow chiming
    From field unto field speeding,
That those who still in chains are pining
    It may awake to freedom.

Kandrat Krapiva

THE NETTLE

In Art's noble kitchen garden,
Vain and worthless weed I lie,
Of what kind? Fit but for laughter!
I am the stinging nettle – I.

Here beneath the fence I flourish,
No great time have grown as yet,
But a host of knaves I've worried,
Arms and legs with stings beset.

Who comes here after cucumbers,
Let that man my blisters wear –
Pluck me, friend, but well remember –
Careful, if your hands are bare!

Who shall meet with me, then let him
Touch me once or twice and try!
Then he'll know, and not forget me;
I am the stinging nettle – I!

GRANDPA AND GRANDMA

(*A fable*)

Grandpa to the market rode,
    Grandma with him in the waggon,
Horse looks useless for the load
    With but feeble effort dragging.

Two years and no more he's grown,
    So the neighbours all are saying,
Grandma all of nineteen stone
    And no less than that is weighing.

In the mud or up the hill,
    Horse with all its might is dragging,
Grandma's helping with a will,
    Though still sitting in the waggon.

What's this, then, a two-year old!
    And she starts her feet a-tapping,
On the footboard kicking bold,
    Might and main she banging, rapping.

'Stop it, and come down, you fool!'
    Grandpa says to Grandma, scoffing,
'You help the horse, but by that rule
    Illnesses are helped by coughing!'

'Ah, you ancient dunderhead!'
    Grandma says, at Grandpa scolding,
'Stop there till you burn,' she said,
    'Little do I need!' she told him.

But at last she did alight,
    By the roadside sat down squarely,
Like a field the horse took flight,
    Just as fast as legs could bear him.

Often in some jobs you see
    'Grandmas' like this if you seek them,
They work at something, certainly,
    But the enterprise goes weakly.

And things will not move this way.
    We must tell them, 'Work is flagging;
Would it not be lighter, say,
    Without you? Come quit the waggon!'

THE RAM WITH A DIPLOMA

(*A fable*)

In a village, (no matter where),
A Ram among the crowd lived there.
In general, learned rams are met with only rarely;
But this was a fool beyond comparing –
His own yard-gate he'd never learned;
His head must have been weak; however,
His forehead back to front was turned.
And such a forehead I had never met, no never.
Since there, it chanced, no other ram did dwell, so
Our friend a duel could fight,
He used to charge against the wall, outright.

Another's soul would sure have taken flight,
But not this fellow
So foolish, they were able
To give him once the name of 'scholar' for a jape;
So he would not escape,
About his neck they hung a label:
'Look! Your diploma! Here you are!'
The Ram about diplomas knew not 'ma-ah' nor 'ba-ah!',
But before the Cat he started prinking:
'Well, Sister Puss, what are you thinking?
Have I no reason to go proudly?
I've a diploma, my brain gained it!
Don't think yourself my equal, lady!
Far better to be quiet about it!'
But said the Cat, replying:
'If you were wiser, only slightly,
Your sheep-like brain would be some good at thinking,
And you would see there is no cause for prinking!
For this diploma you have gained
With forehead, not with brain!'

Other rams say not 'ma-ah' nor 'ba-ah'
But love their names to echo far!

THE OWL, THE ASS AND THE SUN

(*A fable*)

The White Owl flew forth in the night,
Death to the bird-folk she was bringing,
She sang them dirges in her flight,
And as she plucked them, she bewailed them with her singing.
And thus she did not see day had already come,
And the ray of the bright Sun
Blinded her eyes at last from seeing.
The Owl longs to be fleeing,
But strength for flight she cannot muster,
No hollow tree at hand where she might go.
The Owl weeps in her woe –
Who is there to assist her?
But kind fate sent her in this pass
A well-known Ass.
And he said: 'Sister, do not weep, but end your
Worries and your concern –

We'll solve this plight of yours together,
And to the Sun we need not make surrender.
My long ears set to face against the Sun I'll turn,
My ears shall shade it over.
And when the dark the wide land covers,
And when this hateful brilliance wanes,
Back to your hollow tree again
You'll fly and hover.'
And our Ass started keenly on his labour;
His grey ears, wide as he was able,
He stretched and spread, all that he could,
Against the Sun he stood.
But, on the left, a ray was peeping,
A beam of light came brightly creeping.
So, to the left he hopped!
Then – on the right – illumination!
So back again he popped!
At last he sees the situation
Is hopeless, jumping to and fro,
But does it touch the Sun – O no!
He doesn't help the Owl one whit!
And blinds his own eyes doing it!
At last the Ass the truth clearly discovers:
An Ass's ears are far too small the Sun to cover.

The truth in these sharp words displayed
I bring, perturbed, to Owls who are of Fascist trade,
And asses – those who lend them aid.

Ŭladzimir Dubouka

O BIEŁARUŚ, MY BRIAR-ROSE CHERISHED . . .

O Biełaruś, my briar-rose cherished,
O leaf of green, O flower of red,
In the wild wind you shall not perish,
Nor choke, by rank weeds overspread.

For I, myself, shall be your petals,
I'll pierce my heart upon the pikes
Of your dear eyes, the hue of metal,
The rays I love, burnished and bright.

Never shall the wild-blowing breezes
Unloose your maiden plaits so fair,
Through the world's striving, you strive ceaseless.
That joy may blossom everywhere.

Foes shall not cause your path to perish,
In hardship is the spirit bred,
O Biełaruś, my briar-rose cherished,
O leaf of green, O flower of red.

Janka Kupała

FOR ALL

For all my people gave me,
All that today is mine,
A corner in my native
Land, bread and salt untyned,

I have repayed my people
With whatsoe'er I might,
From slavery called to freedom,
From darkness called to light.

For the land of my fathers
And all her fallen might,
Among crosses and graveyards
A victory hymn I write.

I warred with the aggressor
For people's happiness,
Oft writing in dejection
In blood from my own breast.

And thus a fate I brought them,
Mine, for the good of all,
And more . . . But what more can you
From a poor songster call?

Aleś Dudar

THE TOWER

The tower sleeps? What is it dreaming?
It rises, gloomy, like a ghost.
A prison here? A belfry seeming?
Who is there that can guess its past?

And grizzled time roams round about it,
Like hours' tramp, like a minute sped . . .
And the long centuries uncounted
Have made of the grey stones a bed.

The years built, without work nor effort,
A nest of legends, tales of yore . . .
. . . .
And now, today, these men in heavy
Boots tramp the drawbridge-plank once more.

They swathed the tower with forms mysterious;
None will untie the ends once more,
Not mighty Scandinavian heroes,
Nor merchants from the Golden Horn.

And to the tower wires now can anchor
Distance so fast the mind must reel . . .
Foresires, could you but understand the
Truth of antennae of chilled steel.

You cannot comprehend, forefathers,
Your tower now has a task renowned,
For from infinity it gathers
Voices into its shining crown.

Janka Kupała

THOU PASSEST, VILLAGE, FROM BRIGHT STORY

Like a dream of unwished dejection,
Thou passest, Village, from bright story,
And thy folk, faithful in subjection,
Casting their fetters in rejection,
Strive to new fate and to new glory.

Thy people, forth to the field going,
With new tools, a new rule of living,
Will communally do their sowing,
Breasts all exploiter's fang unknowing,
One thought, one rule the victory giving.

Thy offspring on pathways Siberian
With beggar's bag no more goes roaming,
Seeking a haven, wanderer weary,
These shards of history's flotsam dreary –
To dust wild days' command will doom them!

The hills of thy dumb gravemounds (under
Lie slumbering slaves and princes' power),
As knife rips sheep, so steel will sunder,
Flame burn away the tumult's thunder,
Where mud lies muddy flowers will flower.

Where hamlet on hamlet once lay drowsing,
Great giants will raise their flag rebelling,
And, rainbows of bright blossom rousing,
The smoke of dips and torches dowsing,
Electric light will flash compelling.

The plaintive notes from thy flutes flowing
Are crushed by tractor-wheels, swift-turning,
Thy sower, erstwhile lonely sowing,
Drying his sweat in sunshine, going
No more beneath his cross in mourning.

Thy waggon-wheels, rotten, decaying,
The car with petrol sends to ashes,
Bareheaded mower, come from haying,
Will break his scythe, harsh, callouse-making,
Will stoop no more to home-field patches.

Thy maiden, at the raw flax spinning,
No more shall blind bright eyes with working;
The iron distaff, toil beginning,
Grants share of wool and silken linen
To its own peasants, its own workers.

Across thy myths and legends hoary,
The radio shall pour forth, drowing,
And, tuned it to will play, star-soaring,
Forgetting wrongs and serfdom's story,
The age-old forest, age-old Nioman.

Wood-goblin and rusałka frighten
No more the sleepy dwellings; deep in
The undertow, woodsprites, benighted,
Perish, from cottage windows brightened,
Cobwebs fall, silver sunlight leaps in.

Above thy temple-spires, high looming
The factory chimney rises lordly,
Thy bells that ring confusedly booming,
That spring of life, the factory-hooter
Will drown with sounding hooting-order.

And each year, bids new custom for us,
All shall, with piety most zealous,
Keep All-Souls of October Glorious,
And every year, in more victorious
Mood, keep the feast of wills rebellious.

Thou passest, Village, from bright story,
Like a dream of unwished dejection,
For thy folk, faithful in subjection.
Casting their fetters in rejection,
Set out for better fate and glory.

ALESIA

The cuckoo called ever,
In the greenwood, incessant,
A mother watched over
Her daughter, Alesia.

The pinewoods were singing,
At morn and eve sighing,
Over cradle of linden
She sang, lullabying.

'Hushabye, 'tis the hour,
When the songbirds all slumber,
Hushabye, dearest flower,
Lullabye, lulla-lulla!

Do not stir, slumber sweetly,
The hour comes soon after,
When you'll stand on your feet,
My own dearest daughter.

You will spin finest linen,
At the loom will weave gaily,
Gaze in your young springtime
At good fortune, daily!'

The cuckoo called ever
In the greenwood, incessant,
And mother dreamed never
What life held for Alesia.

How when full strength had come to
Her mother's dear daughter,
She flew to the sun, on
A bird's plumage soaring.

The maiden flew swiftly,
In her fleet aircraft going,
O'er a smiling land lifted,
Her own land, below her.

And she opened the doors to
The heavenly highway,
And like hawk, down from soaring
Comes the parachute flying.

To the sun in an instant,
And high, higher ever,
In her aeroplane winging
The stormclouds she severed.

Night and day, mother waiting
Vainly grieves at the window,
From the sun flies the maiden
Never back to her spindle.

The cuckoo called ever
In the greenwood, incessant,
But mother dreamed never
What life held for Alesia.

NOTES

(Owing to the accelerated pace of Byelorussian life and cultural background in the 1920s, in this section the poems are arranged in approximate date-order, and not, as heretofore, poet by poet).

p. 97: *To work*
Written in 1917, this poem is contemporary with some of the latest of the poems in the preceding section. It is included here, however, since it belongs more naturally with the writings of the immediately post-revolutionary period.

p. 97: An earlier version of this translation appeared in *Collected Poems* (Venture Press, 1962). *Symon the Musician*, the other great epic of Kołas, was commenced, discontinued and resumed at approximately the same times as *The New Land*. However, whereas in *The New Land* the stylistic development of Kołas shows itself largely in the deeper richness and poetic quality of language in the later sections, *Symon the Musician* reveals a considerable difference of approach; the first two books being naturalistic, whereas the treatment from Book III onwards is increasingly symbolic.

It is noteworthy that this invocation to the land of Biełaruś occurs at the beginning of Book III, one of the traditional points at which an epic poet invokes his Muse (cf. for example, the 'Hail, Holy Light . . .' passage in *Paradise Lost*).

p. 100: Part XVI of *The New Land* was written shortly after the Peace of Riga (1921), by which Byelorussia was partitioned, the Western part being incorporated into the re-established Polish state.

p. 102 ff: *part XXX, paragraph 4*. 'Three words', i.e. 'My native nook' – the opening words of the poem (see p. 67).

paragraph 5. The 'striving' is the effort to purchase 'the new land' – the search for which is the major theme of the epic.

paragraph 5. 'Seals of death'. This may be a reference to Revelations vi–viii, or, more probably, it is an image of an official seal on a legal document (the red colour of the wax being evoked by the thick red colour of the blood, which is the final, and condemning symptom of the illness). If the latter alternative is the poet's intention, then, since such a wax seal would have appeared, in particular, on the deed of purchase of the 'new land', we have a strong example of tragic irony.

paragraph 6. Michaś. Diminutive from Michał.

paragraph 7. 'The blest candle'. A candle, blessed in church on Candlemas day (February 2nd) and kept in the home for such an emergency. In this case, the candle would be placed in the hand of the dying man.

paragraph 8. *In the field* . . . An echo of folksong.

p. 107: *To the eaglets*
'Eagles' or 'falcons' are frequent folksong terms for warrior-heroes.

p. 110: *The nettle*
The poet's pseudonym, *Krapiva*, does, in fact, mean 'nettle'.

p. 110: *Grandma and Grandpa*
A sly dig at the new Soviet bureaucracy.

stanza 2. literally 'grandma weighs seven *puds*'. A *pud* being 16·38 kg, this works out, in round figures at nineteen stone avoirdupois.

p. 111: *The Owl, the Ass and the Sun*
The use of the word 'Fascist' in the 'moral' of this poem (dated 1927) seems at first a little surprising, and makes one suspect later 'retouching' of the poem by the author. Reference, however, to the Soviet press of the period confirms that, already by this date, the word 'Fascist' was used, not only in the strict relevance to contemporary Italian politics, but also, by extension, as a synonym for 'anti-Communist'.

p. 114: *O Biełaruś, my briar-rose cherished . . .*
As has been stated above, the 'national' flower of Byelorussian, in the symbolism of *Naša Niva*, was the cornflower. Although stylized rose-patterns do appear in Byelorussian folk art (though with nothing like so great a frequency as do the several variations of the typical 'cornflower cross' pattern) this choice of symbolism seems to have been made by Duboŭka and Duboŭka alone. It is interesting that when the white-red-white flag of the National Republic of 1918 (which was still in use in the Byelorussian SSR as late as, the Byelorussian Academic Conference of 1926) was finally replaced with the new flag of Soviet Byelorussia (introduced in 1951) the colours chosen for the latter were predominantly red and green (with a white band bearing a traditional 'embroidery' design in red at the hoist). Of this choice of colours, Edgar H. Lehrman writes 'It all seems to agree with the Byelorussian nationalists of the middle 1930s who found expression in the poem of that fine writer Ŭładzimier Duboŭka, entitled, "Oh, Byelorussia, My Sweet-briar". The green is here associated with the green leaf, symbolizing the revival of life in young Byelorussia. The red is linked with the flowering of Byelorussian culture and the attainment of national self-determination.' Apart from the error in date – the poem was written in the mid 1920s and by 1930 Duboŭka had disappeared from the literary scene in one of the first Stalinist purges – there is nothing impossible in Lehrman's supposition that the choice of flag was strongly influenced by this poem. If this, in fact, be the truth of the matter, it must be an event virtually unique in literary history, that a single poem has decided the design of a country's flag.

p. 116: *The Tower*
stanza 4. A somewhat compressed image. The scaffolding is seen first as some kind of textile swathing to the tower, this evokes the image of the Gordian knot (an image only just below the threshold of consciousness among many Byelorussian poets – perhaps largely due to the existence of a medieval Byelorussian narrative epos of Alexander the Great), this then evokes the concept of the far-voyaging hero who is to untie the knot, which in its turn is connected in the poet's mind with the ancient Scandinavian trade routes of river and portage, from the Baltic to the Black Sea, crossing Byelorussia by way of the Western Dzvina and the Biarezina.

p. 117: *Thou passest, Village, from bright story . . .*
This is an interesting poem, showing as it does Kupała's wrestling with a subject

about which he held highly ambivalent views. On the one hand, he sees and appreciates the virtues of the technological age, and even goes out of his way to stress that the old, traditional ways were even harmful; on the other, as one of the founding members of the *Naša Niva* movement, he cannot but mourn for the passing of the village life that had given to Byelorussian literature so many potent symbols. Furthermore, the words and concepts of the new technology had not yet acquired any poetic overtones, and without skilful handling, a poem of this type would be only too apt to break down into bathos. Kupała tackled the problem by considerable technical expertise, by combining expressions of hope and progress with the 'dead march' rhythm (which he had last used in the dark days of the Stolypin reaction, in 'In the kingdom of the Night'), by using, as far as possible, abstract ideas and avoiding the current slogans of collectivization. The poem, although 'interesting' rather than 'great', is a good example of 'laureate'-work; a poet dealing with a commissioned subject not entirely to his taste, nor within his preferred range of subjects.

stanza 12. 'All-Souls of October'. The word rendered here by 'All-Souls' (*Dziady*) refers to the old Byelorussian midwinter ancestor feast, originally, presumably kept at the winter solstice, but incorporated into the Christian rituals of Christmas and celebrated on Christmas Eve. (This feast is the background of Mickiewicz's poem *Dziady*, a number of English translations of which exist, under such names as 'Forefathers' Eve'.) Kupała here seems to hint that the new feasts of Communism, in particular the anniversary of the October Revolution, will not oust the old traditions, but will merely become an addition to the festal calendar – the sharp juxtaposition of the oldest and newest feasts indicating at once the vast range of tradition, and the survival power of that tradition which can incorporate and blend the food in that which is new into the corpus of that which is old.

p. 118: *Alesia*

The cuckoo motif here is bound up with the folk-belief, which occurs in many Slav countries and traditions, that it is possible to forecast the length of one's lifetime by counting how many times the cuckoo calls. Thus the sound of the cuckoo's voice quite naturally sets the mother thinking of the future. Thus the typical 'folklore' introduction not only is an effective contrast for what is to follow; it is bound up with the structural motivation of the whole poem.

INTERLUDE–WESTERN BYELORUSSIA

1921–1939

By the Peace of Riga (1921), Byelorussia was partitioned, so that some 38,600 square miles of Byelorussian territory, with a population of 5,000,000 was incorporated into the newly re-established state of Poland. The rights of minority communities in Poland were guaranteed by the League of Nations, as at first it seemed that harmony between the Byelorussians and Poles might well be attained. In the elections of 1922 to the Polish Sejm (Parliament) there were no less than three Byelorussian Senators and twelve Byelorussian Deputies. However, partly due to traditional enmities between Poland and Russia (now represented by the ever-more-powerful Soviet Union), partly as a result of inter-party conflicts in Poland, and partly due to the fact that the restoration of the Polish state evoked not only a new surge of patriotism but also, at least in some Polish hearts, dreams of a restoration of the old Polish empire 'from sea to sea', as time wore on, there were ever greater and greater measures taken to 'unify' the Polish Republic, and to defend the 'national interests' of Poland – at the expense of the rights of her minorities.

The effect upon Byelorussian life was twofold. On the one hand, many patriots turned their eyes eastward and were attracted into membership of the Communist Party of West Byelorussia (organized separately from the Communist Party within the Byelorussian SSR). That this sudden surge of Party membership was due to a devotion to Byelorussia rather than to the theories of International Communism is easily seen from the fact that in pro-Byelorussian demonstrations, the Red flag would be carried alongside the White-Red-White flag of the short-lived Byelorussian National Republic of 1918. On the other hand, although all Byelorussian political activity was gradually suppressed (the last Byelorussian member of the Sejm lost his seat in the elections of 1934), literary and cultural activity could still continue subject to censorship and restriction. Mindful of the League guarantees, the Polish government was cautious concerning any suppression of cultural rights – although many writers were imprisoned, the formal charges were not that they were Byelorussian writers, but that they were, for example, members of the forbidden Communist Party of West Byelorussia. Thus, literary activity continued, and the Byelorussian poetry which flourished among conditions of adversity does much to supplement the literary dearth from Soviet Byelorussia during much of this time. Further, since such activity was tolerated under sufferance by the authorities, the general perversity of human nature in general, and the stubbornness of the Byelorussian temperament in particular, evoked among vast numbers of the population of West Byelorussia, who might otherwise have remained indifferent and passive towards national activities and their native literature, a keen and burning interest in that poetry and prose which fostered and expressed those national hopes and aspirations once more denied them in the political sphere.

Pilip Piestrak

POETRY

You beg at the door to come in my poor home here,
In a windy dark night of autumn . . .
Or not, indeed?
Maybe it is my sick mother groaning,
Who there in the weary murk of the corner,
Lulling pain in half-sleep,
Huddled against the children is lying?
The wind at the window savagely sings,
Through peartrees and thatch, howling and crying,
And beats
Its wings.

The singing pours forth, deafly and lonely,
It grows quiet, then surges,
Then with far grief moaning
It bursts forth, new-rushing,
Then in memories, drowsy,
With the wind it merges . . .
Maybe this is my father's song, after carousing,
There, from the highroad, 'Oak-grove, do not rustle! . . .'
Night clings to the pane, through the window it peers . . .
It was so recently – in past years . . .
And, from fate's dreary spurring,
In me
The heart longs to be sundered;
Under rough prickly burlap
(Nothing else keeps me warm)
Joined with this autumn night, I weep for my mother,
I am a boy-bard, lost, forlorn.

Night clings to the pane,
                                        flapping its wing . . .
Yes! It was this, this same thing . . .

No more need, no more need, no more need now
Of these grim, inescapable chains!
No longer to heaven I plead now,
In my own soul I seek might and main.

O, Poetry, grant a sword radiant,
A word tempered, word-warcry, word-fight!
Grant an eagle's flight to me, that flaming
In a fire-song will beat at the sky.

Grant that I hurl on those vandals
Those nights' curses eternal in thunder,
Those who shod our life into bast-sandals,
Grant that their blood-black horde I may sunder.

Maksim Tank

THE VISIT

'Well, tell me then, what news d'you bring?'
The old man starts with haymaking,
To rye and oats his memory veers,
And the eyes are wet with tears.

And then I said: 'All's well! I've passed
Through the long weary year at last.
But not alone! We're quite a crowd,
We've grown used to the bars, somehow!
Well, how are mother and sister now?
The time's come for the winter plough!
And how is grandpa getting on?
Greetings to him from everyone!'

'All's well! We're living, after all,
But you are withering behind walls.
I've brought a bag of rusks, see here!'
And the eyes are wet with tears!

'Don't weep! We'll come back with the spring,
Forth to the field in one great string.
We'll meet a new dawn's risen glow.
Don't weep, old chap, don't worry so!
From these bars in bright spring again
We'll go with seedbag filled with grain,
A crowd we'll go forth, like dark woods,
Out upon the black furrow's clods!'

The old man trusts my promising,
And he too speaks about the spring,
Stronger and taller he appears,
Although the eyes are wet with tears.

THE SONG OF THE SNIPE

There is a smell of tar, of sweat and russet sheepskin,
Silence to the old bent cottage now has come,
Slowly the night burns like flame down wood-torch creeping
Spreading forth its pine-smoke and its fragrant gum.

From time to time the wind catches the wood, hooks in it,
And for a long time saws it with sickle of the moon,
Warping across the fence, snow thread of finest linen,
With a long snowy song beyond blind windows' gloom.
In the stove is burning firewood and root-tinder,
The shadows on the wall are lying down like hares,
Angrily the potatoes foam and boil within the
Blackened cauldron, raging like a snowstorm there.

'Well, sit down with us,' says the grey grandfather
Setting on the table a morsel of black bread,
'The snow is winnowed like a mountain of chaff; over
The field you'll never cross – you cannot cross its spread.
You come from far, it seems, you are not of this region
Not beneath, perhaps, thatched roofs like ours you bide.
Your clothes are thin, out there the field will surely freeze you
The bench is hard, for sure, but stay with us the night!
You see, there's hunger here, our life's not easy, brother,
Bread is on the table only a guest to please.
It's good if we've potatoes enough to last us over
Until the spring, until the first migrating geese.

The times are not good. Since the days when frost first gathered
They took several young folk, put them into prison.
Many times for sure, the grey birch trees swept over
Their tracks in the field with a white wind risen
That we might learn to know our native tongue more fully
From our hearts we ever make our plea.
I shall soon be at rest under the green pine, surely,
But what will happen to our children – answer me?

In the corner on the plank-bed on an old book poring
A quiet voice is lilting, tufts of white hair flow;
With the young wife who sits by a small cradle mourning,
Joined in song, the wild white snowstorm sobbing low.
'Hushabye, my baby . . .'
'Is your husband working?
You say he's in prison? That he's got ten years?'
'Husha, little falcon . . .'
like a hot rain burning,
From the mother's eyes are falling bitter tears.

'I, old man, was also under thatched roof biding,
I was where your son is suffering today . . .
I lost many tracks upon the muddy highway,
On the scraping strings of white sleds swept away . . .'

'Hushabye, my baby! Little falcon, husha!
Be good now! Stop crying!
                                        Listen! By the creek!
It is not the snowstorm, sobbing where fields slumber;
Snipe are surely wandering in the mist and bleak!'

And the old man lifts eyes rheumy with age and faded:
'Well, how long will things go on as now they go?
We sow the seed always, from morn to midnight labour,
Yet never find escape from suffering and woe.
And always we have gloom and darkness, only sometimes
Now and again the sun between our rooftops peeps;
And half a year we sit, with *kvass* before us hungry,
And in the field across our paths the snowdrift sweeps.
You say that very soon we shall straighten shoulders squarely,
You speak of broader fields, you talk of spring anew;
It seems that even I shall go forth, boldly faring
From stove-side ingle, let the young but call me too!'

Beyond the broken pane the wind is groaning harshly,
Tearing the threads of spinning, on the posts it twists.
'Hushabye my baby, hush . . . no, listen rather,
How, wandering somewhere, the snipe weep in the mist!'

There is a smell of tar, of sweat and russet sheepskin,
Silence to the old bent cottage now has come,
Quietly night burns out, like flame down wood-torch creeping,
Spreading forth its pinesmoke and its fragrant gum.

Under flowing song, hot clouds of sleep are rising . . .
'Hushabye . . . good baby . . . listen . . . by the creek . . .'

And, it seems to me that, in the darkness hiding,
It is not the snowstorm but the snipe that weep.

THE LYRE PLAYER

An old lyre-player died
In the womb of the birches,
Where green leaves and breezes
Whispering, murmured.

So that his songs
Would not hide, by stone hampered,
Nor be torn apart
By hands and feet trampled.

Gave back strings to the stars,
Grief to guelders and willows,
Joy to the lakes, echoes
To valley hollows.

And his eyes of crystal,
To the sun, high high over,
Were borne by a falcon
From banks of the Nioman.

Today we go walking,
Walk the country over,
Star-chime, joy, sorrow,
And echoes we gather.

Valancin Taŭlaj

LAST WORDS

What do I seek? To ask me this is silly.
For you without an answer have bestowed
Fetters upon me, granted prison skilly.
Not just for one long year have caged me so.

In the Republic's name you do your judging.
It is for you to judge now, ours to break the jail,
And under these our lean arms' forceful urging
These cold walls yet will crumble and will quail.

I am a Communist! There are many like me
In this our land that from the dawn of time has groaned.
Never shall magnates crush us, though they strike us,
By jail and gallows we're not overthrown!

The Tsars' gold and their treachery have now departed,
And your dominion will one day be gone.
Are you the first to judge the truth, I ask you?
Am I the first that you passed judgment on?

And there before you, on the green baize cover,
Lie laws with the Tsar's signature below.
You judge by unenlightened laws, thrown over
And smashed by the people's thunder long ago.

Sirs, I have finished! My turn to hear sentence meted.
I go to prison, and believe, there'll come
A year when this my speech will be completed
By barricade, inspiring, mighty guns.

VERSES FROM ŁUKIŠKI

When thunder fills my heart, and when
Łukiški is set shaking,
Verses I write without a pen,
Nor in a notebook make them.

Here the least stub of pencil is
More than taboo forbidden;
If they should find one, know but this:
The hinges' answer given.

But why should my soul deviate?
Their hands will never find verse!
Under the lightning flash, full-spate,
In memory I inscribe verse.

Let the noose menace, let cold frown,
Let punishment cell threaten . . .
The lightning flash will burn them down,
To embers cold and deadened.

Myself I can sit here awhile;
For verse there's shame in staying:
For it should rustle, banner-style,
The proud war-columns swaying.

Look through the judas night and day,
You fiend, sharp-eyed, accursed,
You'll not see how I file away
The bars, to free my verses.

NOTES

p. 129: *The visit*
stanza 3 ff. Note the *Naša Niva* image of the spring represents national resurgence, with perhaps a hint of the associated image of migrating birds as political exiles (here, those 'exiled' by imprisonment).

p. 129: *The song of the snipe*
line 3. 'wood-torch'. A long thin 'spill' of resinous wood, used as a method of lighting a cottage.

line 23. 'It's good if we've potatoes . . .' The growing of potatoes was introduced into the Russian empire at the beginning of the nineteenth century, in face of considerable opposition from 'anti-Westernizing' groups who considered them an un-Russian influence. In Byelorussia, the soil and general climate of which much resembles Ireland, the potato became very rapidly the national food of the peasantry. Symbolically, here, the poet seems to be saying, that provided only the bare minimum of life is provided for physical survival, the Byelorussian people (symbolized by the bereaved peasant family of grandfather, daughter-in-law and infant) will 'hang on' until the coming of national revival and the return of the exiled menfolk.

p. 133: *Last words*
This poem, when the author was only fifteen years of age, in spite of several technical infelicities, is a good example of the 'protest' poetry of the younger Byelorussian poets of this period.

stanza 2. 'The Republic'. Taŭłaj's expression is *Reč Paspalita*, equivalent to the Polish *Rzeczpospolita.* The semantics of this expression deserve comment. The word, of course, like the English word 'republic' derives from the Latin *res publica.* However, in Polish, this expression does not necessarily signify a state governed by an elected president. With its capital 'R', it signified Poland, and more particularly, has strong connotations of the old 'commonwealth' of Poland and Lithuania, and of the aspirations of Poland *od morza do morza* (from sea to sea – i.e. extending from the Baltic to the Black Sea). I have rendered this into English by 'Republic' since, at the time Taŭłaj was writing, Poland was a republic in the normal sense of the word, and since the only alternative rendering in English, 'commonwealth' is probably more open to incorrect connotations than even 'republic'. It is, perhaps, significant, that in the full designation of the present day 'People's Republic of Poland', the word used is not *Rzeczpospolita* but *Republika.*

stanza 3. 'magnates' (Polish *magnaty*), a conventional term in Ukrainian and Byelorussian literature for Polish lords, especially in an unsympathetic sense. Cf. Shevčenko:

> The magnates labour, whetting sabres,
> Setting fire to houses.
> *The Haydamaky*, lines 291–92.

In Polish, the word has no specific Polish connotations, but is used in the normal sense of the English word (and, sometimes sarcastically, as in *magnat bawełniany* – cotton baron). In its Byelorussian context here, however, the word reinforces the overtones of *Rzeczpospolita.*

stanza 5. 'Laws with the Tsar's signature below.' True, but for this the Polish government was not to blame! The re-established Republic of Poland was formed out of a number of territories, each with its own legal code, viz.

(a) the old 'kingdom of Poland' (whose 'king', since the Congress of Vienna, had, of course, been the Tsar);
(b) in the West, the 'cradle of Poland', which had been most recently part of the kingdom of Prussia (Prussian code);
(c) in the far south, lands ceded by the former kingdom of Hungary, to which they had been pawned in the early fifteenth century (Hungarian code);
(d) in the south-east, Western Ukraine, formerly Austrian Galicia (Austrian code);
(e) in the east and north-east, parts of the former 'North-Western Province' of the Russian Empire, Byelorussia and Lithuania (Tsarist code).

To avoid a state of juridical chaos, for the first few years of its existence, the Republic of Poland operated throughout its territories those legal codes and procedures which had been in operation in the various regions immediately prior to the Treaties of Versailles and Riga. The Sejm then appointed a commission to investigate the discrepancies in these codes and procedures, and to draw up a new unified code to apply throughout the entire Polish state – in the usual way of such Commissions, however, this particular Commission took a number of years over its task. The new criminal procedure was introduced on March 19th, 1928; the new criminal code, however, did not come into force until July 11, 1932. (For those not expert in legal terminology, it should be explained that the *procedure* covers such matters as rules of evidence, rights of defendant, etc., whereas the *code* specifies the nature of the offence, the appropriate penalties, and also matters of who is, or is not, a responsible person.)

Thus, when Taŭłaj was arrested in 1929, he was tried according to the new Polish criminal procedure ('In the Republic's name you do your judging'), but the criminal code was still that of 'laws with the Tsar's signature below' (i.e. the Tsarist code of 1903). This, in fact, had a considerable effect on Taŭłaj's case, since he was, at the time, not yet sixteen years of age. Under the Tsarist criminal code, a boy of this age was considered to be an adult, could be put on trial, and, if convicted, sentenced to imprisonment. Under the Polish criminal code of 1932, however, the age of responsibility was fixed at eighteen years; had this code been in operation, therefore, at the time of Taŭłaj's trial, such a trial, in fact, would never have taken place!

p. 133: *Verses from Lukiški*
Lukiški is a suburb of Vilna (now Vil'nyus) where is situated the prison in which Taŭłaj and other Byelorussian poets (who were likewise members of the illegal Byelorussian Communist Party), Piestrak, for example, were incarcerated. It may be noted that this poem, written in 1935, in spite of a few remaining infelicities and obscurities (e.g. line 8) shows a considerable improvement in style in comparison with *Last Words*.

UNIFICATION AND WAR (1939–1945)

As we have said, the thirties, marked as they were with the rise of Stalinism, proved inimicable to the development of poetry in the Byelorussian SSR, and although the unification of the country in 1939, under the terms of the Moscow-Ribbentrop pact, produced an atmosphere of excitement that might well have caused a new flowering of poetry, this impetus was soon masked by a greater one, as Hitler turned on his former allies, and the might of Nazi militarism rolled eastward. As the war raged back and forth across the landscape of Byelorussia – a war in which one in four of the population were to perish – once again, the voice of the Byelorussian poets became the warcry and inspiration of the Byelorussian people. Much war poetry, read afterwards in an atmosphere of peace, gives an impression of somewhat embarrassing naïvety – but in the Byelorussian poetry of the Second World War, this is not often the case. Here, conventional patriotism of the 'war-laureate' type takes on something of the air of a heroic ballad, with its clearcut conflict of good and evil, its simple and archetypal motifs. And here too are the personal poems, the impressions of a sensitive and mature nature against the horror of modern warfare, no longer heroic magnificence but the relentless mechanized juggernaut of the twentieth century. And, at the end, the peace, not of triumph, but of utter warweariness when the fighting must cease since there is nothing left but death, desolation, weariness and dreams of a lost home.

Arkadź Kulašoŭ

MY BIESIADŹ

They say that the rivers by birds were first hollowed out –
Though they appear so small at first sight –
They dug them, bore off in their bills to the forestland,
Little bags with earth stowed,
Then returned in their flight.

But the peewit wheeled round and bathed them with mockery,
And on her the birds an eternal curse laid;
Over the rivers now, still she flies hovering,
Seeking a sip
To drink till this day.

Pining in summer, through the hot glowing days,
On the rare drops she must exist ever,
Which the cloud, in rainshowers, rustling the foliage
Sometimes sends down to her from the heavens.

Obstinate, though, I'll not shed my first causes,
I dig the sands, I crush the hard stone,
Under scorn of amateurs' easy glories.
I'll dig the bed of my river, my own.

With hope I gaze at the well-spring I encounter there,
I wish it flow strong, as a river expand,
Not a mighty Volga,
Not a Kama's bounty there –
Like the Biesiadź in my own native land.

For often a thirst to work seizes, importunes me,
And a verse-craving singes my heart, sans relief,
For I cannot live
Like the peewit unfortunate,
On a drop of rain drunk from a green forest leaf.

MOSCOW STREET

I live on Moscow Street, I have my home there,
Under the springtime thunders
And rain showers,
In the slippery surface mirrored down there,
See it stand, the multi-surfaced house.

Having made my bow to spring and Maytime,
Hearing across the river the cuckoo's din,
Every year I
Drive to the village gaily,
To breathe the air the countryfolk breathe in.

Someone among the group of friends around me
Comes and asks me: 'Where do you live now?'
And I reply:
'On Moscow Street' . . . (Undoubted
The very one the poem is about!)

And hearing the street's name I give him,
He looks and smiles, that moustache grey,
He thinks, it seems,
That I am living,
From Moscow just a little way.

The countryfolk greet me with honour, shyly;
What do I think?
I catch myself out, too!
I walk, I walk along a well-known highway,
And I am known
A Moscow-townsman true!

With interest Moscow-style I try the ringing
Tone of the pipe with childlike whistle through;
Or else with my steel scythe boldly swinging,
I mow the field . . .
A Moscow-townsman true!

Later I think,
As weariness comes stealing,
That here beneath this roof of azure-blue,
That in a street and house I still am dwelling
That is somehow not far from Moscow too!

*   *   *

Gliding the cloud came, she kissed with the earth,
Sickles from the harvest departed,
For they had perceived how there flashed from her girth,
Lightning
On the lowlands of harvest.

To the place where she brings honey down for the bee,
There where she makes the road lighter,
All the rivers began to draw her longingly,
But the cloud floated down to the widest.

She wanted to see herself, mirrored there bright,
She grew quiet,
Stood tall upon tiptoe,
Looked down on its darkened expanse from the height,
Looked down, but its spread was too little.

Once more she grew angry, it seems, from grief's smart,
Hurling her lightnings far under,
She wanted to press the banks further apart,
She wanted
The boundaries to sunder.

This was not the first time that in such unrest
She aimless sailed into the distance,
And in her wake,
As if behind their fate, pressed
Flocks of small cloudlets, insistent.

They look down, in the watery glass they can see,
From the sky, in that mirrorframe shining,
All of their beauty, their azure.
But me –
To be such as those clouds I'm not pining.

Like a cloud in unrest I would hurl thunders forth,
Wrapped in my lightnings about me,
So that it is hard to perceive, first, the truth,
To grasp what you are, without doubting.

To know peace not by night nor by day I desire,
Ceasing from weariness never,
In a mighty love with rain,
And with fire,
On the highway to kiss the earth ever.

Vasil Vitka

NICCOLO PAGANINI

A radiant bow slashes across deaf night,
Invasion comes. The lapwing, all despairing
Calls to her family. The lightning, searing
Has flashed, and struck down to the ocean bed.

Risen from the depths, the waters turning
In pliant circles, greyly, greyly glimmered.
To us there flashed, through the long years returning,
A trembling sail, to true remembrance shimmered.

And on time's shore waves rushed, insistent,
Sank down in doubt, force spent and failing,
And to our dawnlight from an age-old distance,
On the heart's course, a ship was sailing.

Valancin Taŭłaj

ON MY POEMS

Mayakovskii in friendship advised me:
'Don't send poems out, hot from the pen!'
Put them in a drawer!' he wrote, 'You'll find them
Later – you can judge and print them then!'

I would not forget the plan he showed me,
And the Poles 'helped' me to keep it too,
They locked up the drawer with the poems,
And the author – into jail they threw!

Yes, they judged them – you cannot conceal it –
And informers, take which one you might,
One and all swore on the Cross, revealing,
These were not poems but – dynamite.

The Procurator, reading through the codex,
Article by article, he peered,
At each line, his pointing finger showing,
Valued them: for every line – a year!

Sent me again to lie on prison boards where
Poems and my sides I polished, shined,
Sometimes, too, my thoughts to printing soared then:
There lived Skaryna, once upon a time! . . .

And all grieved, the weary while we lay there,
For poems, bard, the nation's reading mind.
Many of my poems grew quite grey there,
Many of them I could never find.

But there is this – and one cannot forget it:
Like my chain-links, I polished every line;
In those days I was hung with chiming fetters,
Maybe from this my poems also chime.

Anatol Astrejka

NIOMAN

O Nioman, O my father Nioman,
Like the sun, like the day dear to me!
With the bones and rank tatters of foemen
Your banks are now strewn utterly.

Your warrior sons strove in their courses,
With their last drop of strength you to save,
So that the foe's murky forces
Would not speed their boats on your waves.

Truth winged us forth into battle,
Our mother gave us our swords,
Look, on your slopes there lie scattered
Nazi locusts, how mighty a horde.

We from your banks have withdrawn now,
Ah, Nioman, it had to be done,
I know well the drear bitter torment
To leave one's own village, one's home.

We shall swiftly return from this parting,
Stay evermore by your flood.
The ill-doer shall pay for our heartache,
Payment of his own Fascist blood.

Rage, then, my tumultuous Nioman,
Rise and roar in revenge for your shame;
To your bed, to a watery grave throw them,
Those aliens who unbidden came.

Jakub Kołas

THE VOICE OF THE LAND

I hear a voice that naught can silence –
My own land calling me away;
It cuts wounds on my heart, beguiling
It chimes like scythe-bell in the hay.
The sigh of oakgroves, forests' moaning,
Sobbing of rivers, well-springs' tears,
And muddy thickets dumbly looming,
They bear me news of strangers here.

I see before me Teuton figures,
The faces cold, the eyes of beasts,
They feel no law, they feel no pity,
And steel-forged hoofs have they for feet.

Ah, had I but the arms, land, for it,
I'd embrace thee with all my might,
I'd silence all your woe and torment,
And give my strength into the fight.

O my dear land, O my dear country,
I hear your bell, its calling lure,
Accept a son's words, offered humbly,
Not long shall slavery endure,

Thy forests are astir with anger,
Thy woods with vengeance are ashake,
Thy day the cloudy dusk will scatter,
Thou still hast warriors awake.

Janka Kupała

TO BYELORUSSIAN PARTISANS

Partisans, O valiant fighters
Sons of Byelorussian plains,
Chains and slavery requiting,
Carve the evil Hitlerites, so
That they never rise again.

On ruins and burnt devastation
Where their bloodstained footprints lie,
Counting their bones' enumeration,
Let raven call to celebration
The owl, and there hold revels high.

Vampire-Hitler, let them take him,
Pick his heart out drain his blood:
With human fat he's saturated
With blood whirlpools inebriated –
Perish the arch-beast for good!

He gouged out the eyes of grandsires
Babies and mothers he would knife
A wild scarecrow, spectre, blackened
Day with darkest night unslackened –
Perish so the villain's life.

Partisans, O valiant fighters
Sons of Byelorussian plains,
Chains and slavery requiting
Carve the evil Hitlerites, so
That they never rise again.

I call you forth to victory's wonder,
Let your days with fortune shine
Slash the cannibals asunder,
So that not a trace lies under –
Foot on our soil's holy shrine.

The shades of slain babes and mothers
Of your grandfathers and sires,
The broad fields, bloodspattered over,
Call to revenge of blood that never
Have past ages matched in ire.

Do not permit these snakes their hateful
Powers over you to spread,
Dig the graves, ready and waiting,
Tear out their veins, still palpitating,
Blood for blood and dead for dead.

Partisans, O valiant fighters
Sons of Byelorussian plains,
Chains and slavery requiting
Carve the Hitlerites, so
That they never rise again.

Let your victory not leave you,
Nowhere let it go from you,
Never let alarms grieve you,
Your pure road will not deceive you,
It will lead to victory true.

Then from the unclean pollution
We shall cleanse the woods, the fields,
Crush Fascist curs in retribution,
Then as of old, will bow the beauty
To us of grain ears rich in yield.

Partisans, O valiant fighters
Sons of Byelorussian plains,
Chains and slavery requiting
Carve the evil Hitlerites, so
That they never rise again.

Piatro Hłebka

THE PARTISANS

Before the sun's setting,
The moment grows tense,
The rushes, unending,
Whisper on, dull of sense.

The autumn fields over,
Ending the day,
There fall the last cover
Of the twilight shades.

Across the trees lightly,
Over wrinkled bark flow
The winds, from the right to
The left; cease to blow.

A yellow leaf, without purpose
From the branch torn,
Without aim, slowly circles,
In the world one, alone.

Letting fall from exhaustion
Its arms, the wood grieves
Without stir, without motion,
Over villages' graves.

In the silence it ponders
The days, weariness filled;
Not a sigh nor sound yonder,
All is still, all is still . . .

A silence so dumb that
At first you might start,
Hearing over the country
The cry of each heart.

The breast feels suffocation,
By black despair choked,
They will not rise, my nation,
They will not rise, my folk.

Suddenly, steps, insistent,
Through the death-silence ring,
As from, far in the distance,
Man and horse, galloping.

Maple to the elm leaning,
With its boughs whispers blithe,
Its news . . . Sudden-seeming,
The earth is alive.

To the rides and the clearings,
From dark thickets and lairs,
Partisans are appearing,
To Assembly draw near.

Thick as soot, the night shields them,
From all bullets' offence,
Will not sell, will not squeal on
Who they are, and from whence.

Only we and our country
And the marsh-thickets might
Know the name of each comer,
Recall many by sight.

These are our neighbours,
That one lived next door,
While with this, sometimes, maybe,
We went drinking of yore.

It would be fine to chat now,
But this is not the place,
For the Brigade commander
Time marches apace!

That old man, too – we know him,
Maybe kinsman of ours,
Carefully, as at home, he
Is hitching the horse.

The boys from the first squadron,
Youth's friends, dear to my heart,
Two machine-guns are loading
On the old grandpa's cart.

The grown men bring, bending
The ground with the load,
The mines, fierce, incendiary,
The TNT stowed.

A young woman is checking
The trigger and catch,
While a young village shepherd
In the distance, a lad,

Contempt for fear showing,
Like an old trooper staid,
In his belt he is stowing
Five hot hand-grenades.

I know not whether powder
Or hate lurks inside,
But the foeman shall know it,
On his head, raised in pride.

Revenge now is goodly!
Having heard the task planned,
They go, one and all, boldly,
The partisan band.

Some kilometres further
From the forest's deaf gloom,
Through the air there go hurling
Bridge and engines to doom.

Fierce explosions are crashing
Like thunder and storm,
On each window-pane splashing,
And set trembling each home.

Half the sky is bright-kindled,
And, roused by the fuss,
Now whisper the children:
'Daddy's working for us!'

Grandmother, all shaking,
As from tears unexpressed,
The Sign of the Cross making;
Prays: 'God grant them success!'

To the gate goes the mother,
Hears, as long minutes pass,
Machine-guns' even stutter,
Whisper of growing grass.

Later, in the blue shimmer
Of the radiant dawn,
Men and horses fade in the
Forest thickets – are gone.

Thick as soot, the night shields them,
From all bullets' offence,
Will not sell, will not squeal on
Who they are and from whence.

Only we and our country
And the marsh-thickets might
Know the name of each comer,
Recall many by sight.

Arkadź Kulašoŭ

From THE FLAG OF THE BRIGADE

I

As from its native branch a little oakleaf may be riven,
I left my native Minsk, by German bombs I was driven.

Through the trees, through the trees,
I walked into the night, and behind now
My native town seethes
With fire; no heart's peace can I find now.
Walked to standstill, I sat by a cottage,
Waiting sunlight's returning,
In a notebook I started the jottings
Of a wanderer's journal.
Yesterday, evening,
Night and today's greyish daybreak,
All the partings and meetings,
I set down on paper.
....
How did my things greet me,
When I left the flat, what were they saying?

Everything in my home
I looked at with long silent grieving,
For they begged me, each one,
That I might take them too, would not leave them.
Not a spoon, not a skillet,
Wished to stay behind, if I were going.
The books were unwilling
To be burned in the square by the foeman.
The horse, shaped by an artist
From pasteboard, with wooden wheels under:
'Are you going?' he asked me,
'To leave us, abandoned, for plunder?
Take me, too, Master, here it is sure
I shall perish forlornly!
D'you forget how from corner to corner I bore
Your small son, from corner to corner?
When war first began, Master, you were away in the country.
And today you have come back to town, for your family hunting.
But the Mistress departed
Yesterday, with the babes, to the station;
And left me, brokenhearted,
To the train with them she would not take me.

He did not want to leave me, your son,
When they left the apartment,
Did not wish me to live here alone,
Live untended, discarded.
'We're off to find Daddy; you see,
Daddy will buy you a new one!'
The Mistress said to him.
And he
Left me here, by the door, truly.
'Don't buy a new one for him, Master, let's set out together,
On the road to your son, you and I; if you're weary, however
Heavy, I'll give
You a lift, from sincerest emotion;
I served your son truly, I'll give
Gladly to you my devotion!'
The doll made her oration:
'I too did not go to the station . . .
Watchful through long nights, I
Did not close once an eye,
Watchful peeping,
Guard on your daughter's dreams was I not keeping,
When she was sleeping?
Give your hand, master, to me,
Do not stand in the doorway,
Like a daughter, lead me
On the road where the folk crowd so sorely.
The children's feet ache, they find the road harsh, unforgiving,
I shall go uncomplaining with you, because I am unliving,
Children ask you for food and for drink,
To choke their mouths dry dust is driving,
I shall ask nothing, think!?
I am only a doll, and unliving.
Swarming in fly the aeroplanes here,
To the children death-giving;
Bullets I do not fear,
I do not fear, I am not living! . . .
If you feel you must rest on the roadway,
We'll go into a thicket.
I'll watch your sleep wakefully, guard you,
Will not blink for a minute! . . .'
I glanced at my things, then departed,
And I took, when I started,
Only the spoon,
Thrust it down
In the flap of my right boot,
Although it was much in the way for me,
I would need it when marching . . .

When I met the street, what did it say to me
When I was departing?

We had lived there in harmony with it, like friends and companions,
Breadth and length of it I'd measured out, with my legs I had spanned it;
When it heard my steps, it would reply, a good friend, with its echo,
Into the eighth entry of the apartment-block beckoned.

I would see window-panes
Pleasantly lit for me, ready,
And through them would see, plain,
My children preparing for bedtime.
But this road had grown strange now,
A narrower, far longer highway,
As when a landslide rains down
On a road through a mountain pass winding.
From the flats no lights came
As of old, from the windows quiet shining,
But great tongues of flame
Lick at the sweet leaves of the limetrees.
I did not know, indeed,
My own street, the limes and horse-chestnuts;
Tramp of thousands of feet
Struck me, unaware, into deafness.
It roused me, my sorrowful mourning,
Alarming and yearnings,
From the city it bore me,
My feet upon broken glass turning.
Just as in a tempest
A leaf from the tree will be riven,
I the city relinquished,
By the merciless fires I was driven.
To the long trek I'm starting now
To grow used,
There'll be many such for me.
A long time, while departing now,
My own street lights the darkness before me.
And by that light I'm
Able to note, with heart's anguish,
The exact hour, the time,
When it must, unforgettably, perish.
I offer these lines to those dear
Names, unknown to me,
Who on cobbles lie, maimed, lifeless here,
Under maples and chestnut-trees strewn here.

I pray that the years
Of black aces in their fires consume them.

Burn that slayer, his sons
And all his descendants,
Who dropped the first bomb
From his wings, on our cobbles descending.
Let them perish in doom,
That slayer (and with him the score of
Kith and kin), he who'll drop the last bomb,
Let them perish in torment!

In the name of those once
In our New Moscow Street dwelling,
I speak: we have all gone
Into the Red Army. I tell you
That although you are razed, as I see you,
Your memory will fade for us never,
For the sound of your hot ashes' seething
In our hearts will live ever.
I swear to you by this your ash, vow and say
That in the dark night I shall not lose my way,
I'll return, I'll return home some day! . . .

BY A GRAVE OF BROTHERS

Near Staraya Ruś
– The Russian village of Lažyna.
There as in Biełaruś
Rowans are growing and willows.
They glow in gold lustre,
Loveliest
Shine there
In the village meadows,
Foes helmets rust there,
Ugliest,
dwine there,
As in Biełaruś shed there.
There is a brotherly grave out beyond
    Lažyna, there in the meadow.
In honour our bold Byelorussian boys
    Laid down their heads there.
We entombed them unweeping,
Memories keeping
Of their duty unfailing,
Manly rifles and helmets would be
    Shamed by tears and bewailing.

We do not weep, though we know,
    With cold gravel we cover,
Not simply warriors' bones,
    But something other.
We covered over their faces,
    Their eyes and moustaches,
The sweet kisses of children
    And wives not yet cold on those faces.
We heaped gravel on arms
    Which had held those babes in their embraces,
We heaped gravel on feet
    Which had walked half a world in their paces.
Those feet long to stand,
    No weariness from the road pulls them,
To the grave, though, compelling,
Strength felling,
Came enemy bullets.
Those arms still desire
    To clasp to the breast their dear orphans,
But the enemy's favours of evil
    To a narrow grave force them.
Although this earth welcomes them kindly,
    Like her sons, worn from travail,
Their eyes still beseech
    A handful of Palessian gravel.
But where to find such?
    When from Biełaruś they departed,
They took for the road
No small bags, with earth stowed,
When they started.
What good is a handful?
    They crave all of thee, dearest country,
But in a knapsack
    No one can place all thy bounty.
Try to take for the road
    Meadows and ploughlands and well-springs,
And deep forests, these can
    In the heart only find dwelling.
Biełaruś, my dear land,
    See, once more I commence my endeavour
To measure thee out in my march,
    With thy savory blue and thy heather . . .
My heart seeks for paths
    That lie in my boots' heavy compass;
I long to behold the light mists
    Of thy wind and thy dustclouds;
To behold them for self and for those who no more

Will rise up from non-being;
The eyes seek to thy heavens to soar,
Thy blue not enough for their needing.
We cover with earth our friends true and good,
Men from Leningrad, Uzbeks and Tartars,
Vowing long draughts of the enemy's blood
To Biełaruś and her swift waters.
We give the salute,
    Our own duty recalling,
Weeping not, for stern helmets
Are shamed by tears falling.

Pimien Pančanka

MY COUNTRY

O thou my joy, my country beloved,
O thou my song of youth's dawning,
Over thy ploughlands, over thy groves,
The heart of a son lingers mourning.

Often as a dream thou dost come to me, now,
Thou dost flow like a wave, forth upon me,
Thou dost perch like a bird on the quiet maple bough,
In the chime of the rain fallest on me.

To the last detail my memory plays,
Over all things bound up in my country,
How the rye rustles, how the dawn's blaze,
Smoulders out on the lake bed, far under.

How in blazing summer, day after day,
We wandered across fields of stubble,
We wounded our feet on the stones of the way,
Yet never by pain were we troubled.

And there was nothing shimmered more bright
Than the sun in our own heavens,
And there was nothing more tasty and light
Than bread by a mother given.

The waters that in a roadside brook splash,
For us past all honey were sweeter,
O thou my country, my mother, alas,
Thy time is heavy and bitter!

They have trampled upon, they have tortured thy land,
Monsters in rabid-mad seizure,
My blood to the uttermost drop I would spend,
If only thus I could ease thee.

I long for no glory nor treasures; and sweet
It would be, though I passed life obscurely,
To feel my own land once more under my feet,
To breathe my own air, blowing purely.

*   *   *

The gardens forever will bloom,
The white-breasted swallows will fly there,
And a girl's foot will tap out the gleam
Of king-cups gold shining.

Not even in dreams, of the spring
Is anyone able to think now;
Today war to memory brings
Woe for its drink now.

The dewdrops fall from the quiet grass
On my army boots brushing;
They are roused, they are stirring at last,
Trees and flowers, with a gentle caressing.

I thought – only blood, only war,
Only harsh words, thoughts of horror;
But sudden she chimes from afar,
Like echo calling to sorrow.

It seems she is walking with me,
Her girlish jokes ringing out plainly:
'Look! the hornbeam has kissed the birch, see!'
Or 'I need a scarf; pick me a rainbow!'

No, no! She cannot come to the woods:
From her home by the Front I am sundered . . .
And the voices of birds go unheard,
Drowned by the roar of the gunfire.

BLITZ BABIES

They heard no mother's sweet lullabying,
They did not listen to grandfather's tales,
Only harsh voices of tanks terrified them,
Alarmed by widows' heartrending wails.

They wept not through sleepless nights of the battle,
Carried safe down to the cellars from bed,
And the first words which they learned to prattle
Were about Nazi and fighting and bread.

The strife will grow quiet. The foeman be humbled.
The children all long for that day, one and all,
When from the clouds, like warm raindrops tumbling,
Down on war's ashes thick silence will fall.

They will venture from home to the fields, shyly doubtful,
So that, the first time in their lives, they in peace
Can delight in their own native landscape about them,
And hear the bell of a brook in the reeds.

The scent of the fields, the woods' beauty delight you,
But their hearts will still tremble from fear many days,
They will see in the first stork an aeroplane flying,
They will see in first dawn-light a city ablaze.

The thunder beyond the far woods gently booming
Will bring back the terror of bombing once more,
And often, yes often, through their pure dreams looming,
Loudly the voices of battle will roar.

THOU, MY DEAR BIEŁARUŚ

Copper-trunked rise the pine-trees, as if metal-cast,
In the clearings, blue savory flowers in the grass,
The sun looks at itself in the lakes' mirror-glass,
This thou art, my Biełaruś.

A maiden is reaping beneath dawn-blue sky,
A young moon on her shoulder, a silvery blade,
And, all around, the ripe orchards lie,
Amber apples, there in the dew,
This thou art, my Biełaruś.

Many a road to the war I have trekked,
Yet have I saved thee, the unique . . .
Fight on, bolder!
I shall come soon and press
Myself to thy sore-wounded breast,
Pay my respects to woods and broad furrows,
Yet those last steps will be laden with sorrow,
Back to thee, my Biełaruś.

Dread it is for me to think of that moment,
When I shall see, face to face, my dear homeland.
I shall seek for a house – and find ruins only,
I shall call to my mother – a grave will re-echo
In an old clearing under a willow decrepit.
Whatever thou may be – at night or at morning,
I shall know thee, I shall not betray thee.
For, having endured every sorrow and torment,
Thou hast grown dearer and nearer to me.

I shall dry all thy tears,
I shall tend thy wounds for thee,
With my hand I'll replace every leaf in due order.
I shall raise up thy cities from burnt desolation,
I shall set round each village a young new plantation,
That thou flower for aye so,
And in happiness grow,
Thou, my dear Biełaruś.

Mikoła Aŭramčyk

PIGEONS

In the village, midst gardens and flowers,
There where we were passing our green years,
To old tales we listened for long hours
That grandfathers poured into our ears.

The pigeons without song, so gently cooing,
And the pigeon-fledglings' timid flight . . .
In our pigeon morning naught we knew then,
No alarm, no sorrow, no affright.

High above the house the tumblers circled,
And our childhood years, one after one,
Like clouds particoloured flew their circuit
Round us, clouds of pigeons, feathery, young.

Tales are all forgotten in affright now,
No time for adventures, this is war . . .
On our heads, helmets we wear as fighters,
An unknown campaign calls us afar.

Here are roads and tracks bitter as wormwood,
And the steppe-grass cuts us like a knife . . .
The feet torn, the throat bitter and burning,
This can be no story, this is life!

Yet if you should chance to drowse a moment,
Pigeons in your dreams fly as they flew . . .
Maybe a girl somewhere (yes, you know her)
Likewise now is thinking about you.

See, a pilot makes heads rise in terror,
Now no cooing – groaning with fear . . .
And alas, no carrier pigeon ever
Seems to bring your letters to me here.

I would gladly die in combat, truly,
If a century hence, children might
Hear pigeons without song, so gently cooing,
Grow up without sorrow or affright.

THE THREE

They put them behind wire in freezing winter,
Each one, already, solemnly had vowed
To break out of captivity, to win a
Way through the woods to their own folk, somehow.

Cold stormwinds over the whole camp were wailing,
Corpses lay by the wall, strewn in a string . . .
Strength was departing from the body daily,
The eldest one could not live out the spring.

With grief and vengeance in the heart deep hidden,
All his companions could not help but grieve . . .
Like them, their friend against his death had striven,
Once more to help the foe this world to leave.

In that night, the two fled from the barracks,
Broke through the circuit-fence close to the gate,
And with them, very carefully they carried
And brought out, from beyond the wire, their mate.

In the darkness a spring wind was breathing . . .
And sitting on the grass, safely arrived,
The two felt that, now that he was in freedom
Once more, the third should straightaway revive.

Piatruś Broŭka

BIEŁARUŚ (extracts)

My native nook,
Dear land that bred me!
Jakub Kołas

I

My land, Biełaruś! Pinewood and oak-spinneys,
The lifegiving ryefields, the silk of the hay,
The rowan rays that in the evening west shimmer,
The clacking of storks, streamlets' chatter, the ribbons
Of roads that through rustling groves make their way.

My land, Biełaruś! With lake eyes aquiver
Thou dost gaze at the zenith, transparent and blue,
In the night, thick as apples, come stars falling ever,
To vanish in dark meres, be lost in the rivers
Or on the grass, sprinkled with droplets of dew.

Lays of past ages, bequest of past times there,
Like boats that are drenched with the sun, ever glide,
Over the green land, expanse unconfined there,
From Nioman to Sož, from the Buh to the Hajna,
On waves of Dniapro, on the Dzvina's broad tide.

And, on their banks, lays of our fathers' past glory,
The pine-woods, those tellers of tales, ever tell,
Połack and its towers ever speak of their story,
My own native Minsk with its battlements hoary,
Turaŭ's walls, Biełavieža with leaf-rustling dells.

II

My land, Biełaruś! In the flame of the fighting,
Striving in the stern conflict of nationhood's war,
Thou hast risen, once more thou hast armed thyself mighty,
Thy sons, steadfast in battle, with foes' blood requiting,
Gave drink to their swords, quenched their thirsts and yet more.

Their strength is the strength of the oaks of Palessia,
Tall in stature, broad-shouldered, as numerous to count
As there are in the woods pine-trees, fragrant with resin,
As stars, scattering the sky with the moon's luminiscence,
As grass in the meads that spread wide without bound.

For freedom and honour – a cause true and holy –
The mighty innumerable host makes its way.
'Death to the dread monster!' This cry echoes solely,
Through Hrodna and Minsk, Brest and Pinsk it is rolling,
Through all Biełaruś it is thundering today.

Inexorable vengeance the highways is pounding,
From late night until the dawn's early glow.
And, as evil winds cannot scatter tall mountains,
Nor flames of hate parch up the rivers and fountains,
So the might of the nation shall not be brought low.

III

Our grandsires of old fought the Prussians rapacious,
No long time in fetters were they doomed to spend;
At Grunwald they fought, on the ice of Lake Peipus,
With Ukrainian brothers, with Russians, tenacious
They fought on, their own Biełaruś to defend.

Against onslaught of divers foes ever they strove on,
Through the plains of Smalensk and Poltava did ride,
As Cossacks they went, through the steppes Zaporozhian,
And firmly believed: no man might overthrow them,
For in truth eternal their land did abide!

Go, ask any pine, any birch, do not doubt it,
They'll tell you true: in the great days of yore,
Vaščyła, Chvieśko, Kalinoŭski came proudly
They led their detachments to deeds bold and doughty,
High over the earth, like the sun, their fame soars.

Foes never were able to crush, overthrow them,
They found refuge and fortress among forest pines;
Dawnlight shone on their brows from over the Nioman,
To their steely breasts well-springs gave draughts, swiftly-flowing,
To mark out their path did a million stars shine.

IV

In days of yore, even, when wood-torches glinted,
The fame of the city of Połack was heard,
Thence came the great printer, Hieorhij Skaryna,
Who over his native land scattered, by printing,
The radiance of learning in crystalline words.

And from his well-spring drank many a nation
And took from his wisdom an eternal flame,
In his first letters found strength, inspiration . . .
Glorious thou art, that for all generations
Thou didst give birth to a son of such fame.

On thy breast, like a treasurehouse of living power,
From out of the ancient mists prows gently glide,
Where the grey mansions of Hrodna town glower,
Walls of Novahrudek, or Sofia's towers,
The castles of Zasłaŭ with steep rampart-sides.

The murmuring flax-plants tell of the folk's glory,
And the thoughts of the nation are hidden away
By lakes, like pure pearls, and by well-springs outpouring,
And the sky sparkles with bright rainbows for them,
To light out their path in the thick of the fray.
....

VIII

Folk of my Biełaruś! As heroes we knew you
Long enough you in want and in slavery pined –
You have washed your face now in a water-spring flowing,
Wiped it dry with a silken dawn, easterly glowing,
Boldly looked to the future with glance unconfined.

You have straightened your shoulders, tall-statured and mighty,
Among native vales, tall as a giant you have loomed.
Like a pine forest lifted your head to clouds, highly
Above spaces where ryefields spread rustling and widely,
And your lips have, like fires of cranberries, bloomed.

Your brethren have from your misfortune unlocked you,
Brushing the dark clouds away from your gaze;
Like the strong waves in a stormy flood flocking,
Like stormy winds that set the waves rocking
In a free land you have the broad ploughlands embraced.

Like the voice of a well-spring, or water-brook ringing,
Like the splash of blue lakes that stretch boundless, afar,
Like the sound in the oakgroves of leaves in the spring-time,
Thus your free words go forth, chiming and singing
Borne on a wave to the sun and the stars.
....

XXV

My land, Biełaruś! Motherland of true heroes,
Today boundless spaces are caught in the strife,
Thou will bring down the foe, for there stand ever near you
The Soviet peoples, united and fearless.
Thou shalt find joyous peace and a happier life.

But while on thy peaceful fields in war come crowding,
Together the criminal gang of thy foes,
Beneath the Red flag, standing tally and proudly
Rending the chains of captivity boldly,
Through the days of war thou shalt, a partisan, go.

My land, Biełaruś! Through fields and woods passing,
All through thy expanse liberation shall roll.
Through the storm-whirlwind, through snowdrifts advancing,
Troop upon troop come the Guards, swiftly marching
They shall be met by some million souls.

They come, and the sun rises high, flashes ever
From village to village, from township to town,
Through all Biełaruś, every child, every mother,
This day from sincere heart says, all the land over:
'To Nation and Party all praise and renown!'

NADZIA-NADZIEJKA

Orphan flute sobs in the forest are breaking . . .
You have grown silent,
Grown dumb, our Nadziejka.
Who would have dreamed the working of fortune:
Your eyes to be closed by cloudy autumn,
Your tresses unplaited,
Cheeks sunken palely,
Hands drooping frailly.

'*Nadzia-Nadziejka!*' the flute's sobs are breaking.
Never again your hands
Shall reap the rye more,
Shall reap the rye more,
Nor the sheaves tie more.
For the third night the young girl is hanging
On the white birch-tree, near her home standing.
A searing-grief chains the heart over,
What is this, birch-tree, could you not save her?

With yellowed leaves come tears bitter and paining,
From the white birch-tree, falling and raining:
'O you good people, I pray that you set me
Free from my grief, fell me, it were fare better!
From very childhood this maid I remember . . .
Gold of the far sand,
Green of a garland.
Blue her eyes, seeming
Like cornflowers gleaming . . .'

Gusty the winds, and wild the storms blowing . . .
Sad through the forest a young lad is going.
'*Nadzia-Nadziejka!*' the flute's sobs are breaking.
With yellowed leaves come tears bitter and paining,
From the white birch-tree falling and raining:
'Young lad, your eyes heavy with sorrow,
Hew me down, white, in night's blackness, for terror
It is to endure this young maiden's horror.
I recall you two laughing,
Dancing and singing
Ballads of springtime
Till dawn-light glimmered . . .'

The lad carries his grief the broad ploughland over,
Seeks in his pain from the birch to discover:
'Why couldn't your branches hide my beloved?'
'*Nadzia-Nadziejka!*' The flute's sobs are breaking . . .

With yellowed leaves come tears bitter and paining,
From the white birch-tree falling and raining
'When there came flying the darkness-attacker,
Serpents crawled in, with bite of an adder,
They breathed forth smoke – I became blackened.
With uproar, commotion,
Alarm, devastation,
Beauty they ruined.
The maiden – they slew her!'

Through woodland and forest and oak-grove goes sternly
A lad fired with anger, a lad grim-determined:
'Soon I'll be returning
With my companions,
With lightning's clamour,
And thunder's hammer,
With iron generation, we'll roast out these adders,
We'll cleanse the sky, every cloud we shall scatter,

We shall honour this maiden,
The branches we'll straighten,
We'll sprinkle the grasses with pure tear-drops over,
With pure tear-drops over,
Like dewdrop cover . . .'
'*Nadzia-Nadziejka!*' the flute's cry is waking.

Piatro Hłebka

NATIVE BREAD

The fire burns. Round the trenches massing
For home yearn our countrymen,
And the partisan young lasses
Bake and dry flat loaves again.

May that bread be blessed ever,
Bread which in the field they make,
Bread unsalted, bread unleavened,
For our weighty needing baked.

From a threshold burned and yawning,
Messenger of all our woes,
With this bread a lad, at dawning,
Leaves his troop and takes the road.

All the way from Hrodna marching
On to Moscow he will strive,
Often weary, hungry, parching,
Hardly living, will arrive.

But from the last crust (in this bag it
Slowly falls away to crumbs),
He'll not break himself a fragment,
Nor touch it, whoever comes.

But when he's finished with escaping,
With friends at table takes his place,
He'll think of bread on hot coals baking,
Flavoured with smoke and cumin-taste.

And, as by the Byelorussian custom
To bring a gift each traveller must,
From his bag he'll bring out a rusk of
Bread gone hard, a dried-up crust.

He will break the bread as need be,
And 'Before we drink,' he'll say,
'Lads, let's taste our own bread, kneaded,
In our own land, far away!'

And, dearest God, the air is sated
With that earth's scent so fragrant, fine!
And all will be intoxicated,
Straightway, but not with bitter wine.

Drunk with memories unfading
Of our own dear native land,
Of a country and a cradle,
And our mother's tender hand.

Where gathered round the trenches massing
Each evening mourn our countrymen
Where the Partisan young lasses
Bake and dry flat loaves again.

DEATH OF A SOLDIER

Upon the battle field a soldier dies,
To his last shot he fought in bold endeavour,
Already his companions sleep forever
And, side by side, in rank with them, he lies.

But he did not yield up his life in vain,
Having shot down some dozens of black helmets,
And carrying out every duty well, now
Quietly he into non-existence wanes.

He longed for one thing only, earnestly:
Upon green fields to let his glances linger,
For one last time run grass-blades through his fingers,
To hear the solemn sound of native trees.

But everything was desert, all around,
The fir-trees burned to charcoal, the grass blackened,
The spruces lying, mown down, crushed and flattened,
And bitter smoke was rolling on the ground.

Like old-time warrior of heroic race
Though on the grave's dark threshold he now hovered,
The last remaining shreds of strength he gathered
And, with an effort, upward turned his face.

Thick azure turned to dark above his head.
The day was burning out, the sun was dying,
Slowly beyond the rim of earth was gliding,
As if beneath a tombstone's shade it sped.

But the sun with its immortal light,
Was tinting white clouds red, incarnadining,
Was spreading gold along the distant skyline
Touching each shoot, each grain of sand with bright.

At last the sun's disc was a quarter down,
The soldier looked, with eyes wide open round him,
'What beauty, dearest land of mine, surrounds thee,
When even death wears such a noble gown!

In my own home I shall no more abide,
But life will not burn out in them, no never.
Dear land, in happiness, then, flower thou ever!'
Thus the soldier spoke before he died.

Slowly, to non-existence, all our ways
Must lead; then fate, a death heroic bring me!
And grant that, beneath death's eyes, I may sing thee
A hymn to life, a last paean of praise!

Anatol Astrejka

MY HUT

In a glade beneath a birch-tree,
Safe away from every eye,
In no house, nor dug-out murky,
In a forest hut live I.

Seven poles with fork-joints, covered
In with osiers entwined,
Like a gravemound, mossed all over,
This partisan home of mine.

A plank for a little table,
And a bed five branches make,
Hay on top, and one is able
To sleep there without an ache.

I am used to its routine now,
Where I lie down, that's my bed,
When it rains, I spread a screen of
Waterproof above my head.

When no trace of war will meet you,
To deep forest glades once more
I'll return, again to greet it,
My partisan hut of yore.

Valancin Taŭłaj

TO MY LITTLE SISTER

While you are growing, at the time
You first tread out life's pathway, dearest,
Fix in your memory these lines
That I compose from words sincerest.

Maybe you will not comprehend –
I write them as a man mature, dear,
I know: this day must have its end,
From which these lines today matured dear.

Maybe this poem and no more,
Living in memory you'll keep then,
Like a far echo of the hours
That spur my heart, that wound it deeply.

Then, little sister, call to mind
All those who came not back from warring,
Fighting that days for which we pined
Might flow o'er Biełaruś once more then.

Pimien Pančanka

THE SNIPER'S EYE

In a sniper's eye, as in a mansion gleaming,
There are trees and clouds and starry evening,
And the light shadow of a bird in flight
Whose wing in passing cuts across the sight.

I long to be a sniper, who can garner
In a small falling star friends one and all,
Beloved cities with their lofty walls,
Lakes and well-springs, meadowland and gardens.

But now the white ravine,
Around, snows keep it,
But from the scrub eyes catch a black snake creeping,
At once, like tongs, the eyelashes have seized
And gripped the serpent.
Swift the lightning ran.
And the blue snows of January freeze
Over two hundred fallen Aryans . . .

Once more the sniper's eye is open, poring
On birds and trees, friends and the stars' high soaring.

THE HERO

He angrily said 'Troops! Get up. Hustle!
This is no beach, this is war! Don't slack!'
And he lay on the snaked coils of wire. And, mustered,
Two hundred soldiers boots, worn and dusty
Passed on over his back.

Not he, but others attacked, were hurling
Grenades into concrete pillboxes there,
They ran through Fritzes, set tanks burning
And hoisted the victory flag in the morning
Over the conquered frontier.

But he, from the rusted barbs releasing,
Plucked his bones without groaning, with his own hand,
Collapsed in the grass, as a pain unceasing
To grasses, to dewdrops and soothing breezes
Which from the Valdai lakes gently fanned.

Kastuś Kirenka

THE FIELD

Thunders had struck the field. Stormwinds of fiery flame
In blood had raged there,
like fiends kneading clay madly.
And my friends had given it a name,
Called it Death Valley.

How many mass graves have been hollowed here,
With monuments or untended,
Burying grief for a hundred-fold years,
And joys of true friendship.

By leaden hailstones this field was scored.
But days pass away. Far the front-line advances.
And the farmer-soldier has come back from war,
To the ploughland's expanses.

From the earth, silently, he has dug up his plough,
Angry, as in the last battle's hell-striving,
He has cut in the field the first furrow, somehow,
One-armed driving.

On the free tillage he scattered his grain,
Pure as the tears of a mother,
And the field has put on, beneath the warm rain,
Robes of green lustre.

It resounded with chiming bee-notes again;
To it the soldier came out, and
Spoke the words which long caused him pain
'Beloved ploughland!'

But sudden his glance was caught and held
By the quiet mass-graves around there.
The soldier convulsively shuddered and felt
His heart wildly pounding.

He thought of his friends, heroic and good,
The infantryman's joys and yearning,
He longed to be far from these green oak woods,
To the fifth troop returning,

To bear arms and go forth in the battle to toil,
To pour far and widely spilt blood of foemen,
For brave hearts of soldiers under the soil,
For his native ploughland.

Vasil Vitka

FATHER

Because the house grew brighter, bolder,
And mother from sheer joy was sobbing,
I recognized the new-come soldier,
Him for whom we for years were longing.

From the kit-bag of a foot-slogger,
Grown sour with salt dust, he unpacked the
Children's present – just some sugar
Somehow mixed up with tobacco.

I did not see that the next instant
He'd turned aside, as if in thinking;
I did not see the dewdrop glisten,
On Father's stern eyelashes winking.

Being so young, I had not learned then:
Maybe naught harder to fulfil than
To bring through war, safe home returning,
Joy in a kit-bag for the children.

Pimien Pančanka

*   *   *

You hear honking cries – Are you glad, are you sad?
Between waves of dense azure fly forth
The cranes, high above and beyond Ararat,
The cranes flying home to the north.

You are used, at this time, to greet them, welcoming,
Under the first dawn of spring.
But here the cranes, with their great wing-flaps, depart,
In migration, flight breaking a way through the heart.

You forget you are thousands of miles from your home,
Wish, in anger, to cry out and curse:
'Hey, who's showing this film, so poignantly known,
And has rigged it to run in reverse?'

The cranes fly beyond Kazbek and El'brus,
Heart contracts with its yearning and need.
Soon she will greet them, my Biełaruś,
In the warm green of the meads.

I never have envied birds, never have longed
For wings; better without them, say I;
Yet now I stand mute, stricken by some deaf wrong,
And cannot tear my gaze from the sky.

Iran, 1944

Anatol Vialuhin

BALLAD OF THE URAL TANK

Far in the Urals
Beyond cedars' cloud-fastness,
The miners went down
Into murkiest darkness.

And through the long nights
Men dreamed at the stopings,
Of a tank for dread battle,
Never seen yet, long hoped for.

The golden earth yielded
Her ore to their toiling,
That blast-furnace might seethe
With a metal flood boiling.

The hands of the workers
And tools handled rightly
Part by part have assembled
A giant great and mighty.

Cast and moulded in anger
From Uralian bedrock,
It rose up, for warfare
And battle charge ready.

A young craftsman toiling,
As the sleepless shift passes,
Colours it over,
As green as the grass is.

Sits on the machine-guns,
With tobacco-mists twining,
Paints on the turrets
Stars brightly shining.

At such a great labour
– Two nights, sleeping never –
His stern eyes are weary,
Lids sleep-glued together.

Yet, by the new guns,
(He had driven out slumber)
To his memory come
His home and his mother,

Whom he had left
In that dread summer,
Now in captivity
Half a world from him . . .

And the lad wrote (hope filled him),
Above the gun-slits there,
'Give back my village,
My own dear Sunicy!'

At the call of the orders,
Mighty, green and impressive,
The tank ran through the hubbub
Of guns ranged to test it.

And then locomotives
Pulled it and towed it
On a mountainous, resinous
Cross-taiga roadway.

With its echelon it was
Gulped down by tunnels,
Across rolling Volga
On bridges it rattled.

At a dark whistle-stop
Beyond Smalensk smoky,
On to the field, warriors
The machine unloaded.

On the armour clad branches
Of fir-tree they set there,
Drivers gave to the engines
A good drink of petrol.

The general read over
The mighty gun-slits there:
'Give back my village,
My own dear Sunicy!'

At the call of the orders,
Its part playing rightly,
The tank ran through the field with
Its missile shells smiting.

In the field many
To toil at avenging,
It crushed the machine-guns,
Concrete pill-boxes rending.

Defended by fire,
The foeman's fierce shooting
Against them there thundered
The thunders
Of shooting.

Although on the Urals' son
The gunfire smote, pealing,
The warrior armour
To no missile yielded!

Over infantry ranks rolled
The tank, onward flying,
And the green companies
From fear were crying.

On the armour were tatters
Of uniform clinging . . .
....
He was the first into
The street of the village.

The sweat-soaked tank driver
Stood up from the turret.
A village of grief this,
No windows. No hubbub.

But a grandma crossed herself,
For the stars and gun-slits there . . .
'What is this village called?'
'Son, this is Sunicy! . . .'

Alaksiej Zarycki

THE HEART

For Pimien Pančanka

A miser I,
The greatest of misers –
All that I can find in
My heart I am hiding.
Dreams from youth rising,
Battle's loud thunder,
Fortune's bright wonder,
Greatness of our country,
Her dear bounty,
The light of her glory poured –
All this in my heart I have stored.

Yet my heart knows not stillness
Being so wilful.
Fall asleep, and it is gone,
Alone,
Through fields of rye going,
Orchards blowing,
Through groves growing,
It crosses town bridges (each showing
Waves beneath with nocturnal lights glowing,
Evenly rocking and flowing).
It goes out on the banks.
Where lumber-jacks spread their campfires,
Near blast-furnaces running,
While sun upon sun the
Steel-masters smelt there,
Tireless.

It taps on a girl's window-pane,
And again
To a new house
Goes on boldly,
To a soldier,
Then, next, a young man it finds, and
Leaves behind it
Everywhere warm golden nuggets
For others.
I am a miser – a finder
And hider.

But my heart, overflowing,
Like wind through grain blowing,
Through the wide world that treasure is sowing.

Until the first dawn-light it wanders,
And then it returns, jumps up on my verandah,
Comes, knocks upon the breast, shakes it,
And wakes it.
And I awaken then,
Greet the morning
And our bright sun's
Burning colours,
Once more gathering, storing,
Treasures new for a thousand
Hearts of others.

HOMELAND SWALLOW

We were marching through Germany,
Wearily,
We took a short nap by a spinney.
A swallow,
A swallow (dreams revealed it)
Above Dniapro wheeling,
Scooping spray with its wingbeats.
I awoke – a strange vista appears,
Yet the twitter of swallows I hear.
So, under this pine I'll still lie,
In dreams, maybe, swallows will fly.

THE EAGLE WELL-SPRING

To the memory of Captain Hastel

Eagle, not to you will it be given
To hear in August fields whistling winds ever,
Poplars whispering, murmuring rivers:
Wakeless is your sleep, immobile slumber . . .
Where are you eagle, where, bold and beloved,
Do you sleep? What vale is its beacon?
Beneath what fir-tree, whisperedly-speaking?
. . . For the eagle's grave come not seeking!

There where Hasteł's heart ceased, no more to
Beat after all its striving – men tell it –
On that spot there flows, ever-pouring
From the plumbless depths, a clear well-spring.
Willows raise their vesture high over,
And young eaglets drink from it ever.

THAT THEY MIGHT KNOW

On a high gravemound is growing a pine,
That they might know;
Down to the depths the swollen roots twine,
That they might know;
And its tip brushes the stars as they shine
That they might know;
Like a taut string with the breezes it chimes,
That they might know,
The mothers
Where falcon-sons slumbering remain,
The winds
Where with loud bow to play, unrestrained,
The stars
Where to fall, like droplets of rain,
The birds in migration –
Their own home again.

Pimien Pančanka

THE CARAVAN

Praise to you, soldier's rest, strong and deep!
Free from dreams without sense!
An unclear ringing roused me from sleep,
Dull bells of a sadness intense.
In narrow passes lay a blue smoke,
On the peaks lay a pink smoke
After the leader, the chief, grey and ruddy,
The camels were plodding.
And the look in their eyes such a grief was expressing,
And their humps were so weary and worn.
It seemed: from the era of Cyrus, unresting,
They trudge, until Nothingness dawns.
The caravan-master, an aged man, leads,
Foreign caravan to Mecca city
Through a desert of yellow,
No rivers, no trees –
For this man I feel pity.
At Mecca arriving
He'll find no luck thriving . . .
Surely it's not a lie radio was invented
And aeroplanes?
And I say sadly,
Come, my Minsk morning, give this foreign country
One short hour of gladness.
By the Sož, by the Prypiać today gather in,
The down of the stars,
Scent of fir-trees and mint.
In a red tablecloth bring to us hither.
Birdsongs from above Nioman's tide,
And with grains of clear dew sow the desert, far, wide.
Maybe that will ease this country's poor pining,
Maybe, in a dream, the grey leader will guess
That somewhere above Minsk,
Beneath the sun's shining,
Are crane's voices calling of happiness.

POTATOES

To journey to the west in such a fashion,
Only once in an epoch comes to pass.
Everyone was dying for their rations,
But cook and stove were in the mud, alas.

Tightening their belts with a sharp tugging,
We lay to rest, with dark blue firs above us,
On the dry roadside, repose complete,
Cigarette for the soul, heaven for feet.

Then a quarrel broke out, unexpected,
What's the tastiest of all known food?
'Chaš i łoba,' Vano interjected,
'I'd like seven plates-ful, now, I would!'

'Pilau,' said Achmed, 'At home, I remember . . .'
And unexpectedly his lips he licked,
'But,' said Gurgen, 'do you know, however
Erevan and its juiciest shashliks!'

I grew angry, and no joke, I'll tell you:
'I'd not underrate your dishes, no!
Certainly, these foods have no small value,
Gourmets praise them highly, I heard so!

It's a shame, though, not to know the finest,'
(I rushed at the soldiers in attack!)
'If for a tasty breakfast you are pining,
Order up potatoes and salt sprats!

Baked potatoes are a tale of magic!
Scrape 'em with a knife – then eat your fill!
Golden as a cake the roasted jacket,
You will eat enough for three, you will!

When you meet a housewife good and kindly,
Ask her, friend, to be so kind and make
Potato pancakes with fresh cream as side dish,
Potato scones, and dumplings, even cakes.

From the good potatoes of our nation
A thousand dishes come, no less, my friends! . . .'
I jumped up and sang with inspiration
The Potato Polka to the end.

I see my speech has swayed them, for enlivened
They yell, 'Where are they? Bring them here! No lag!'
It's a good thing the cook was just arriving
Plodding on a sweating ginger nag.

Mikoła Aŭramčyk

THE SOLDIER'S TEAR

Many a friend of his death's scythe had taken
Among burned homes and ruins of their kin,
But he, broad-shouldered champion unshaken
Of Biełaruś, strove on towards Berlin.

Many a mile his boots already trekked now,
Till to the foreign border he had won,
Where first his cheeks – no more with bitter sweat now –
Glittered with a tear-drop in the sun.

He leapt into the battle. Without resting
Across the muddied osiers he crawled . . .
. . . And there trembled in his tear, incessant,
Images of trees and brickwork walls.

Anatol Vialuhin

THE BULL-FINCHES

White ploughlands, deep in slumber, drowse now.
Frost through the yard came clattering.
Look through the window:
There, like flowers now,
Bull-finches on blue willows swing.

The birds' breasts puff with pride and splendour . . .
In the stern hubbub's noise, in truth,
Never, friend, will you not remember
These, the bull-finch days of youth.

A bird-trap near the oak-grove waits them.
Run then, eager as you are . . .
Agile, fiery-powdered, take them,
Living fragments of a star!

Alaksiej Rusiecki

MAY

The world would wither up from year to year
Without the sap without the Maytime colours,
When it from the deep dreams of seed appears
Piercing with its verdant plumes the furrows;
When, on the branches, twisted, knotted tight,
It bursts forth, in the air expands, and shivers
With a transparent foliage, like light
From spirit-lamp, thin fire on the breeze quivers;
When, like small curled mustachios, it creeps
Like fleshy hop-bines on oak hop-poles twisting,
Sprinkles the rays in dewdrops, where sparks leap,
And in a bright-hued dust on colours glistens,
Upon the osier bush, like dawn it gleams,
Chimes with the nightingales beside the river,
In the grass, in a darling's hair its sheen –
Then come, my shoulders bear their burden ever.
A mighty hour. Softer than lightest silk
Resin has clotted the wounds upon the fir-trees,
Beneath burnt remnants strong sap pounds, unkilled,
To be reborn in new, abundant verdure.
Over the channels, trenches, earthworks, waver
Rye, in a running undulation surging
In sunlight the house springs up, as alive,
Though its blind windows speak of brickbats hurling.
I often dreamed of such a spring in nights
When torn by iron, my skin like treebark on one,
Now I can feel it spread in me, while white
Apple trees in a vernal flood are thronging.
Space for the heart, as for a cloud, again,
All is clear-cut, I find, with inspiration,
Thought answering to thought, and grain to grain
And brick for brick in new regeneration.
And, from their sources every living thing
Will rise again with force unbowed, undying,
To the sun's Maytime zenith summoning,
But they'll not heed who in the graves are lying.
Dearest friends, young heroes, brave and true
I shall not forget the place where heavy
Sands were piled deeply to cover you,
In darkness to bury you for ever.
Different fate divided me from you,

Though to battle we in step were marching,
For the peaceful glitter of green dews,
For bright day, above our homeland arching.
May the sun's thin rays creep down to you
Piercing down into your deepest dreaming,
With the fragrances from quiet fields streaming
Just as to living men in hour of gloom
Was your own life-affirming spirit gleaming!
Springtime colours settle all around,
On yellowed hillock, over grey stone playing,
May they know, these ones deep underground,
How with our wreaths we our own hearts are laying.
Blaze, mighty radiance of the spring once more,
Shine burning colours in a rainbow glorious,
Above those who could not come back from war,
Above these who foreknew this May victorious.

NOTES

Again, in this section, the poems are arranged in approximately chronological order.

p. 139: *My Biesiadź*
As the conventional 'they say' of the opening line indicates (*kažuć*), the motif of the peewit is based on a Byelorussian folk-tale, the 'moral' of which is akin to that of the grasshopper and the ant. The poet, however, imbues the whole theme of the poem with his own personal insight; in particular, seeming to equate, at least partially, the 'little bags, with earth stowed' carried by the birds, with the small bag of native soil traditionally carried by a wanderer or exile. (The identical expression appears in *By a grave of brothers* – see p. 155.)

The peewit's cry, to Byelorussian ears, sound like *pić* (pronounced *peets*), cf. Janka Kupała, *Burial Mound*, stanza 12, meaning 'to drink'. This effect cannot be fully rendered in English; the present version, however, attempts to indicate the pun and the supporting alliteration of *i prosic pić* by 'seeking a sip'.

p. 139: *Moscow Street*
Although Kułasoŭ was not, himself, from West Byelorussia, the reunion of the country led, for a time, to a general wave of pro-Russian feeling. This poem, although at first typical-seeming of this honeymoon period, seems at second glance, to be not so much a straightforward eulogium, but a gently humorous 'send-up' of the enthusiasm of the period.

stanza 3. The 'poem' mentioned does not seem readily identifiable – the reference to it, however, seems to intensify the 'send-up' effect.

stanza 5. 'A Moscow-townsman.' The poet does not call himself a Muscovite (Maskał) since this would imply merely a Russian – he calls himself 'Maskvič', a dweller-in-the-city-of-Moscow. (Motoring enthusiasts will better recognize this name, in its Russian form of Moskvič!)

p. 140: *Gliding the cloud came . . .*
Byelorussian, having the full three-gender system, permits personification of natural objects and phenomena in a manner altogether lacking the somewhat eighteenth-century atmosphere of personifications in English. Accordingly, to render *jana* (referring to a cloud) as 'she' would normally be somewhat suspect; particularly at so late a date as 1940. Nevertheless, the picture of the cloud in this poem is so anthropomorphic that it seems the personification may validly be rendered in English.

p. 142: *Niccolo Paganini*
Niccolo Paganini (1782–1840), the Italian violinist and composer, in addition to his undoubted position as the principal nineteenth-century virtuoso of the violin, also acquired, in his own day, the personal aura of a 'Byronic' figure, outwardly Mephistophelean, inwardly consumed with melancholy and depression, yet enamoured withal of the delights of gambling and romantic lover. (This reputation may have been, at least in part, self-cultivated; the fact that his protégé, Berlioz, composed his *Harold en Italie* 'for' Paganini, suggests that the Byronic reputation did not come to the latter entirely unsought!) In all events, the aura of

Byronism connected with the composer seems to have permeated the concept which Vitka received of Paganini's music; an aura the more powerful when one recalls that in Eastern Europe the name of Byron is far more revered than it has ever been within the British Isles – Byron having benefited both from the happy accident of good translators and a posthumously-acquired reputation of a champion of the Orthodox faith, the Greek struggle for independence being seen, not so much as a political confrontation of Hellene and Turk as a religious conflict of Orthodox versus Infidel (since the need to 'protect' their Orthodox brethren was the public excuse of successive Tsars for their attempts at dabbling in Balkan politics).

stanza 1. Ornithologically, of course, the 'lapwing' mentioned here is identical with the 'peewit' (*Konia*) of *My Biesiadz* and *Burial Mound.* The word used here, however, is *čajka*, a perfectly acceptable variant in Byelorussian, but the standard form in Ukrainian. The 'lapwing' image, here, is indeed a strong echo of the Ukrainian 'folk-song' (the words of which are attributed to Hetman Ivan Mazeppa, *O woe to the lapwing . . .* (see *The Ukrainian Review*, 3, 1959, p. 47).

p. 143: *On my poems*
stanza 1. Vladimir Vladimirovič Mayakovskii (1893–1930), the well-known 'Futurist' poet of the early Soviet period. It should, perhaps, be pointed out, that at the time of Mayakovskii's suicide in 1930, Taŭłaj was only 16 years of age; it should not therefore be assumed that the advice mentioned was necessarily Mayakovskii's personal practice; it is redolent, rather of the standard advice any established writer gives to any beginner, however talented.

stanza 5. Francysk Skaryna was born *c.* 1490 in Połack. He studied at the Universities of Kraków and then at Padua (receiving from the latter the degree of Doctor of Medical Science). He then proceeded to the Bohemian capital of Praha, where he mastered the printing trade, and became the first printer of Byelorussian books, at first in Praha, (1517) and then in Vilna. He died not earlier than 1535. Skaryna's books are distinguished by his own personal colophon of the sun and moon; this with its strong stylistic connections with the illustrations of alchemical manuscripts and the early printed alchemical books, suggests that at least part of his time in Praha was spent in the company of the practitioners of the Golden Lane! (A supposition not unlikely, when one recalls the strong connections between the early book-trade and the iatrochemical/alchemical profession – Dante Alighieri himself, for example, was enrolled as a member of the Guild of Physicians and Apothecaries in 1295–6.) Although I know of no alchemical work which exactly reproduces the Skaryna colophon, a number come very close to it; the nearest, to my knowledge, being in the *Philosophorum Praeclara Monita*, in the St Andrews' collection, in the representation of the Hermetic Androgyne. (The illustration in question being conveniently reproduced as plate 16 of John Read's *Prelude to Chemistry*, London, 1936.) It should be noted, however, that in this manuscript, the moon is in the waning (right-facing) position, whereas in the Skaryna colophon it is in the auspicious waxing position with the 'horns' pointing towards the left.

stanza 7. The American poet, Menke Katz (of Byelorussian-Jewish origin), has drawn my attention, in this context, to a line which he states to be by Longfellow, but which I have so far been unable to identify, that rhyme is a 'prisoner dancing to the music of his chains'. One wonders if such an image, recast and inverted by Taŭłaj, lies at the back of this stanza.

p. 144: *Nioman*
The Nioman, as the largest of Byelorussian rivers, typifies and symbolizes in this poem the essence of Byelorussia. It may be noted, that, although the word for 'river' in Byelorussian (*raka*), and, indeed, its analogues in the other Slavonic languages, is feminine, that the mighty river Nioman (like, for example, the Thames, Tiber and Mississippi) is masculine, and may be personified as a father-figure.

stanza 4. The 'withdrawal' was necessitated by the manner (or lack of manner) of the declaration of war. It will be recalled that Nazi Germany had entered into a non-aggression pact with the USSR. In the early morning of June 22, 1941, this was rudely broken when the panzer divisions moved across the Byelorussian and Ukrainian borders. This advance, and the accompanying bombardment of major cities, was so complete a surprise, that Hitler's armies were well into Byelorussia before any concerted action to halt them could be embarked on.

p. 145: *The Voice of the land*
stanza 3. 'Teuton' figures. Much of the poetry of this period uses the evocative key-words of Nazi pride of race, turning them into words of derision. But here, too, is a veiled allusion to the Teutonic knights, so long an implacable enemy of the Grand Duchy of Lithuania, to escape whose 'crusades' the (ethnic) Lithuanian princes embraced Christianity in 1386.

p. 146: *To Byelorussian Partisans*
Perhaps the most bloodthirsty of all Byelorussian war poetry. It should be remembered, however, that this was literally a fight for the survival of the Byelorussian nation, Hitler's plans for *lebensraum* including, *inter alia*, the takeover of 'Poland, White Russia and the Ukraine. To obtain this would involve a major war, and, incidentally, *the extermination of the people then living in these parts*.' (Winston S. Churchill, *The Gathering Storm*, Ch. 15, my italics.)

p. 152: *The Flag of the Brigade*
A long narrative, beginning on the very first day of the onslaught of war (see note to *Nioman, supra*), and tracing the history of the war from the point of view of the narrator Aleś Rybka. The poem was awarded a Stalin prize for literature in 1946. Only the first part of the poem is given in this selection.

It should be recalled, in the latter part of this extract, describing New Moscow Street, that, the month being June, the horsechestnuts would be in flower and the leaves of the lime-trees 'sweet' with a coating of stick sap.

p. 155: *By a grave of brothers*
The Byelorussian expression 'A grave of brothers' (*Brackija mahiła*) means, in fact, a mass grave. I have ventured to translate the idiom literally, as being more meaningful and emotive than the standard English expression.

line 1. Staraya Ruś is a village in Russia, a little to the north of the Byelorussian frontier.

p. 159: *The gardens forever will bloom . . .*
line 3. Like Olwen in Welsh folklore, Lada, the Byelorussian goddess of spring, was so beautiful that wherever her foot touched the soil, flowers sprang up (though, in the traditions unlike those of Olwen, no specific colour or genus of flower are mentioned in connection with Lada). Here the image of Lada (and all

the overtones of spring represent liberation) merge with the image of the beloved, left behind, beyond the lines, in the Occupied regions.

p. 159: *Blitz babies*
Strictly speaking, the title of this poem *Dzieci vajny* should be translated 'Children of the War'. However, since the former rendering has strong emotive overtones in English (particularly in so far as the psychological after-effect of war is concerned) whereas the literal rendering is entirely colourless, I have here proceeded 'andgit of andgiete' in the Alfredian phrase.

p. 162: *Pigeons*
Perhaps one of the poignant features of this poem is that under the German occupation, the keeping of tame pigeons (whether for racing, or simply as pets) was strictly forbidden, and all such birds were immediately ordered to be destroyed lest they be used for partisan purposes as carriers.

p. 163: *The three*
line 8. 'Could not live out the spring', *'pieražyc viasny'*. So the text, although in the context of the poem, one might expect something on the lines of *'pieražyc da viasny'*, 'Could not endure till spring' – the sick prisoner dying on the last day of winter, and laid dead on the grass in the dawn of the first day of spring (with an irony somewhat akin to that of the Czech Jiři Wolker's *Ballad from Hospital* – for an English translation, see E. Osers and J. K. Montgomery, *Modern Czech Poetry*). If, however, the reading is correct, and the rhythm would tend to confirm this, then either this is a strong meiosis 'could not live out the spring' – 'could live only to the first day of spring', or the poet is deliberately rejecting the Wolker-type effect as being too 'obvious' or 'theatrical' in this given context.

p. 164: *Biełaruś*
An interesting example of an 'occasional' poem, clearly written to inspire patriotism and resistance, with an approach to the subject matter that is imaginative and loosely symbolic, rather than noted for its historical precision.

The epigraph is, of course, the opening line of *The New Land.*

section I, stanza 4. The Biełavieža forest, the last European home of the wild bison, is the only wild-life preserve in Europe owned and administered jointly by two countries – Poland and the Byelorussian SSR. There is in existence (though now out of print) a very beautiful bilingual Byelorussian/English illustrated book (of the 'coffee-table' genus), entitled *Bielaviežskaja Pušča* (The Bielavieža forest) published in Minsk in 1964, to which the English-speaking reader is warmly recommended.

section III, stanza 1. The Prussians, i.e. the Teutonic Knights, defeated by the forces of the Grand Duchy of Lithuania (which, of course, included Byelorussia) under Jagajlo in 1410).

section III, stanza 1. 'Lake Peipus' (Broŭka uses the alternative name of Čudski). The site of Alexander Nevskii's 'Battle on the Ice' (April 5, 1242), when the heavily armoured German knights came to grief, after an initial successful charge, as the rotten ice gave way under their weight.

The concept of unity through the ages between Russians, Ukrainians and Byelorussians, while perhaps a laudable ideal in the context of such a poem is simply not borne out by historical fact.

stanza 2. 'Smalensk' (Russian: Smolensk), situated on the borders of Russia and Byelorussia, has frequently been the scene of battles in the course of its long and tumultuous history, being attacked in 1340 by Muscovites and Tartars, besieged in 1408 by Lithuanians, captured by Muscovy in 1514, taken by the Poles in 1611 (during the 'Time of Troubles') and ceded to Muscovy in 1667. The coupling of Smalensk and Poltava in the same line, however, suggests the campaigns of Charles XII of Sweden in 1708–9. In which case, the Byelorussians being at that time incorporated into the Polish–Lithuanian state which was an active ally of the Swedes, the poet has here cited an incident in which Byelorussians and Russians were fighting on opposing sides. A contemporary account of the somewhat complex manœuvres in the Smalensk area at this time is to be found in the letters of Captain James Jeffereyes (edited by R. M. Hatton in *Historiske Handlingar, 35* (1), 1954. For perhaps the best survey of this campaign from the point of view of a modern historian, see the relevant chapters in R. M. Hatton: *Charles XII of Sweden* (London, 1968).

'Poltava'. The celebrated defeat, on June 27 (O.S.) 1709, of the Swedish armies and their allies, the Ukrainian Cossacks, under Hetman Ivan Mazeppa by the armies of Peter I ('the Great') of Russia – 'dread Pultowa's day' as Byron has it – which marked the turning-point in the Russo–Swedish 'Northern War'. It should be noted that, even more unequivocably than in the preceding case, Broŭka cites an instance when the 'brotherhood' of Russian, Ukrainian and Byelorussian peoples was divided against itself in war.

'the steppes Zapcrozhian', i.e. the plains of the lower Dnieper. The old Cossack headquarters (the *Sič*) was on the island of Khortytsya in the Dnieper 'beyond the rapids' (in Ukrainian *za porohami*), i.e. downstream from the nine great rapids formed where the Dnieper turns from an easterly to a southerly course. The Sič was destroyed by Catherine II ('the Great') in 1775. The name of the Zaporozhian Cossacks is preserved in that of the city of Zaporizhzhiya (pre-revolutionary Aleksandrovsk), which is close to the site of the original Sič.

stanza 3. 'Vaščyła': a somewhat obscure hero, whose name is connected with the ancient heroic period of the *bylyny.*

'Chvieśko': another somewhat obscure character of the seventeenth century.

Kalinoŭski. Kastuś Kalinoŭski was, at least in the subsequent 'folklore' of the times, the principal Byelorussian leader of the Polish–Lithuanian–Byelorussian rising of 1863. He was publisher and editor of the (illegal) newspaper *Mužyckaja-pravda.* After the failure of the rising, Kalinoŭski was hanged by the Russians in Vilna in March, 1864.

The Rising of 1863, largely concerned with the injustices arising as an aftermath of the General Emancipation of the serfs of the Russian Empire in 1861, attracted considerable attention in Britain (see, for example, *The Times* for February and March, 1863, also *Punch*, February 21, 1863).

A brief biography of Kalinoŭski appears in *JBS*, Vol. 1, No. 1, 1965, pp. 30–5; for a detailed discussion of the background to the Rising, see Robert F. Leslie; *Reform and Insurrection in Russian Poland, 1856–1865* (University of London Historical Studies, No. 13, 1963).

section IV, stanza 1. 'Połack': a city standing on the Western Dzvina, at the confluence with the Połota; it is first mentioned in the chronicles of 862. In the tenth century, it was ruled by an immigrant Scandinavian prince, Rohvalad (Rognvald and although he was ultimately defeated in battle by Volodymyr I of Kiev (later to become a saint, but then still in his unregenerate pagan period), Połack preserved a good measure of independence right through the Kievan period. After the Tartar invasion (1240–41) and the destruction of Kievan power, Połack came under the control of the Grand Dukes of Lithuania, and by the end of the century was of sufficient importance to be mentioned in an Icelandic list of the principal cities of the world (see Hauksbók, MS. AM544 folio 3v). Połack achieved self-government in 1498, but was captured by Tsar Ivan IV ('the Terrible') of Russia in 1563 and retaken by Stepan Batory for Poland in 1579 (a contemporary English account of this capture: A TRUE REPORTE OF THE TAKING OF THE GREATE TOWNE AND CASTELL OF POLOTZKO BY THE KING OF POLONIA *with the manner of the Assaults, Batteries, Underminninges, Skirmishes and Fyreworkes that were there used from the 11. of August to the 30. of the same month 1579,* is published in *JBS*, Vol. 1, No. 1, pp. 19–22). Finally, under the First Partition of Poland, Połack passed under the rule of the Russian Empire.

Skaryna: see note to Taułaj's *On My Poems*, in this section, *supra.* In fact, although born in Połack, Skaryna does not seem to have had any close connection with the city in adult life.

stanza 3. 'Hrodna' (Russian Grodno), a city on the Nioman, first mentioned in the Chronicles under the annal for 1126. It was sacked by the Tartars in 1241 and the Teutonic knights in 1284, and 1391. Under the name of Gaudinas, it was in the thirteenth century, the capital of the Grand Duchy of Lithuania, and later it came under the rule of Poland, the Polish king, Stepan Batory died there in 1586. Hrodna passed to Russia under the terms of the Third Partition of Poland (1795), After the First World War, it became part of Poland and was reunited to Eastern Byelorussia (the Byelorussian SSR) in 1939.

The 'mansions' here referred to would include such historical relics as the twelfth-century Princes' Chapel, The Church of Sts Boris and Gleb, the castle of Stepan Batory (*c.* 1580) and the eighteenth-century castle of Augustus III.

Novahrudek, situated on the hills which take from it their name of the Novarudek heights, was first mentioned in 1227. It was sacked by the Tartars in 1240, and later was for a time the capital of the Grand Duchy of Lithuania. It was ceded to Russia by the Third Partition (1795), and given to Poland under the terms of the treaty of Versailles, in 1919. It was incorporated into the Byelorussian SSR in 1939. The walls referred to here are those of the ruined castle, which on its hill dominates the city. Novahrudek's principal claim to renown is as the birthplace of the poet, Adam Mickiewicz, who, although writing in the Polish language, considered himself rather as a native of the Grand Duchy. (His epic, *Pan Tadeusz,* begins: *Litwo! Ojczyzno moja!* – Lithuania, land of my fathers!)

Sofia's towers. The cathedral of St Sofia in Połack, built 1044–66 was founded and endowed by the then Prince of Połack, Vsesłav 'the Magician', who beautified the cathedral at the expense of neighbouring cities. Thus the Novgorod Chronicle records for 1066 that in this year Vsesłav sacked Novgorod 'O great was the distress at that time!' and removed the lustres from the church. Połack cathedral, however, was entirely rebuilt in baroque style during the seventeenth century, and it is to the towers of this later edifice that the poet refers.

Zasłaŭ – the Izviasłav of the ancient chronicles – was in the eleventh to thirteenth centuries a well-fortified town of the Połack principality, which in the fourteenth century came under Lithuanian rule. In the city and its immediate vicinity, there are preserved from antiquity three hill-forts, in addition to several unfortified settlements and a number of groups of gravemounds (the grave-goods in which indicate that the original inhabitants were of the tribe of the *Kryvyčy* – see note to *Song to the Sun*, p. 56).

p. 167: *Nadzia-Nadziejka*
The name of the heroine of this poem is Nadzia, of which *Nadziejka* is a diminutive. It adds considerably to the poignancy of the human tragedy of this poem to realize that the name Nadzia means 'hope'. The image of the weeping birch-tree goes back to a poem of Jan Čačot (see Introduction), of a birch-tree weeping after thoughtless lads have slashed the bark to draw off the sweet sap to drink:

> The birch-tree was weeping, sadly she murmured:
> How then have I wronged you, that I deserve it
> That you so cut me and slash me,
> And to suck my blood gash me? . . .
> For you by the roadside I stand as a maid,
> For you in the springtime my plaits I unbraid,
> Here the birds flock, sweetly singing,
> Gentle shade for men is clinging.
>
> Why then without fault of mine do you slash me?
> To sip at my sweet blood cruelly gash me?
> Thus before my time I dwine now,
> For I shed my blood and pine now.
>
> In the road the blood flows like a river,
> No one comes with stoup to catch it ever.
> You have slashed me in cruel mischief,
> Only sipped, to drain not wishful . . .

Thus the image of the weeping birch immediately evokes overtones of wanton destruction, which add greatly to the poignancy of this poem.

p. 175: *The sniper's eye*
line 15. 'Blue snows of January.' The adjective *'ściudzionyja'* means, basically, 'freezing cold'. However (like all Slavonic languages with the exception of Russian), Byelorussian names its months after natural phenomena – January being called *studzień* – the 'freezing month' (from an alternative form – *studzany* – of the adjective). Since, in any case, freezing cold is, at least artistically, implicit in the concept of January, it seemed poetically 'right' to take the temporal, rather than the purely thermal, adjective.

line 16. 'Aryans', i.e. Germans. Strictly speaking, both the Byelorussian language and the Byelorussian nation may perfectly validly be described as 'Aryan', in the academic sense of an Indo-European language spoken by a nation belonging to the Indo-European 'family'. Here, of course, the poet uses the term with sarcasm, and in inverted commas, as it were, in the sense of the racialist 'historians' Arthur de Gobineau, Houston Stewart Chamberlain and Alfred Rosenberg, upon whose 'philosophy' of racial 'purity' Hitler's Nazism was founded.

p. 175: *The hero*
It should be remembered, in the context of this poem, that the Nazi attack on the Soviet Union (to which the Nazis were formally allied in a non-aggression pact) took the Soviet High Command completely unaware, with the result that many essential war supplies fell into enemy hands before any attempt at evacuation could be made. For this reason, in spite of the British Murmansk convoys and American Lend-Lease, the Red Army remained throughout the War dangerously short of essential supplies, so that a small breakdown in the logistics of supply could result in a complete lack of essentials, such as, in this case, wire-cutters, resulting in the improvisation of often desperate expedients.

line 15. The Valdai lakes. The Valdai hills, which begin just outside Byelorussian territory are the highest part of the North Russian plain; they lie between Moscow and Leningrad, extending from just north of Smalensk in a north-north-east direction as far as the river Tikhvina. There are innumerable lakes among these hills, lake Seliger being the largest.

p. 179: *You hear honking cries*
line 3. Mount Ararat stands just inside Turkish territory, overlooking the point where the frontiers of Turkey, Iran and Soviet Armenia converge.

line 13. Mount Kazbek (16,558 ft) in the Georgian SSR is one of the highest mountains in the Caucausus.

The El'brus (in Russian) or Elburz (in Persian) is a mountain range in Northern Iran, separating the Caspian depression from the Iranian plateau. The El'brus comes to an end almost exactly at the Soviet border. The highest peak of the El'brus is Mt Demavend (18,580 ft).

p. 180: *Ballad of the Ural Tank*
Owing to the German advance (which ultimately reached to the Volga), all war-production had to be evacuated to the Urals or even farther east.

For the rhymes of this poem, it should be remembered that the name of the village – *Sunicy* – is pronounced Suni*tsy*, with the stress on the second syllable.

p. 184: *The Eagle-Well-spring*
Dedication. Mikałaj Hasteł, an Air Force Pilot-Captain, was one of the first 'heroes', to be acclaimed by the press of the Soviet Union during the first months of the Second World War. His exploits, and later his death in combat, caught the popular imagination, and a number of biographies of him were published during and shortly after the war.

p. 187: *The caravan*
line 7. The camel is described as being grey and *'rudy'* – *rudy* being the colour-adjective normally used to describe only 'ginger' or 'red' hair. Among desert-peoples, and other connoisseurs of the camel as a working transport animal, this type of colouring (described by P. C. Wren, in *Beau Geste* as 'tawny reddish buff' are particularly prized for speed and endurance.

line 11. Cyrus. Either Cyrus the Great of Media (reigned 559–30 B.C.) perhaps best known for his action in freeing the Jews from the Babylonian captivity (see II Chronicles xxxvi, 22–3) or else Cyrus the Younger (died 401 B.C.) whose expedition to replace his brother Artaxerxes II on the throne of Persia is told in Xenophon's *Anabasis*. In either case, the significance of the time of Cyrus, as typifying the dawn of Persian history, is clear. It should be noted in this context that Mecca was a cult-centre long before the time of Mohammed, and that the incorporation of the Mecca pilgrimage into the rituals of Islam, was an attempt to turn to the service of Allah what was already well-established as a pagan practice (see, for example, J. B. Glubb: *a short history of the arab peoples,* 1969, p. 26). Thus the poet's vision of the pilgrimage as trudging 'from the era of Cyrus' is not as anachronistic as at first it might seem; although before Mohammed, the Mecca-cult must have been of far more local a nature.

line 12. 'until nothingness dawns'. The Byelorussian *'u niabyt'* – 'into non-existence' seems highly reminiscent of the Fitzgerald version of Omar Khayyám:

'. . . the Caravan
Starts for the Dawn of Nothing . . .'

Although there is nothing corresponding to this expression in the Persian original of the relevant stanza of the Rubáiyát (*stanza 38*), and although indeed there seems no such corresponding idiom in Persian which Fitzgerald might have learned in his reading and worked into this stanza, a deliberate echo of the Fitzgerald version does seem here in order, both on account of the Persian atmosphere and as a means of elucidating an idiom for the end of the world, that, both in Byelorussian and in English, seems more than a little strange at first reading.

p. 188: *Potatoes*
stanza 3. 'Chaš i łoba.' This baffles me completely. The name *Vano* seems to be either Estonian or Finnish (in the latter case, Vaino would be the correct spelling). But *Chaš i łoba* as the name of either an Estonian or a Finnish dish seems impossible – since neither the Estonian nor Finnish languages contain the letter 'b'. However, since the spelling of the names of the other dishes is somewhat garbled (*Płoŭ* for 'pilau'), it is possible that some mismemory has occurred in the poet's mind. In view of this, and remembering that both Finland and (to a lesser extent) Estonia, have been strongly influenced by Sweden, I would tentatively suggest the Scandinavian *Labskaus* as a possible solution. This is a savoury hash compounded of beef or mutton, together with salt pork, potatoes and onion.

stanza 4. 'Pilaŭ', of course, is the savoury rice dish, well-known to all patrons of oriental restaurants, *shashliks* – the Caucasian version of kebabs – are chunks of lamb, sometimes interspersed with vegetables to taste, impaled along the length of a skewer, and grilled until 'rare'.

stanza 9. 'The Potato Polka' (the Byelorussian name is simply *Bulba* – 'Potatoes'), is one of the most popular Byelorussian folk songs and dances; on gramophone records of 'Songs and Dances of the USSR' Byelorussia is usually represented either by Bulba or by the equally popular *Lavonicha* (*not* to be confused with the poem of Bandanovič of this name!)

THE YEARS OF RECONSTRUCTION

1945–1953

The end of the Second World War found Byelorussia in a state of almost total devastation. One in four of her population dead. Thousands more scattered throughout the world by the shifting tides of war. Her cities in ruins, and her survivors living in dug-outs and hutments. Her livestock slaughtered – 75 per cent of her horses, 71 per cent of her cattle, 92 per cent of her pigs, 83 per cent of her sheep and 100 per cent of her poultry and bees obliterated. Her plough-land reverted to fallow. Her industries wrecked almost beyond hope of repair. And many of the youngest and finest of her sons, her one hope for reconstruction, scattered about Europe in the occupation forces of the Red Army. And in literature, the fiery impetus of the war, the ideal and inspiration of four years of poetry – had vanished. Now there was only work, the unremitting ceaseless work of reconstruction. Like the grim 'utility' years in Britain, this period shows a characteristic drawing in of resources – even in literature, there is little time now for looking beyond one's own borders – there is a country to be rebuilt, and in this rebuilding the poets play a vital and vigour-giving part.

Michaś Kałačynski

BURGENLAND

And all is clear that yesterday was seeming
Far and remote, in distance deaf and dead.
The vale of Burgenland a coloured, gleaming
Pattern of carpeting for us has spread.

The terrifying dawn has burned to embers.
Manors on hillocks by the river laze.
There crouch as if painted in oils and umber
Islands of villages in fields of maize.

Upon the thatch, late melons ripely growing,
Beans by the window hanging up to dry.
All is in order.
But from deaf farms come blowing
Into the twentieth century – times gone by.

A two-wheeled cart creeps, cuts the heart with squeaking,
The hornbeam axle weeps against the grease.
The verges seem green serpents that are seeking
To crush earth and man's fate in close embrace.

The oxen plod; behind the ploughshare follows
Plodding, beneath his rustic hat, a man.
You look and think that there upon the furrow
Some age from a museum-case you scan.

Maksim Łužanin

THE LANDRAIL

Living in a strange land, maybe, rootlessly yearning,
Without aim, yet you cannot fight back, though you wail –
There is a strange song within the ears burning,
To me memories of a small bird are returning,
The landrail.

He's no master of flight, but spring spurs him to hurry
Back to the same places where he lived before,
Where he ran, where to hide in the green rye he burrowed,
Upon the same ploughland, upon the same furrow,
To the nest on the verges, familiar of yore.

Losing no time, he prepares to trek, running
Through Europe on foot in the space of a night,
To us, to his own native verges returning,
Lifts his head, in a monotonous-churning
Ludicrous harsh song forgets himself quite.

Often from you were we led by our duty,
Fields of our Biełaruś, and their limitless space,
Often were led to be awed by new beauty,
But I say the truth, gladly will I dispute it:
In spring we must go home to our native place.

We have looked on the world, wide and far in our going,
But the heart yet remembers our earliest steps;
Here our mother bore us, and here we were growing,
Here we our finest of songs were composing,
Here friends will weep, bearing us to our last rest.

May I be granted to say:
'Good-day, my fellows!'
To watch how the sky in the little streams glides,
And then, for a year! . . . but we'll come back together,
Landrail and I.

To be there for a day, for one short hour abide there,
To be drunken with joy, lift my head bold and free,
With a song to the sun, like that little bird's tidings . . .
What is that? Can it be that the cranes will come gliding
To our land, without me?

Not of my own will to words am I excited,
Yet I say,
    I am drowsing, in dreams – though you wail –
The song may commence and that small bird be sighted
Which lives in our Biełaruś under the title
Landrail.

1946
Germany

Maksim Tank

IT WOULD BE WELL

It would be well someone else start this song,
For they are calling me, all the night long,
The pines, close to the cross-roads, which I could not
Manage to save from bullets and shot,
The ploughlands that I, when evil storms pressed,
Could not achieve to shield with my breast,
The stars which from fires of war I have failed
With these my hands to cover and veil,
The ash of our country, and brotherly shades
Call me from under grave-hills, new-made.

But everyone has so much business today:
The ear shall bring forth a good handful of grain,
The sun shall raise up the crushed grasses to stand,
The winds level over war-trenches with sand,
The clouds shall give rain to quench the land's thirst,
The bird, back from the Southland, shall weave her a nest.
And everything I must begin again, make
Everything new, from pine house-frame and strakes,
Right to the wide wedding-tables and so
Right to the tipsy cymbalom and bow.

This has befallen me not the first time,
But I am true to the old order, thus:
So that sheaves in the barn will not dwindle and dwine,
Bees in the beehives and guests in my house –
On the burned sites, loftier than of old
I'll raise walls, set the gable-ends wider and bold,
I have called to the neighbours to lend me a hand.
Many, though, did not come. They could not rise again
It seemed, from beneath the scorched grass of steppe-lands,
Nor to return from Carpathian glens.
For us it will be harder without them to start
Work and feast, and to raise up a toast from the heart.

Maybe some of them yet the way homeward will trace,
That they might gaze on the fields' open space,
That they might gaze on the rich harvest there,
That they might gaze upon plough, upon share,
That they might ask for their orphans, their kin,
That the nation embrace them and welcome them in.

Maybe some of them yet the way homeward will trace,
Surely some of them yet . . . And so we shall assign
For our friends at each table a duly-laid place,
Lay a goblet for each, sparkling brimful of wine,
And a favourite song, and when the night comes,
Lest their steps go astray, on the road home,
All the house windows like starlight shall shine.

Arkadź Kułašoŭ

THE EAR OF GRAIN

The ear shall bring forth a good handful of grain.
Maksim Tank

The oats are rustling, barley chimes,
And to believe you're able
That the ears all the long day-time
Are blooming without trouble.

With toiling you began the day,
Sweated in sunshine baking,
But on the ear no worries prey
It seems. You are mistaken!

On your way home from work, look! see!
How the ear has been toiling,
Its beard can move but wearily,
Soaked with the sweat of moiling.

It does not watch the sky above,
View the clouds, bright and fleecy,
But up and down and down and up,
It drives its sap, unceasing.

It drives up droplets from the earth
And in the sunshine warms them,
For it must bear a handful's worth
Of grain within it forming.

It catches the sun's every ray,
Glad in the sky's sweet water,
It works so hard throughout the day
It is wet all night after.

Neither by day nor night-time now
No rest from labour knowing,
Each dawn the sweat from off its brow
It wipes in the sun's glowing.

Vasil Vitka

AT HOME

Across the fence the cherry droops,
Acacia gleams with yellow,
The pumpkin on the forcing heap
Grows warm, thrusts up its belly.

Surely a bat some twilight came
And with its wing has brushed me,
In the trenches I have not lain,
Knew not the whirlwind's rushing.

In no attacks nor battle-charge
In no forced march half-failing,
The well-beam, like a crane, stands guard
Over our well's oak-railing.

No billycan now in my hand,
But well-known pail, I'm rubbing
The towel with embroidered band
On my face with its rough stubble.

A stack of pancakes from the pan
Mother has tossed already,
And once more in this house I can
See myself, a boy, threading.

Listening I'd sit, in winter time,
On the stove, behind the chimney,
To how the frosty evening chimed
As with thin threads of linen.

At New Year in the pail I'd put
A *hrivna* in the water,
So that our house, stored full of goods
Would almost crack, next August.

In spring, when the first thunder spoke,
I would run through the puddles,
To touch my brow against an oak,
To have strength in abundance.

Always to see good fate I knew
A way most sure and proven,
From the fields I would have first dew
And my eyes wash and bathe then.

From then my native nook shines clear
Under a bright sky ever,
From them I yearn, through parting drear,
For the bread of my mother.

Surely a bat some twilight came,
Brushed me with its wing's shadow . . .
Before me stands my long-loved home,
The brook, and there the meadow.

This I recalled in wartime days
When for our country fighting;
My land now turns on me her gaze,
Her eyes are wide and smiling.

Maksim Tank

GOOD MORNING

Good morning, out in the wide fields to
The wind, blowing sweetly,
To the tall grain-ears, rich yielding,
To the girls reaping.

Good day to larks in the clear heavens
To kvass, coolly flowing,
To bread, earned by honest toil ever,
To the farm, the fields growing.

Good evening to tracks leading homeward,
To the cart, gaily driving,
To the lights twinkling out in friends' homes, and
To dew and stars shining.

Goodnight to the clubhouse accordion,
Nightingales in woods winging,
And to all who, till dawn, find melodious
Their singing.

Vasil Vitka

MIRACLE

I bought my daughter a nightingale,
Made of clay
Dried and hardened.
To life it stirred,
My little bird,
To magic it hearkened.

She whispered, my child,
One word, no more –
From the house, through the window
The nightingale soared,
And in its freedom began singing,
Out
In our orchard
On lilac boughs swinging.

And the word quivers –
Living
Warm in the
Throat of the songster,
A sweet-calling
Drop, falling.

Folk gather to listen.
But I
Stand wondering: What word
Was it you said,
Daughter of mine,
To the bird?

Kastuś Kirenka

THE SHIPS

The winds and the spring sun, united together,
Have chased from the earth snowy drifts.
Look, in all Biełaruś, on the streams, just as ever,
Once more there sail little ships.

Wood and paper, yet 'ships of the line' you will call them,
'Launch her!' The boys shout, and bright
In their thoughts, in their visions are shining before them
The spaces of sea, harbour lights.

Under the sails, sounding waters foam ever,
Childhood. . . . Yet each year, of yore,
The moment the streams arose from their ice-cover,
We shipwrights built our fleet once more.

Reared among woodlands, from when came this panting,
In our quiet land, without shore,
Marine imaginings, and the fleet chantys,
Yearnings to sail ships? Wherefore?

Surely we have such a soul in us. May be
At childhood's first spring we hear,
Not of Biełaruś alone the sons we be,
But of one Motherland dear.

A Motherland which has seas many and distant,
Paths with good fortune agleam.
Build then your ships, through the waves strive, insistent,
Toward new lighthouses' beams.

Mikola Auramčyk

BYELORUSSIAN PINE

Scented with Biełaruś, the mines breathe now
From her forest
Resinous pines;
The underground path, narrow, easeless,
Seems a woodland ride, deep in the mine.

Above low coal stopings, roof-cover
Rests on pit-props by the score.
One of them creaks
High above you,
Like the pine with its branches
Of yore.

Above it the heavy rock presses.
The undermined soil on it rests.
Strata thousands of years old compress it,
Half a kilometre thick, no less.

It can bear such a burden no longer,
Resin oozes from it like a sweat,
Yet the pine
Stands there uprightly, strongly,
Longs to strive once again to the light.

And you cleave the coal, steadfastly, doughty,
Sparks are flying from each hammer-blow . . .
Heavy laden, the pines of our country
Let no harm reach their countryman, no!

Anatol Vialuhin

MOUNTAIN ROAD

Lowlands and poplars and *vallées*
Covered by cloud, greyly looming,
Struck in the face by a sally
From the ridge, of the wind's chilly plumage.

Peaks on high
Smothered
By snowing.
Motors ply,
The winds covered
Them, blowing.

Such a vista
Is past imagination.
Road twisting
In spiral gyration.
Granite heights.
And caverns
Fanged with stalactites
Snarl and raven,
Then sudden
In the darkness, a tunnel.
A two-vierst-long chasm
At the side plunges.

Peaks on high
Smothered
By snowing,
Motors ply,
The winds covered
Them, blowing.

And wings read, alarmed, wary,
On the old vault, this inscription:
'Wayfarer,
Take care, now!
Like teardrop on lash thy position!'

But onwards our motors yet fly,
Noisily kilometres are going,
As we speed,
Tyres tread
On clouds, peaks on high
And winds blowing.

Michaś Kałačynski

THE APPLE

In spring, in heat and rains that fell,
'Neath wings of branches hanging,
An apple grew, as if yeast-swelled,
Both day and night expanding.

The branches no more could suspend
The apple's weight, so plunging
Down to the earth the branches bent
All in the fires of sunshine.

But some Mičurynite came by,
And a strong prop brought he,
He lifted the young apple high
And the branch supported.

In it the fields reflected shone,
Houses and fence were gleaming,
And up and down the veins all run,
Like meridians seeming.

From all good things that earth supplies
The apple wove a vesture,
The apple-tree held the fruit high
Like a globe terrestrial.

Kastuś Kirenka

THE LETTER

Mother sent a letter away to the Front,
To Ukraine, to near Sumy, saying:
'Fly letter dear,
To my son, letter dear,
A mother's thought conveying!'

The letter hurried to Sumy. But there
Joy had long reached the people, however.
The Front had advanced.
To the letter they said:
'The addressee's across Dnipro river!'

The post took the letter further. And see,
Here the winged Dnipro is gliding.
But once again the soldier has gone:
'Freeing the Carpathians you'll find him!'

So, after the army, along native paths
To the mountains the letter went speeding.
But the farmers are ploughing the tillage anew,
And their wives are whitewashing and cleaning.

And the mountain slopes ring with a song of praise
For the warrior-lad and his boldness.
And the letter can learn from these songs.
'He is greeted in Praha!' they told him.

A day comes, a second passes.
The squares of Praha lie open.
The spring wind above the earth
Rinses red sails, high over.

The city re-echoes. The people rejoice.
In free Praha they celebrate. Uttered
On the lips of the Czechs is one name alone:
The name of their Russian brother.

The name of him the letter had
For so long been seeking.
And to the post-office,
Glad on the track,
The addressee's track it was speeding.

But once again the soldier has gone,
Only his track through the lowland,
Over mountains and rivers
That track led on,
Led on, to Berlin it was going.

Now the spring scatters its bells far and wide
In a Russian marching-song. In it
Is so much emotion
That the breast aches,
And the heart grows tight within it.

There in the ruins which once were Berlin,
Where Victory was established,
The lads are singing of their native land,
And of the road to battle.

And to it in answer from eastward afar,
Another song flies to meet it.
The letter can learn:
'This is a mother
Her own dear hero-son greeting!'

He has given his weapons of war to his friends,
To bring their land fame multiplying.
But he has gone home,
To build towns, to grow bread,
The needs of his homeland supplying.

On wings flew the letter back home once more.
It rapped on the window-pane:
'Mother!
I have sought for your son all over the earth,
But I could catch up with him never.'

And the mother came out, took the three-cornered envelope,
And then she tenderly kissed it.
'And well-done, then . . .'
And to the joyful full-blowing
Wind, her face she lifted.

And there her son speeds over his native fields,
On a tractor, grinding, grating.
And such a young man, what letter, what song
Can ever overtake him?'

MY REPUBLIC (extract)

Do not say my Republic is
A country of dark woods.
Look and see –
Above it the fires of
The factory-workshops brood.

Do not say my Republic is
A country of quiet vales!
Listen, hear –
Above it, like thunder,
The mighty turbines wail.

Do not say my Republic is
A country of hogs and fallow!
With orchards it is
Heavy-laden,
With ryefields it is
Swaying,
And roads run there, straight as an arrow.
In today's view of my country
Seek for no griefs past and gone.
Like a wonderful book of the sunshine
It is here for your eyes: read you on . . .

Kandrat Krapiva

THE CHILD, THE HEDGEHOG AND THE SNAKE

In a pine-copse, one holiday,
A mother with her Child was playing,
Then drowsing in the sun she lay there,
But danger threatened, while she stayed there,
Her little Girl. Not far away
Down from the hill a path is tending,
And there the little Girl is wending,
Chasing the butterflies.
And there beside a sapling pine-tree,
An Adder basks in the sun's shining,
With patterned scales it gleaming lies.
She tries to touch it, little Girlie,
Delighted: 'Pretty Dolly!' lisps she,
But the 'Dolly!' starts uncurling,
Quietly, insidious he whispers:
'Child, I want to be your friend. I'll kiss you,
Curling you in my love, caressing, true.
You'll see my love so sweet for you!'
But at the Child's feet, of a sudden,
A Hedgehog, angry, grunted,
And upon the Snake himself he threw.
The Snake, like flash of lightning, turns then,
To sink his fangs he's yearning,
Instantly rays from his scales dart,
But Hedgehog, with needles armoured sternly
Fears not the snake-fangs burning,
And swift he tears Adder apart.
The Child is cross. To shake her fists she starts,
Shouts at the Hedgehog: 'Look, you've gone and spoiled my Dolly,
You silly, clumsy brute.
I'll beat you for this. Yes, I'll do it!
You're just a bully!'
'Child', the Hedgehog answered to her,
'Though I'm a bully, ugly, prickly truly,
Yet to your death I've put an end.
When you grow up, then you will make amend,
And understand, and thank me as a friend!'

A child's a child – and childish likewise is its mind.
But about children I'm not talking,
But upon earth are folk of grown-up kind
Awalking.
Who are quite ready to embrace a snake,
Since flattery it well knows how to make,
A snake, insidious, crawling to their mind is
Dearer than a true friend – though spiny.

Arkadź Kulašoŭ

YOU, DEAR, AND I

You were a girl when I first saw you,
I a youth glad and free.
You were the dearest earth for me,
I was your sea.

You strove for the far-distant spaces
Of the infinite seas,
But I – to your heart
Hidden in the deep woods, secretly.

But over the wild ocean waves
No pathway you knew,
Through the primaeval wood
To your heart I could never win through.

Why could you not be, in youth's morning,
A river's swift, wide?
All of my waves I'd have given
To mingle your tide.

Why was I not as a flame
When I was young,
All through your forest with seething
Fire I'd have run.

Days of youth, like swift sails, pass away,
From the eyes disappear,
No, no longer those waves now,
And the sea becomes calmer each year.

Becomes calmer each year,
Clearer now as the years unfold
There arises the shoreline
Of the coasts long-desired of old.

You are earth again, I am sea for you,
Time could not part us, my sweet,
I in the free spaces before you
Have lain happily down at your feet.

I am evermore in your memory,
You are evermore my heart's dream,
And I lie now before you,
Here, as your mirror, to gleam.

Alaksiej Pysin

A BOY HAD PLANTED A YOUNG TREE

A young tree by the schoolhouse Vitya planted,
The first young tree in his life;
Wiped from his hands the black earth they had garnered:
'Well, grow up, and thrive!
In spring catch up your green companions quickly!
Look, isn't space here vast?'
And with a branch the maple nodded meekly:
'I will accept the task!'
With the news a light breeze set off running,
To oaks across the river, fields and
Lea,
A little fairer had the world become then,
A boy had planted a young tree.

Maksim Tank

MOTHER'S HANDS

The earth has kissed them indeed,
With sandy lips it has kissed them,
With the grain-ears;
And with the noon-heat, the winds and the rain-showers
The sky kissed them.

Such toil of spinning
Through sleepless nights has drunk from them
Freshness of morning;
So many times have they kindled the dawn-break,
Stars over us.

How many are there today,
Seen on them, dark and scored deeply,
Scars, lines and wrinkles,
They are the traces forever imprinted
Of our harsh pathway.

And yet, whenever
The family gather at home,
And mother's hands rest on the table,
As if from the sun, light from them fills the house with its radiance,
Fills the heart.

Piatruś Makal

THE APPLE-TREE

Once, at dawn, I planted a young apple,
Close beside the porch I set my sapling,
– May it grow!

To help my work the cloud its aid was lending,
Watering the soil with careful tending.
– May it grow!

I and the sun, during the time of winter,
Warmed the weakly sapling with warm glimmer,
– May it grow!

Soon I have to move away; my neighbour
Will pluck the apples, harvest of my labour.
– May it grow!

But surely, in some other house's garden,
A friend unknown a little tree is planting . . .
– May it grow!

Maksim Tank

GOOD NIGHT AND SWEET DREAMS

Evening of spring. Moon above the grove gleaming.
'Good night', I wish to all things, 'and sweet dreaming!'

'Good night and sweet dreams!' to the booming-voiced river,
So that when I go out none will hear, not a quiver.

To the keen dogs that hear each guest approaching,
Over the lone courtyard carefully watching;

And to the gates by the dark lime I speak it,
That I may open them without their squeaking.

And 'Good night and sweet dreams' most of all to a mother
Who carefully watches her dear daughter over,
That she'll not be awake to hear, understand a
Voice that calls 'Come out, dear, to the verandah!'

Calls to the verandah, my starlight, my dearest;
Life without her I'd find bitter and dreary!

Evening of spring. Moon above the grove gleaming.
'Good night!' I wish to all things, 'and sweet dreaming!'

NOTES

Once again, in this section, the poems are presented in approximately chronological order.

p. 205: *Burgenland*
Burgenland is the most easterly province of Austria (provincial capital – Eisenstadt); during the years of Allied occupation (1945–55) it was under the control of the Soviet forces.

stanza 5. 'some age from a museum case'. A pardonable exaggeration, but since Kałačynski was born in 1917, to suggest that he literally had never seen such a scene before would mean that he had been an unusually unobservant child, since in Byelorussia, the mechanization of agriculture did not really get under way until collectivization began in 1929 – by which time Kałačynski was twelve years of age.

p. 206: *The landrail*
The landrail (*drač*) or corncrake (*dziarhač*) – Byelorussian, like English, has two names for the one bird – is, in fact, a very rare example of a non-flying migrant, as far as Eastern Europe is concerned. (In England, of course, the landrail is a resident.)

stanza 5. Appears to contain echoes of Bujła's *I love our land* (cf. pp. 83–84).

p. 208: *It would be well*
stanza 2. The 'shall' here is gnomic, not compulsive. The use of the 'shall' form is inspired by the resemblance of this passage to the style of the Old English gnomic verses.

'strakes': Byelorussian wooden houses are built first by erecting the framework, then by filling in the sides by courses of wood, 'strakes', laid parallel to the earth, in the same manner as courses of bricks are laid in a brick-built house.

'cymbalom and bow'. It will be recalled from the note to *Play then, play* (p. 40) that the cymbalom and violin are traditionally the instruments of joy.

stanza 3. 'set the gable-ends wider'. The original says simply 'I shall make wider the angles' (*šyru vuhli*). To use *vuhli* to mean gable-ends is odd in Byelorussian, but there does not seem any other angle in the construction of a house that *can* be widened without detriment to the over-all structure.

stanza 4. An interesting use of folklore here. As we have seen (note to *Thou passest, Village, from bright story*, pp. 122–123) the Byelorussian Christmas Eve feast goes back on an original ancestor-feast. Part of the ritual of this feast is the laying of an empty place, which still in Byelorussian and Ukrainian tradition is explained as representing deceased (and, in particular, recently deceased) members of the family. Originally, it would seem, a light was placed in an uncurtained window presumably to guide ancestor-spirits to the feast, but the present writer has never seen this done nowadays.

However, Maksim Tank grew up in West Byelorussia, which was not only under Polish rule during his formative years, but also contained great mixing of populations, Byelorussian and Polish (as is usual in disputed border regions). The Poles also have the same Christmas Eve rituals, with the empty place and the lighted candle, but, under the influence of Latin Catholicism, have interpreted the traditions somewhat differently. Although, in Poland, small children are told that the empty place is laid and the candle is lighted in case, once again, the Holy Family should be seeking shelter for the night, adults 'rationalize' the tradition as meaning that the candle is there to light the lost wayfarer to a welcome, and the empty place is laid for any passing stranger.

Here, in a beautiful and moving way, Tank unites the two branches of the common Slavonic tradition: here the dead relatives *are* the lost wayfarers, struggling home through the winter-darkness, to the feast of the family and the kinfolk they gave their lives to defend.

p. 211: *At home*
stanzas 6–8. The folk-traditions described here seem fairly clear and to need little in the way of commentary. The *hrivna* was an ancient gold coin ('guinea' in English would have the same 'flavour' if not the same exact value), and the placing of it in the bucket, like the silver coin in the Scottish milking-pail, seems to be to placate the house-spirits.

p. 213: *Good morning*
stanza 2. 'farm'. Tank actually says 'collective farm' (*kalhoz*), but in English this seems a politico-technical term only, and would destroy the atmosphere of this poem.

p. 214: *The miracle*
This seems to be founded upon the legend of the Christ-child told in a number of the Apocryphal gospels (notably the pseudo-Thomas), and immortalized in English by Hilaire Belloc in his poem beginning 'When Jesus Christ was four years old'. The application of this legend, however apocryphal, to a human child *could*, in the hands of a lesser poet, seem a lapse of taste (although taste in such matters does vary from country to country, and tradition to tradition – the Ukrainian, Ivan Franko, for example, begins an invocation to his poetic muse 'Blessed art thou amongst women'). Here, however, Vitka, although probably considering himself a non-believer, handles the theme with such artistic taste and reverence, that the poem becomes an affirmation of the numinous 'clouds of glory' surrounding childhood, and could not give offence even to the most ardent devotee of pious legends.

p. 215: *The ships*
The problem posed is a real one; the sea plays a considerable part in Byelorussian literary tradition (as well as in the games of Byelorussian children). However, the answer proposed here does not seem complete: what explanation would Kirenka give to the sea-motifs as *The Chronicler* (p. 74) *Emigrants' Song* (p. 79), and the many other poems, not given in this selection, from the pens of *Naša Niva* poets, to whose thinking the concept of detachment from the Russian 'Motherland' was *de rigueur?*

p. 217: *Mountain road*
line 1. vallées. The Byelorussian has 'duvały', which is not a Byelorussian word, and seems explicable only as an attempt to render the French 'du val' and then to add a plural ending. The alternative French *vallées* seem better sense in English usage, and, further, aids the scansion.

stanza 3. Vierst, a measure of length, officially archaic, but still used colloquially. It is approximately 3,500 ft, a little longer than the kilometre (3,280·8 ft).

p. 219: *The Apple-tree*
Probably a children's piece, it has a slight hint of the 'improving' nature of Victorian schoolbooks.

stanza 3. Ivan Vladimirovič Mičurin (1855–1935), the Russian biologist, is most noted for his work in cross-breeding fruit trees to produce types specially suited for acclimatization to the conditions of Northern and Central Russia. After Mičurin's death, he was claimed by Lysenko as a forerunner of Lysenko's own peculiar views on plant selection, and a Mičurinite would normally mean what would in English be called a Lysenko-ite, one who supported these views in opposition to Mendel's theory of genetic selection. However, at the time this poem was written, preparations were under way, in the Soviet Press for the great August 1948 session of the Lenin All-Union Academy of Agricultural Sciences, which gave the official seal of approval of Stalin's government to 'Mičurinism' (i.e. Lysenkoism). In this context, Mičurinite became the 'in' word for a biologist, and seems to be used here, not in its controversial, but in its fashionable sense. (See also, Zh. A. Medvedev; *The Rise and Fall of T. D. Lysenko*, New York–London, 1969, Chapter 6.)

p. 220: *The letter*
The immediate problem arising from this poem is: could one soldier really have taken part in all the battles mentioned in this poem. As will be seen below, the answer is 'yes (just)', provided that it is assumed that he did not take part in the capture of Berlin, but was only posted there later.

stanza 1. Sumy, a town on the Psiol, a left (i.e. east) tributary of the Dnieper, was captured from the Nazis on September 2, 1943.

stanza 2. The battle of the Dnipro (Dnieper) was fought August–December 1944. Thus, by early 1944, our hero could be 'across Dnipro river'. Note that the peet does not say that he took part in the battle of the Dnipro, he was at least part of the time otherwise engaged in freeing Sumy.

stanza 3. 'winged' (*krylaty*) is a traditional epithet for the Dnipro in Cossack songs.

The Carpathian campaign was fought December 1944–January 1945. By the beginning of February, all principal towns on the Slovak side of the Carpathians were in Russian hands.

stanzas 5–7. Praha, the capital of Czechoslovakia, was the last of the east European capitals to be captured by the Red Army, and did not fall to them until May 9, 1945. Berlin (*stanza 9*) had already fallen on May 2, 1945.

Note that, although the hero of this poem is, presumably, a Byelorussian, being a Red Army soldier, he is to the Czechs, generically, a *Russian* brother!

p. 227: *A boy had planted a young tree*
Vitya – the diminutive form of Viktar (Victor).

p. 228: *Mother's hands*
This version was first published in *Manifold*, No. 13, 1965.

p. 230: *Good night and sweet dreams*
The title of this poem, and the wish repeated throughout, is, literally, 'peaceful night' (*spakojnaj nočy*). This in English, seems to have too many overtones of Christmas carols to be usable in the context – on the other hand, something a little more than the conventional 'Good night' of English usage seems to be indicated.

THE 'THAW' AND AFTER
1954—

The end of the years of austerity in Byelorussia coincided, to a great extent, with the phenomenon known in Soviet literature as 'the thaw'. Authorities differ as to when the beginning of the thaw should be dated – some taking it as early as the death of Stalin in 1953, some as late as the Twentieth Party Congress in 1966. As far as Byelorussia is concerned, the most convenient date is perhaps 1954, since it was in this year that Byelorussian literature began to look again outward, beyond its borders, and copies of Byelorussian literary periodicals began to appear again in libraries abroad. Gradually, too, poets such as Pušča and Duboŭka, silenced in the Stalinist purges of the thirties, appear once again in print. By 1956, the Golden Jubilee of *Naša Niva*, the 'thaw' was in full swing, and since that time, Byelorussian poetry has gone on from strength to strength. Poets such as Tank make tours abroad, others attend the United Nations as their country's delegates. The range of subject and technique is wider and deeper, and hence, in this final section, we shall consider the poems, not by authors, nor by dates, but by themes, to better indicate the breadth and sweep of the whole spectrum of the Byelorussian poetry of this latest, and to date finest, era.

I

'I bid you welcome, life . . .'

Kanstancyja Bujła

* * *

Though I pass to the shades,
I'll not forever perish,
Not simple was my fate, not lightly did I live;
My life-span shall flow on, in sons and grandsons cherished,
For to them I have much of heart and warmth to give.
To people I bequeath all thoughts, all books, all singing,
In poems through the years my voice shall live and ring;
As crayfish rends the ice, sunders the ice-floes clinging,
And bursting through its bonds, once more in freedom swims,
So thought shall live,
and rend the ice of death asunder,
And, living, it shall sparkle, weep, sing merrily;
What then this tomb of ice, that buries the turf under,
When, with a living verse,
from it I shall break free?

Jazep Pusča

GREATLY AM I INDEBTED STILL . . .

Greatly am I indebted still,
And I cannot repay the fill
Of forces my folk gave to me.
The years, like water, run away,
After them I chase eagerly:
O my spring, please answer me!

The spring does not answer me,
And is she wronged then, can it be,
That I'll not cease her song to sing?
But I cannot turn back my spring,
She went away from me, and when
I meet her, she avoids me then.
Sad, but there's nothing that will aid,
She'll not be moved, though long you've prayed,
She'll not return nor come back home,
Whether the day be clear or gloom.

Autumnal sounds, autumnal sounds,
Now battering my soul they pound.
Resound, resound, I am not dumb –
Flying in skeins the wild geese come,
Call with their song the highest blue,
Am I not son of my land true?

Each day thou art before my sight,
Thy image dear to the heart always,
For everything I'll thee requite,
My debts to my folk I'll repay.

As son, poet and man, I so
Love unremembered rivers' flow,
Into an age of light they go.
The ripples spread out far and wide,
Scouring the river-banks beside,
From stains of past years, with their tide.

In dusk-fires where the woodlands loom,
In the wondrous heather-blooms,
The autumn-lass I love and choose,
And this song I will not lose.

As a bequest, I leave it to
The spring, all joyful, young and new,
Let nightingales on every hand
Sing forth through a free, fabled land.

Piatruś Broŭka

*   *   *

Such an hour also has come to me, truly,
In the heart you will ponder it when you look back –
You have lived through it all, as they say, have endured it,
In this world you have seen of curios no lack.

But now, if they asked me what I am desiring,
What do I envy, most wish for in life?
I would give answer: a child's eyes enquiring,
Which to win through to the truth ever strive.

For, to him, through all the years of childish weeping,
Having started his long road on earth, it would seem
That for his wonder are stored in safe-keeping,
Such marvels of which we but thirstily dream.

It would be good to voyage with a new being,
Find in our work again pleasure and zest,
That from this half the twentieth century to see in
The century to come a brief vista at least.

Piatro Hłebka

THE WAVE

(A ballad)

On a starry night, in the deaf depths of the ocean,
Like a housewife, a wave slept, worn out from her motion;
At dawn she arose for her bath but, poor lady,
To revel and play thus not long would her fate be,
For as soon as she showed to the world her nude wonder,
A radiant star had cleft her asunder.

From the fragment with such anguish from the wave torn there,
A new little wavelet was straightaway born there;
And she ran and ran, as the children play, running,
And the wind, new-awakened, behind her was coming,
And in the wind's wake, the clouds flew forth, insistent . . .
But the little wave now was far off in the distance.

The old powerful wave grew sorrowful, grieving,
She charges the shore, she draws back to the sealine,
She breaks on the crags, rolls the pebbles and shingle,
She cries to the little wave, calls, never lingering,
But she has not learned, has not grasped yet, however,
That she will catch up with the little wave never.

And the little one grows to full height, swiftly running,
With her restless stormy companions far-roaming,
Till she too must pause, in brief rest from her motion,
There in the broad, boundless as the world, ocean.

Arkadź Kulašou

*   *   *

Quiet happiness I wish
    No man to suffer,
What use to the storm is
    Lightning without thunder,
What use is a brook
    When no parched thirst needs quenching,
Or chilly attention
    That's worth no attention,
Or wishes, the wings of
    Desire folding for rest,
Forest without cuckoo,
    Or cuckooless forest?

ELEGY

My life's a heavy battle with the years,
And each rest-halt is longer than the former,
And verses skid about like tip-up lorries,
And yet I know that moment will appear

When it will not be firs with forest dreaming
That will enclose my road's inquietude,
But, bending, evil-counselling, will brood
All my long-bearded years, above me looming.

Why did they come here, seeking for what wonders?
And what is it they wish me, what strange dream?
I shall get up, upon a staff will lean,
And I shall rend those dotard's beards asunder.

For all years from the years I shall take tribute,
With the road count the days I yet may keep,
And, like a bone, the rest to death attribute,
Upon the threshold of eternal sleep.

*   *   *

From happiness the heart leaps like a child,
From sorrow, like a mill, in the night groaning,
With its heavy stones forever turning,
The total of life's bitterness it compiles.

But the heart as a clock should not be reckoned:
When it has stopped, I shall not wind it, no,
It will not have the power to mark the seconds
When Death shall come and scythe my pathway low.

Into repair (although need says I must then)
I'll not send it to the most skilled of men,
Nor shall I sell it like an old clock when
The times are hard, barter it for a crust then.

So with this heart I yet shall journey on,
And step-by-step to walk with it I'm ready
Until its life-long winding, reckoned steady
For all my path at last has quite run down.

*   *   *

Time affirms: that life is changing ever,
Death comes – for all men the law reads one way,
And yet, in life's arena, men, however,
May sometimes live at setting of the day.

You write an exclamation, life! A query
I put; what if my generation famed
Shall break the law, and some researcher daring
A living protein, water-borne, obtain,
That like a wondrous living tribe, far-reaching,
Shall spread forth wildly over continents?

And what if we shall show it by our teaching
To live, to walk upright, to view with sense
The world, we shall pass on, from hand to hand,
The axe, we shall pass on the books of learning,
All our achievements, work and knowledge gleaning?
. . . Time, try to argue with this or withstand!

*   *   *

To live each year for me, it is ordained,
In this our twentieth century some new motion
Of life . . . And I am but a rye-field ocean . . .
In mine are millions of fates contained,
Yet still undrained the dregs of all fate's notions.

Neither a boss nor a gold-miner I –
Atom, by twentieth century liberated,
And space for life I borrow from the skies,
To be their friend and brother estimated.
But even this is not the last fate by
The twentieth century to me now fated.

For I shall yet evolve anew, anew,
Idea to matter, one life to another . . .
I live, and such deep feelings in me quiver,
As if not only fifty years I knew,
But have lived five long centuries, or over.

* * *

By mills and factories wormwood is not needed.
Gift of ill fate, the age-old means of needy
Harvest women, who by its bitterness
Would turn away their babies from the breast.
So that they stood on their own feet more quickly,
And could reveal, aiding with their own hands
Worn thresholds of homes with no proper chimney . . .

With it I passed through life – in childhood's span –
From first steps under work-bench of my father,
To battle-banners that we bore on ever
With glory, not relinquishing them in war –
Grateful are we to wormwood, more and more!

Wormwood and mother's care, and the road winding,
And tears, and memories of an orphan's verge,
And bitterness of that milk, which abiding
On the lips is not wiped by any thirst.

Alaksiej Zarycki

*   *   *

In fire was I,
'Neath fire, indeed,
On the steed high,
Beneath the steed.
To clouds soared free,
In the depths lay,
And death to me
Stared in the face.
I in battle hot
Slew friends, it seems,
Yet forget not
Their youthful dreams
And their young
Thoughts, high, profound,
I hear them come
Like the spring sound
Of groves and rivers . . .
In me they appear,
In dream, quite clear,
For ever and ever!

Maksim Tank

I AM GLAD TO BE A MAN

Good to be wave of the sea
Sandgrain, a well-spring, wind blowing,
Crag rising unscalably,
Snowflake that lives for a moment;
Good to be grass or a flower
The rainbow ribbon, the sunshine
Or, where pine-forest depths glower,
Bird, or a beast swiftly running.

Only I, having lived through a past
Of prison, hard frost, loss of freedom,
Villages ruined to ash,
Road to the front grimly leading,
Furrows' heat the blast shattered and rove,
The taste of cherries, full-ripened,
Friendship, the gleam of true love,
The power of song, grand and mighty,
I am glad I am a man,
This I'd choose, never repenting;
And to all else, friend, you can
Know, I'd not give my consenting.

HAPPINESS

Happiness of humankind is
Simple, such as yours and mine is,

Surely from salt it's compounded,
And bread reaped in fields abounding,

From sweat, the dust of the highway,
Woven from our native skyline,

From friendship, than stern death far stronger,
From song . . . So, when on this I ponder,

I think: if from aught else compounded,
Will it be happiness? I doubt it'

THE SUN-CLOCK

Everyone buys a timepiece,
So he will not be late, meeting his sweetheart,
For work and for duty.
I have a sun-given timepiece,
Which has, by now, for many a year,
Without repairs served me.
You cannot put it in a pocket, that's true,
Neither can you strap it on to your wrist,
But it is remarkably accurate.
When someone asks me:
'What o'clock is it?'
I stop,
Like my grandsire and father,
I pace out my shadow and tell
The time, accurate to the minute.
The time of spring floods, when to sow,
To gather the rye,
The time of first ice, and
Of weddings.
There is nowhere a timepiece –
Nor of gold nor of silver –
That can equal or vie
With this sun-given timepiece of mine,
Because it marks for me
The time of my birth, and
The time of my final departing,
When my shadow will leave
And disappear from its
Evergreen clock-face.

Siarhiej Hrachoŭski

GOODNESS

It is not easy to have trust, sincereness,
It is not easy to forget old wrongs,
They hang about the person, interfering
With trust and love like weights, heavy and strong.

Not easy to be good.
                                        Yet we've no need for
Bread that is won too easily and cheaply,
Facile achievements, discounts, false success,
Nor problems solved by other people's guess,

Nor those praises given far too lightly
At the dinner-table by our friends,
Nor scandal-mongering, which, like snakes, wreathes tightly
Breathing out wrong and evil without end.

Everything passes, like uneven rainfall,
Anguish and anger and cheap ugliness,
But one thing, chief and weighty is remaining,
– Goodness, that talent brighter than the rest.

Alaksiej Rusiecki

*   *   *

Year of the quiet sun . . . But I would have
A day of the quiet heart.
You can gaze quite phlegmatically on that orb
Through a telescope,
But just touch a stethoscope's
Bell to the breast – hear the trembling,
And the voices of sickness athrob.
Now, if I feared death,
I would put on a shirt made of steel,
Put a shirt on my heart
A shirt made of steel armour-plate,
So that guns of all calibres,
At my heart pointing,
Might loose all their firepower, full spate.
But on my pounding heart
There is no shirt of armour:
Laughter can reach it,
Wrong can pierce it, like bullet through bull's-eye,
And it shrieks, and it smiles,
And it shrinks into silence,
Filled with tempests,
And this daily.
The sun with its corona
Happy in its quiet year is glowing.
Is not the living heart happy
In this its quiet day.
In new war on the banal and base
In campaign we are going.
Should you not armour the heart?
Do not armour it, nay.

THE DISCOVERY

Recently,
Having taken from my finger blood
And sap from the palm of a maple,
A biochemist
The sign of our true kinship showed:
With our green friends from time past
We are akin,

We are delighted –
With this discovery
And the kinship of our colouring,
For certain
Often by colour-blind eyes well-ascertained,
And life shows us, implicitly.
When the sun's rising, Jack-o'Green
Stretches its breathing tubes open again,
And with oxygen the dews are smoking,
The day of many happenings starts then,
Once more my lung-foliage is beginning
To bloom with its blossoms, fragrant, crimson.
In both the same spirit of burning lives,
In the two usual colours appearing,
But when the strong October frosts are nearing,
Flaming with colour then my green friend thrives,
Like banners, all the trees are now ablaze,
They tell our kinship in their rustling leaves . . .
We all are crimson now,
And, like the elements,
We are unconquerable,
For we are life!

Alaksiej Pysin

*　　*　　*

Much in life forgotten lies,
Swept from the path and washed off cleanly.
I want to walk into the rye,
The rye that is eternal-seeming.

I shall pick a rough ear of grain,
On its watchful straw sound-guide growing –
From far my ancestor will then
Answer to me – an unknown sower;

And unknown reapers' voices heard
Will float above a dry form looming.
The grain-ears are to swaying stirred
By the dense southern haze of noontime.

Here beneath the haze grow ripe
Hopes confluent, wishes blending.
It rustles on, my sound-guide rye,
Joins past days to new times unending.

The distant prospect riper grows,
Like a quivering membrane sounding,
Hands search to find grain, we know
Somewhere too we shall resound then.

Hienadž Baurukin

NOON

I trust in noon.
                    No errors is it keeping,
Because it has within it not a trace
Of mistiness of mornings still half-sleeping,
And the weariness of evening peace.

I trust in noon.
                    It does not chatter fables,
And does not stretch its mouth with yawning yet,
But toils with zest,
                    as hard as it is able,
Silent, and with its sleeve it mops its sweat.

It goes upon its usual way, recalling
One thing alone, that high above there rides
Right in the zenith
                    the stern sun, and all things
It sees, and from that height nothing can hide.

I trust in noon.
                    I trust,
                        for grave deportment
And constancy make it no friend in vain,
And in it nothing is of evening caution,
And in it naught of morning's sudden flame . . .

I trust in noon . . .

Siarhiej Dziarhaj

GNOMICA

The tear is always bitter,
And sweat is salty,
And blood is crimson,
And grief is murky.
There are tears of joy, truly,
And in these tears is sweetness . . .
But are these teardrops, really?
Nonsense!
By no means!
There is a cold sweat also,
The sweat of a coward,
Born of his fear . . .
But can this sweat film his shirt over
With salty silver?
Then there is blood of blue,
Born out of the sick fancy
Of aristocrats enfeebled . . .
Here you can say nothing,
Add nothing.
And there is woe, so tiny,
Like poppy-seed, so little,
It is as unimportant
As white down on the poplar,
Empty, gone in a twinkling,
Like slanting rain in summer . . .
But this is not the same,
Because, indeed, in life:
The tear is always bitter,
And sweat is salty,
And blood is crimson,
And grief is murky.

Jeŭdakija Łoś

I BID YOU WELCOME . . .

I bid you welcome,
                                        life,
Many-voiced and quiet to hear,
You are hard as a steely knife,
Like September heath-smoke you are clear.

You are no day's guest to me,
I reckon you past all count,
And I welcome you,
                                        such as you be,
To give back to me
                                        such as I want.

II

'From fires of war . . .'

Piatruś Broŭka

A DROP OF BLOOD

There is nothing on earth I know more powerful than the one plain word
'Live!'
No weight can outweigh the drop of blood that a soldier gives.

And though in the sternest conflict, not each drop is known aright
Yet how many of the living each ransomed, spilled in the fight.

It shall fade never; for it eternal life is decreed,
It shall be platinum-set, into boundless space shall it speed.

Never shall cease on earth through all generations it grows,
Rustles in grains, its blossom in standard of scarlet blows.

And this flies forth above the earth, saying: 'Work and live!'
What dearer than the drop of blood that a soldier gives!

I WANT NO MORE

I want no more that tombs should arise
In broad fields, nor in the deep woods,
I want no more of weeping-filled skies,
I want no dawns stained with human blood.

I want no more of the sounds of alarm,
Trenches and shelters scoring the earth,
I want no more, that where the storks swarmed
Bombers through the sky make a path.

The blue of the heavens over my head,
And far and forward this cry I pour;
'That this peace should be shattered and shed
I want no more!'

Arkadź Kulašou

ON MARS

On Mars you will find no Martians dwelling,
No work of their hands makes deaf lowlands bright.
Mars, long since, within its gravemound's cell has
Buried them, some dread sin to requite.

Did time slay them, or was their destruction
Wrought by disputes their time could not resolve?
Like furrows on a brown canal constructions
Are turned to us with questions we must solve:

'Tell us, keen astronomer-curator,
And explain to us, O learned sage,
For what cause, wider than a river's gauge,
From the grey pole down to the equator
Do we drive water from age to age?

In the autumn you observed us, staring
Through your optic tube late at night,
Across the planet, hills of dust they bear, those
Tornadoes with their radioactive blight.
Only to reap us too death seems uncaring.'

How is one to answer their insistence?
Maybe, in all truth, their strange existence
Is for other planets needed more,
Maybe, when confrontations rise, persistent,
By handiwork, undying evermore
The Martians yet will warn us, with insistence,
Of woes which did not pass them by of yore?

* * *

Bound to this house by card of registration
Am I, by cradle from the ceiling slung.
Bound to my mother by each line and trace, and
By the wooden spoon, the earthen basin –
All which binds table to what work has won.

I am my mother's song, my mother's caring,
My mother's wrath, upon its own feet faring.
I drove death westward, out from lair to lair.
With eager whip of victory I drove it;
While all the roads of seven Fronts were smoking
Like fuses of dynamite, behind me there.

Having freed the world from such dread intimations,
I'll not let smoke and dust-cloud force earth's doom
To a bomb-shelter, wreak this transformation:
A milliard cards – milliard annihilations,
A milliard cradles to a milliard tombs!

Maksim Tank

IDENTITY DISC

This identity disc cast from a stainless alloy, Number
Seven million three hundred and forty-five,
I found in a field where foeman soldiers in inglorious slumber
Sleep, where the rye, blooming, rustling, thrives.

I wipe it clean of all the sand. And who were you, then, fallen foeman,
Your symbol to your kin I'd like to give,
But I do not know your name, your family and where is your hometown,
Seven million three hundred and forty-five!

I only know: your general, some Kriegswulf or von Spadel's aiming
With his imperialists that war should thrive.
Rise up, and lest the years prepare new death, call to you own by name, friend
Seven million three hundred and forty-five.

Surely you'll not allow your son, having lost his youth and honour,
To tread that one-way road so that they'll fix
Upon his breast another mark of death that bears the number on it:
Seven million three hundred and forty-six.

THE GOBLET

Out of an empty shell, in which death once had its dwelling,
Men a fine goblet have made.
Good it is for many years!
Only whenever I drink out of the yellow-gold shell, in
It I see friends unforgotten, in the sky-vault fires appear,
And even a draught of mead becomes then as bitter as tears.

* * *

The trees have forgotten all tempests and losses,
And earth has healed up her wounds gradually.
Only you can forget nothing, nor toss it
Away, memory!

Coils of barbed wire, the compounds enclosing,
The roads of war and the cannonade's sound,
And burned sites, their crippled pine-trees exposing,
And grave mounds.

Even today, when again at dawn's breaking,
I let my song with the bird-family ring,
I can feel rusty splinters yet aching –
As I sing.

THE PANES OF AN OLD MANSION

Very carefully,
Wipe the window-panes clean
Of this old mansion!
There have survived such a few of them
Of all that were in my city.

They have seen far, far more than
The trees and the monuments.
They have seen far, far more than
The eyes of mere men
Which always grew dim when the shooting
Was over.

Very carefully,
Wipe the window-panes clean
Lest with shadows of smoke
From fires of war
You wipe off the shadows
Of those close to you
Who for the very last time
Once looked out through the panes of these windows.

Vasil Vitka

ROSE AND BAYONET

The watercourse is sere now
Where once a spring ran ever.
Where the stove stood, here now
The bricks are blackened over.

The battle-field's grown over
With a grassy cover,
With grey goose-foot beset now,
And with stinging nettles.

But where you fell and died, friend,
At the house's side, friend,
On your blood-stained track, there,
Grass will not grow back there.

Your monument with graces
Is twisted, past all bribing,
The bayonet in the clay is,
Driven, the helmet lies there.

Memories unperished
Of you, my friend, the bushes
Of briar-roses cherish,
Covered with blossoms lushly.

Let any one extending
His hand attempt to touch it,
Blood on the heart descending
In living dews is rushing.

The iron is grown over
With thorns set sharply, boldly;
And they'll be fresh for ever,
Those memories of a soldier.

Pimien Pančanka

THE UNBURIED COFFINS

'Why, my dear son, does my heart ache and hurt?
I shall go bleach my dear son a shirt!'

A woman in madness was singing this song,
And the war walked, ruined roadways along.

There is not a son, there is not a shirt, no!
Winter has bleached the woman with snow.

In rusty pits on the roadway of war,
The waxen faces of children;
Here only snow and black chimney-stones are,
Snow, and graveyards of the village.

One such I never shall cease to recall;
The aggressors slew here, fiercely rending
People who knew how to love and to toil,
Who were loved with a love true and tender.

And then the orphaned daughters and mothers
Knocked deal-boards together,
But to dig graves for their darlings
Their strength was failing.

In a sad line the coffins must stand,
Forged round with blue icy bands.
They waited, they waited there in the snow,
For war to go.

'People!' I call, and no tiredness abates it,
'Our task's to keep peace! To it hurry!'
Still in my heart stand waiting, stand waiting,
Coffins unburied.

THE ORANGES

Marching towards Dziamiansk.
The rear was trailing.
After the thaw
Like gravel fell the sleet.

Though rarer now and rarer bombs were wailing,
There were still mines,
And not a bite to eat!

Suddenly, near some trenches, then, the soldiers,
Met the chief quartermaster standing there.
As if his own creation, he was holding
Spanish, fantastic fruit, sharp-tasting, rare.

Before the war we never ate an orange . . .
But by a hundred combats rebaptized,
We knew how golden trophies should be honoured,
Not less than Spanish kings these fruits we prized.

In the golden oranges' glad shining
Was a foretaste of victory.
We went on!
In the azure snow, eight *vierstś* behind us,
The blossoms of the orange orchards shone.

And, till the battered town was in our keeping
We fought, west in the stranger's tracks we strove,
While fallen comrades in the snow lay sleeping,
In the white loveliness of orange-groves.

Siarhiaj Dziarhaj

HIROSHIMA

Here on your ruins and stones
Are printed
For aeons eternal
Death and grim torment,
Hiroshima.

The living embers
Fill space unbounded,
And, having sought rest in vain,
Seat themselves in our hearts, O
Hiroshima.

We love and remember,
Hoping and seeking,
Seeking, believing.
Striving.
Hiroshima.

A single minute,
A minute of sorrowful silence,
In memory of that which once was,
It is very little,
Hiroshima.

With silence eternal of guns.
The stillness of peace eternal
We shall honour the memory
Of those victims of thine,
Hiroshima.

Time will come,
All earth will blossom with spring,
And will be born again, rise again,
Your quiet glory,
Hiroshima.

Kastuś Kirenka

PETITION

Dress my wounds for me –
    I have not the power.
Press my heart for me,
    for, see, where are running
Blood path-lets,
    trickling,
    a terrible sound!
And to live I am longing
To live I am longing.

Dress my wounds for me –
    the pain in war won,
But tell no one, I beg,
    what you have heard, after!
Because I have sons,
Because I have sons;
Let them think on,
Let them think on
That suffering
    never
        came to their father!

Mikoła Aŭramčyk

THE CRANE'S KEY-SHAPED FLIGHTS

Jean, *mon ami,*
The wounds of our bodies have healed up already.
Again spring . . .
Again icicles have long since gone.
But under my heart
Their splinters have settled,
And from them a frost on my spirit has come.

The icicle-stalactites of pink salt-crystals
Under the earth
Bring back memories to me
Of late sap on the birches
Which were wounded, sore hurt in
Captivity when spring frosts come
Untimely.

Maybe it is because my body is yet burning
From underground waters, droplets of brine,
That I feel, so it seems,
In my spirit returning,
The fiery pangs of my wounds at that time.

For then,
Even the birds from the woodlands and farmsteads
Fled from the thunder and fire of those years,
In the water
The shoals of fish, wary of harming,
Deep in the depths
Were hiding from fear.

Only people, in spirit and strength then were mighty.
Brothers and friends sent aid to our side . . .
While great shoals of terrible birds, silver-flighted,
With booming of terror soared to the height.

It seemed to me
The clouds were broken asunder,
As wedge upon wedge
From afar on them smote,
And at each blow, the sparks flew forth, under
The impact the earth and sky shook from the blows.

From fear were our watchmen completely dumbfounded,
But spring,
Taking the cranes in the key of their flight,
Unlocked us the doors to light from underground and
After nocturnal dark, drenched us with light.

The cranes from their exile were now flying homeward,
Rousing memories of our dear land in the soul . . .
From their key-shaped flights,
Like an arrow, swift going,
We learned the way to our country, our goal.

I thought about this
When I saw geese extending
Their flights from the southland home in a long chain,
To lakes, water-meadows of Bielaruś tending,
While my daughter drinks neat maple-syrup again.

You thought
That the loon had flown to you forever,
But this was the loon
That from the clouds hurled
On the Sahara a fire-wounding feather,
And spread burning poison
Abroad in the world.

Spring again . . .
You remember the cranes' key-shaped flights . . .
Jean,
But do you sleep easy o' nights?

Anatol Vialuhin

PARTISAN FOREST

(for Platon Varan'ko)

'See, the earth's dreaming sounds
Around
The tree trunk, lichen bound!'

'What is it?'

'The wind:
On tree tops the wind lay there,
It leads patrols storming.
In black pitchy water
The rainclouds
Like pontoons are swaying!'

'Do not look with the eyes of war
At whirlpool mirror, where appear
The fir-bell trees,
And we,
And day's sandstone screes.
High over
With flash of its wings
The swift soars high . . .'

'Thunder will strike:
For rain
Old wounds once more have started aching!'

THE PARTISAN SCHOOL

For scrolls of dry parchment – birch-bark was serving.
Letters crabbed as ants . . . The heart wearily grieving.
Palessian childhood was learning to write
While the Junkers whined down, and set fires seething
In clouds, trees and grass, forty days, forty nights.

Witness to our need – pads of 'tree-shop' providing.
On sunny bark silk, courage is guiding
An unsteady hand to form words as it may.

'Land. Tent. Flag.
                    Slavery. Thirst.' We can find them
Resounding, such words, in the old 'Igor's Lay!'

The oakgrove set type for a primer forever.
Stifling a cough, wrapped in a bedcover,
Homeless war sought for warmth on a fire-blackened field.

Our native tongue shall not die nor yield ever,
Since to so great a fire
                    it did not yield.

Alaksiej Pysin

THE OAK

An old oak in the valley shuddered, flinching,
Where grass has grown across the trenches' sill:
By some strange chance in scars of old mine-splinters
A wood-pecker was tapping with its bill.

MY FRIEND IS IN HOSPITAL

Rainstorms, bypass our land in your flying,
Thunder not under the morning star;
Do not breathe, scorching winds, from afar –
My friend is in hospital lying.

In delirium he thinks that he must be
In the sick-bay, fires through his wounds course;
And he knows not if it was tanks crushed him,
Or trampled by a broad-breasted horse . . .

Come nearer, you well-springs, provide him
A flagon of water, ice-cold;
Orchards, your red apples withhold
Not, my friend is in hospital lying.

Unbearable pains, woe oppressive,
He bites, but the taste does not know.
Like a hand-grenade now he is pressing
The apple, but cannot rise, no.

You winds, scatter the field mists asunder,
And tint the far distances blue:
Soldier will not retreat nor surrender,
He is living, he'll fight on anew.

THE FLAG

Taut stick across my shoulders, I
Hold life's extension in my hands.
Chime forth, my flag, and fluttering fly,
Boldly in rays and winds expand.

Higher my flag than unsuccess,
Higher my flag than any lies.
And in red calico for dress
From head to foot-sole clothed am I.
Corrections were
                    by bullets
                                made,
And then I saw, displayed,
Blossoming thick and crimsonly
My bandages
                on
                    me.
Undying, flag, you shall live on,
We bear you through all strife
In our blood and in our bone,
And yield you but with life.

Piatruś Makal

THE AIR

The people are growing alarmed, poor with terror,
Haunted by atom mushrooms o' nights,
They nourish sorrow, build shelters in horror,
Slaves of their own explosive-forged might.
Some do rebel, and draw up petitions,
To wisdom and leading leaders they pray,
Others arrange practice repetitions
Rehearsing for doomsday . . .
                                        Sense – take it away!
Already the atom has slipped from its leashes,
Drives us underground with its thunders and groans.
And where to hide Shakespeare and Pushkin, whose riches
Make their dwellings in tomes
                                        as their homes?
In black cradles, within a friend buried,
Without knowledge of music and light to them shown,
Homers grow blind and Beethovens deafened,
Earth, with bomb-jungles you are overgrown!
To dust and ash topples many an acropolis;
Rummaging cranny and nook in their search,
Like policemen come the poisonous droplets:
Do any scraps of air linger unhurt?
Some will escape the explosion-waves' pelting,
And the living will look with envy on death . . .
You,
        who lurk like moles in the shelters,
What will you have to use for your breath?
Lest the Last Judgment of atom-bomb dooming
Drag the world into whirl-pools plumbless, without cease,
Build, my countrymen, that shelter, sound in bomb-proofing –
Peace!

Nil Hilevič

THEY HAVE BOMBED THE HOUSE OF A WRITER

In the 'free world' bombs are now bursting,
So as to make it even 'freer'.
The Fascists have miscalculated.
Still he lives, our friend unknown.
Once more the anguish of the word of truth
More forcefully explodes than the bombs.
Once more the anguish of a voice unfearing
Calls men to true brotherhood to come.

They have bombed the house of a writer
Who did not sing obscurantist psalms . . .
Many were the black slayings we knew
From Pushkin to Halan even.
It was not rhymsters they slew,
The quickly-in-and-out of fashion.
They slew the one whose voice over
The barricade fires rang true.

There where the fetters of slavery are bursting,
Where the steps of freedom grow wider –
How many of them today, bold in spirit,
Are there to raise above their head
As they would raise a flag's crimson,
Lorca's heart, riddled with shooting,
Who are ready to write their last line on
The earth in the blood they have shed!

I set these volumes in type very solemnly –
Of the holy and unholy alike,
Grateful, sincerely, to all those whose bounty
For me was lavishly poured.
But a triple bow give I as homage
Low to the earth before all those
Who for the good-fate of their country,
As soldiers have fallen in war.

Ryhor Baradulin

THE WARD OF THE SAPPERS

My old classmate stretches his arm towards me.
I press the poor stump (scars and furrows enwrap it).
And the district hospital smells of HE
And manganese dust
from the ward of the sappers.
Far to the west the thunder pealed out.
We were playing war games –
we and the Germans,
But the war,
having made every bush a redoubt,
Spied out the land all around
dumbly learning.
Early in the wet trenches we grew to be men,
But we did not forget our toys soon. And it happened
Those 'toys' went off bang!
Said the doctor again:
'Reinforcements once more
for the ward of the sappers!'
And it seemed
in the quiet
the earth thumped as it spun,
With its axis,
as peg-leg,
tap-tapping,
After dressings were changed
(Ah, the wounds burned) they sang
'Eaglet'
there in the ward of the sappers.
A gale pressed the leaves close on our window-pane,
Set the rowan's
unwounded arms
bending.
But we could not go back to the classroom again
When (in 'forty-four)
summoned September.
With one sleeve empty the son has gone home.
Mother,
apple-tree white, and grief shattered.
But let powder be smelt –
you'll hear answering soon
The lads
from the ward of the sappers.

Hienadź Buraŭkin

DANCE AT THE RECRUITING CENTRE

Dance at the recruiting centre,
Dance at the recruiting centre . . .
Crop-haired lads in combat-jackets.
And the eyes of young girls
                                        yearn
And the mothers,
                        the old, quiet mothers:
'It is time now for the youngest's
                                                turn.'
And in the waltz couples circle.
Dance at the recruiting centre.
And the lads, crop-headed, clumsy,
Are most carefree in mood . . .
But then
            a stentorian shout,
Through the noisy square, a command,
And smartly-turned-out sergeants
Fall them into line.
The lads will be looked after carefully
Well-fed, feet well-booted,
And they will be issued
Enough of tobacco and dreams.
Mothers,
            why are you weeping,
Why looking with sadness
On the crop-headed, clumsy
Youngest of sons? . . .

Your sons will come back to you quickly,
They'll have a good time in the army.
And the mothers,
                        a little shamefacedly,
Wipe their tears away
                                with wrinkled hand
They are reassured now, for their sons.
What can you do,
                        when such as these
Crop-haired lads, in combat-jackets,
In their fallen fathers' . . .

Anatol Viarcinski

EVERY FOURTH ONE

During the last war, every fourth Byelorussian perished. To date the population has not attained its prewar level.
(From official documents)

Have you seen a wood
cut by great empty clefts?
Seen a pineforest like this one
Which of every second pine is bereft,
Or at least every fourth one?
With my people it came to pass so.
The hatchet of war laid them low.
And there fell, scattered, prone,
Every fourth one.
Then the falling stars fell, thousandfold,
Black had the skyline become.
And on the earth footprints grew cold,
Every fourth one.
Peace shone its torch on us once more,
Thundrously fanfares were rung.
Empty seats, though,
at that festal board,
Every fourth one.
Long years to their hopes widows clung,
Long years mothers waited their sons,
They did not believe dead and gone
Every fourth one.
Never shall we forget our great loss,
Memory, like reeds, murmurs on.
O why are you not here with us –
Every fourth one!

III

'Circling the world . . .'

Maksim Tank

A TOAST TO FRIENDSHIP

If we but lift our hands together,
A million hands, white,
                    yellow,
                              black,
We could raise the sun up, even,
Higher than all mountain peaks.

If we but clasp our hands, to form
A living garland, we'll enclose
With garland of hands, black,
                         white,
                                   and yellow,
This poor rounded world of ours.

But when we clench our fists in menace
Millions of yellow,
                    black,
                              and white,
Then will fall the last of fetters,
Thunder the universe will smite.

Then, brothers, let us charge our glasses.
Bright, foaming, starry wine, no lack!
And raise up, in a toast to friendship,
Our hands of white,
                    yellow,
                              and black.

Pimien Pančanka

THE ESTONIAN'S CAP

There was no tempest nor storm on that day
In Tallin when I was born there,
The ordinary sun in the ordinary way
Rose after one hour of dawning.

But in the south somewhere the war groaned with pain.
My father had gone to the war now.
A Workers' barracks. In our room remained
Of bread just the very last morsel.

And doubtless my mother was wondering how
To take me back to her poor village,
There where you still might get victuals somehow,
If only potatoes, to fill you.

And mother wept longingly, deeply she pined
For the far Minsk region, her homeland . . .
And there came to see us, towards evening time,
Friends of my father, Estonians.

'The people have sent us to visit,' they said,
Their stern faces over me bending,
They blessed my arrival in life without words,
A little praise to me extending.

This was the anxious year of 'seventeen.
The eyes were sunk in from starvation.
'Our work on the docks is honey by no means,
Yet may he work with keen dedication!'

As my mother will tell, I was not quiet and good,
I started to cry without stopping,
I was marking my birthday the best that I could,
Even though I could see nothing of it.

Did not see how the ship-wrights had left a cap filled
With money for us brimming over,
Crumpled one-rouble notes, the shipwrights in their guild
Had held a collection for Mother.

I have praised love, expeditions and war,
The sun in my dear country glowing.
But praise above all praise in my poems for
The simple cap of an Estonian.

Ryhor Baradulin

*   *   *

The goods-waggon chugging and shaking.
The tallow-candle flickers, gleams.
There music deafens all the joking,
Here many have succumbed to dreams.

But the wind, spreading the smoke over
The roof, leads along distant ways.
And, for good luck, pails brimming over,
Great Volga
Crossed our path today.

With star-gold prettily, threshed befittingly,
Milky Way spreads the sky with dust.
Urals like Russian giants hospitable
Unroll an iron towel for us.

On both sides, by the track-lines looping
Telegraph poles, supported, file,
Like two friends who, with shoulders stooping,
Let a third further see awhile.

And, for the rest, free steppe . . .
Sun scorches,
It will show us no pity here.
Now we must synchronize our watches –
The time of virgin soil is near.

Siarhiej Hrachoŭski

ON THE TAIGA ROAD

Round the reddish-brown moaning of curves the wind whines,
The snowstorm is sweeping away the whole highway.
On Siberia's blue *taiga* roads one at times
Can hear very faintly the lone sledges gliding.

From one village on to the next takes a day
And a night – not a living soul; only the gloomy
Shaggy wind drives the last traces away
Of the road which a lonely plough cut in the noonday.

Never silent, the telegraph poles are awhine,
The wind warps white flax on the frame of the snowdrifts.
The snowstorm is raging. You peer as if blind,
At it seems that the gear on the horses is frozen.

The snowstorm is raging, it sweeps and it sweeps –
Forges aspen trees into white ingots of metal.
At the thirty-vierst mark, in the night gloom there peeps
A small glimmer of light from a little house set there.

Above the high drift of the roof's sloping pitch
Naked and greyly a treebranch is leaning.
In the dark of the frigid wastes two windows which
Over the *taiga* till dawn-break are shining.

I went in, but inside there is no one around,
Only a small fire in the stove glimmered faintly;
On the bench a jug filled with well-water I found,
Salt in a glass
And a fresh loaf was waiting.

On the wide clean deal table newspaper was spread,
And on the shelf too, dated First of December,
Someone kindled the stove and then rode on ahead,
Vanished into the snowdrifts and weather.

Someone had left a loaf and chopped wood for the fire,
Kindled the lamp, so that, out in the darkness,
No stranger nor friend should be lost, weary-tired,
Chilled from the night and worn by the road's starkness.

So when I was warm, I too brought in more wood,
Left some bread there and scattered the crumbs round the doorway.
The snowstorm grows silent, the frost is less rude.
And the long road holds no more terrors for me.

Piatruś Broŭka

A FOOTPATH NEAR NEW YORK

All this America to know
I cannot, willy-nilly,
But there's one footpath here that goes
To Oyster Bay, our villa.

I became good friends with it,
After New York's great teeming,
And often I would walk on it,
Often of it was dreaming.

And often in the morning, sad
Along it I'd go walking,
The maples rustled overhead
And the firs were talking.

And it seemed that I could hear
Of my spring in that moment,
The path recalled to me, quite clear
Another in my homeland.

Which longer seems to me, more wide
Than any highway can be,
Nearer to me than aught beside,
Although it is far from me.

Over it dreaming fir-woods sing,
Pines talk with oaks above it,
Among lakes it leads, wandering,
In my dear land beloved.

Like eel that wriggles through the meads,
Through bushes, woodland country,
To that quiet little place it leads
That's called Ušačy county.

Now, as of old, it is to me
Still the one and only,
Along it Mother first took me,
The whole wide world to show me.

But my world had an ending, though
Too near was set the limit.
Who could have thought this path would do
Circling the world within it?

Through villages and towns would lead
(With it the years passed slowly)
That it would bring me here indeed,
Across the ocean's rolling.

And even though today I stroll
This path with interest seeming,
I love but one with all my soul,
Of one alone am dreaming.

Oyster Bay, near New York
October, 1959

Pimien Pančanka

THE BOY FROM THE FARM

In a villa just outside New York we're living
On a plot of land that is our own.
We work on it, and good account shall give when
On an eastbound ship we sail back home.

Next-door a farm stands, simple, rough and ready.
And through a crack in our fence came to look
Each morning a young farm-lad, nothing dreading,
To watch the children and the Soviet folk.

A quiff of hair, a nose, eyes gaily twinkling,
And on the quiff a blue beret is perched.
And we see that he is very willing
Already our sovreignty to encroach.

He has no fear of Senate or commissions,
And without visas, without verbal notes,
On a distinctly peaceable trade-mission
Boldly in across our fence he got.

He swaps some stamps in a most expert manner,
Tries our sweets and praises them: 'OK!'
And through the garden walks resounds the chatter
Of children's international speech today.

With pure hearts and bright laughter, children's fashion,
After a chipmunk through the dew they run.
And now they play at Soviets-versus-Fascists,
And now at cops-and-robbers, turn by turn.

They deal an orange out, segment by segment,
Which the boy had brought with him when he came,
For children find the grasses' fragrance pleasant
In Moscow or Long Island, just the same.

Arkadź Kulašou

*   *   *

On the third day I met storms on the ocean
After I had sailed from the foreign shore
Of North America.

For Inspiration

Flags need the wind, but I need flags the more.
But not those flags which, meeting winter's coldness,
It seems, surrender to the tempest's might.

Not before evil nor to crooked-souled-ness
Have I ever raised a flag of white.
Not before waves that roll with threatened crashing,
Not before death nor before loving passion,
When it desires not as a sailor brave
To see me stand before it, but a slave.

Let the waves rage on. A bold, inciting
Challenge I shall send to meet them, so:
My flag of life is red. As for the white one –
This I gladly leave unto my foes.

Piatruś Makal

THE ROUND TABLE

My homage to thee, festal table round,
For, see, a cheese-cake task-force overran you
And chairs in their orbits gather round,
Circling like satellites about a planet.
I praise those who, in order, sit at thee!
And who to set the table is not ready
When 'mother' will the wisest elder be?
So be it in the General Assembly!
Sons and their wives, daughters and sons-in-law –
Delegates from Čukotka and On-Nioman!
Then solve life's knots of problems, don't burn your
Lips, just use the saucer and be homely!
This is one family from far and near.
Brotherly forum. East and West. You're able
Surely to do the same, earth, just as here?
You too are round,
almost like my own table.
And what man is not awed
when, soaring winged,
He has looked down upon earth's table service,
Back to her own great table she will bring
Us home, from loved heights down to her returning.
As if from bowls, smoke from volcanoes soars,
Fermenting the strong grapes – a glass you wish for?
Snow-peaks as serviettes bedeck the board,
His Highness Caucausus serves out the dishes . . .
Ah, could we only seize their collars,
Shake
Those who in their fanged greediness are able
And ready to kick over and to break
You, just to grab a little more, dear table!
From good dishes and wishes you'll not fall,
With your eternal lamp, the full-moon shinin
You'll pay full measure to men, one and all,
Of bitterness and sweet, in sauce combining.

So, human family, of your table think,
And what it needs in household manner on it,
And to the table,
like an altar, bring
Each day a loaf of bread as crown upon it.

IV

'The new dynasty'

Hienadź Buraŭkin

THE FIRST OF A DYNASTY

Evening at the kindergarten –
doors burst open.
And down towards the weary fathers roll
The loudly-shouting
happy dynasty of
Połack petroleum workers, grimed with toil.

And in the yard they cluster round their fathers.
To hide their nose in father's sleeve they run.
A white-haired lassie
to the Lithuanian,
To the Armenian
a dark-eyed son.

From snowballing
their little gloves are dripping,
Fingers are frozen from the wind – they warm
Their little hands, tomorrow's chemists, slipping
Them in a painter's or a joiner's palm.

They do not understand,
those tousled children,
Who play with dolls and whistles merrily,
That with them
a new dynasty is beginning,
Połack petroleum workers yet to be.

Alaksiej Rusiecki

MUSE IN A WHITE COAT

Once more I must go back to my old toiling,
Once more to care for work-hardened hands,
A muse in a white coat
Pleasantly smiling –
There my lab-girl stands.
On the table there gleams fragile glass and nickel,
Flashes of light on my object-glass flicker.
And the muse drops on a glass slide for me,
Like a jeweller's
Diamond, radiant,
One drop of thunder,
A droplet of rain, carefully.
All is still;
From ether and balsam, light fragrance.
And, as ever, my view through the lens gleams with light,
I fly into the unknown
In the laboratory;
As if from deep space distant stars twinkle bright,
Bustling of micro-beings – stars in glory.
The greatness of this minute world steals the breath,
In this glorious droplet in radiance gleaming. . . .
It is my fate to see, with X-ray eyes, even
Ribs within beauty's breast.
Yet I find no embarrassment in my profession:
There where the sharpness of vision breaks down,
It would seem a new land
And thy wonders are found,
O poetry.

Aleś Zvonak

THE GEOLOGIST

Then I was much younger, and my hand
And my will were harder and far firmer.
I've passed through much on water and dry land,
Geologist, explorer keen for learning.

With a hammer made from special steel
Pieces of bedrock I would cleave; I broke them
Where fossil cleavage and thin veins revealed
To me the breath of ages past laid open.

The promise of success I found in ore
In which were crystals, glittering embedded.
I was far younger. I was looking for
Seams of metal, such as would be needed

By an engineer with unbroken will
To make an alloy to resist all forces.
He was, like me, no doubter. He was still
Winged with imagination in his courses.

At night-time, when the moon's oar dipped to stir
The deathly dankness of silver-lake waters,
I threw in lumps of refractory words,
Heated to a white heat by due forging.

Take it, my sun, I shouted, find and say
Which is the stone that bears the brightest facet,
Burning with sparks of impetus always,
In which dwell unique wonders and their magic?

Take it from my hand, unwearied yet,
Look on the world, and in the bright refraction,
You will see, friend unique, how there is set
On each face wonderment and joy enacted.

Ryhor Baradulin

BOBBINS

'Buy a bobbin, buy a bobbin,
Workmanship of finest jobbing!'
The old man calls, loud and clear.
'You will never find, their equal,
They spin wool like silk, so sleekly . . .
Come and see them, come on here!'

'No one nowadays can use 'em,
Give 'em, Dad, to the Museum!'
Some bright jester gives a shout.
An old woman sighs, half-sobbing,
Memories roused by the bobbins.
But they melt away, the crowd.

Only the boys cluster round him,
Want to spin the bobbins round, and
The old man more gladly calls:
'You will never find their equal,
They spin wool like silk, so sleekly!'
But no buyer comes at all!

'Come and buy now! Fine new bobbins!'
But no one comes here for shopping,
The market's packing up, and there
They stand like orphans, those fine bobbins,
Finest-made, those brand-new bobbins.
'Too late, old man, you brought your wares! . . .'

Anatol Viarcinski

* * *

A little small house,
I see,
was destroyed.
And in this little house
men sang songs of joy.
In this little house
a mother gave birth.
In this little house
guests were welcomed with mirth.
In this little house,
in this house, I say,
Summer and winter
were cosy and gay.
I grieve till I ache,
I grieve till tears flow
For this little house
that has been levelled low.
A thing is not better
because it is newer,
A thing is the better
if nearer and truer.
A thing is not better
because it stands taller,
A thing is the better
if closer, though smaller.
A thing is not better
because it is fairer,
A thing is the better
if dearer and rarer.
And this little house
to someone was close
This little low house
some man loved the most,
With this little house
was someone's fate bound.
And this house today
was razed to the ground.

Ryhor Baradulin

THE CRADLE

Earth is the cradle of mankind, but one cannot live forever in the cradle.
K. E. Tsiolkovskii.

The sky hangs down in a blue canopy.
Cradle, I thank you sincerely
That you raised no weak seeds to pine languidly,
Nor gave earth-room to wraiths or chimeras.

Canopy with a Milky Way tapestry.
In the clouds, the sun dangle-toy hanging.
Non-terrestrial wounds you healed, wrapped for us,
You, of all creation
one sandgrain.

Railed in around by the Carpathians
And by the Himalayas swaddled,
Like the palm of a man you are roughened,
But for man you are now all too little.

And when we, on the eagle-roads zooming,
To the wary planets are riding.
You, fragrant with clay and with cumin,
Will be but a way-star to guide us.

The grey-haired cosmos we shall transform them.
Earth alone shall know sorrow and yearning:
There the lark, in his throat, until autumn,
Cools the drop of bright sun, hot and burning.

Ravens over the forest are cawing.
In the meadows the pasture grows lushly.
The colt tugs the grass in juicy jawfuls,
Nudging aside the foal's thrusting.

But out in that far tousled mistiness,
Where cosmic whirlwinds lie before us,
We'll remember our mother's hands, wistfully,
Hands which rocked our cradle for us.

Those good hands which first did take us,
And lift us up from the earth, highly.
'Look, ladies, they've finished rickmaking . . .
Look above the woods, see the cranes flying . . .'

V

'Pictures beloved of my native country'

Maksim Tank

MY DAILY BREAD

I am unquiet for you, my dear land,
For your harvest, your quiet slumbering,
For every tree that in your groves stands,
resounding songs of the spring,
I am unquiet for you my dear land –
My daily bread.

Sometimes from the dust bitter it was,
Sometimes from fallen tears salty it was,
Sometimes from powder fiery it was,
But also from friendship sweet it was,
My daily bread.

And give me no other bread to take
In my pack, when on my road I must start,
Nor let it in festive tables take part,
Nor place it, when my hands are crossed, on my heart.

Heinadz Buraŭkin

* * *

The starling sings . . .
Its weary wings . . .
widely spread
And from the earthy
spring happiness
its eyes are shutting.

It hid its song long oversea
safe from freezing and sleet –
But in the warm throat
that song is now chiming
and bubbling.

It flutters, it flaps,
it has no use for rest,
As if somewhere it caught on its tongue
embers undwindling,
Preparing
from nectar of buds,
upon each twig expressed,
A hundred of tiny
green fires
to kindle.

Ŭladzimir Duboŭka

THE YOUNG CAPTAINS

In the wide world the rain falls,
Gentle, small and thinly.
By the water, children walk,
Rinsing their boots in it.

They've made little boats of bark,
In the puddles sail them.
Granpa scolds with his remarks,
Shakes a hand that's failing.

He is fearful lest they may
Sail in these boats far distant,
The wind will drive ships far away
Where the wide ocean glistens . . .

To those shoes unattained, now set
Sail, children, without repining!
Grandpa could never reach them – yet
For you the sun is shining!

Larysa Hienijuš

IN THE NIGHT PASTURE

The wind chases billows, bends the willows low,
Roaming through the mist the hobbled horses go,
My bay horses, their hooves smiting
On my heart are ringing quietly,
Ringing so.

Long, long sleepless in this wondrous night I lay,
In the field a small flame wandered, gone astray,
Long the nightingale was singing,
Through the boughs its notes came ringing,
Through the hay.

Long, long, from the villages girls' singing pealed,
Flowing forth until the horned moon, swooning, reeled,
Till the lads fell into slumber
And wind scattered the last embers
Through the field.

The night was like a tale of azure-blue,
Till the stars went out I pondered and I knew
That more fair than stars through branches
Are a certain maiden's glances,
– Mine and true.

Roaming early through the mist the horses go,
Soon the lads will rise and drive them swiftly home.
The wind chases billows, ringing
In my heart with native singing,
Ringing so.

Janka Sipakoŭ

A GREEN CLOUD IN THE MARKET-PLACE

Come, who buys? I bring to sell
Winds that tall grasses have rocked into slumbering!
Come, who buys? I offer as well
Nightingale songs, meadow-stored beyond numbering!

Hurry, hurry . . . for I bring to sell
Maytime, drunk with the spring floods to ebriety!
There you are! I've flower-honey as well
Soaked in the humming of bees to satiety.

Hurry along there! . . . for I bring to sell
Sunshine and lightning (you'll know just by feeling it!)
No need to haggle! A give-away! well,
This green cloud of summer is (there's no concealing it)
A waggon of fragrant new hay!

Anatol Vialuhin

THE RIPE FOREST

Of all cathedrals there is one
That I consent to pray in:
Ripe forest, when ripe summer comes,
Then set your belfry playing.

In sultry fragrance of the lea,
Where youth of old was strolling,
Thorn-apple, cockle, rosemary
Set incenses a-rolling.

Rank upon rank the fungi brood,
Bumblebee's bass is shaking.
Deep is the moss. The leaves show blood
Of the bear-raspberry's making.

The trunks with arrow-tappings bleed,
Marked with the cross of suffering.
And hastening Brother-Badger speeds,
To his dark corner hurrying.

And amber resin's healthful smell.
In the clear height extending
That white down is not clouds, it tells
Of angels hawks were rending.

At every step, is something new.
Thyme makes the air oppressive.
And each pine sings an anthem true,
Its forest's praise expressing.

Ŭladzimir Duboŭka

RAIN IN MAZYR

Slowly and quiet above the land
Like roller shafts the clouds are nearing.
Here single file, and here a band,
Here they come, two by two appearing.

Moon, like a shepherd, has appeared
With his smock flung about his shoulders,
Driving the clouds all to Mazyr,
Relief from thirsting to unfold there.

Maybe, there, thunder thunders back?
Or, perhaps, somewhere querns are turning?
Or, is it, somewhere a whip cracks
Beyond the horizon, blackly-blurring.

And there, too, our moon plunges now,
(His smock up to his ears he's drawing).
And through the murky darkness down
As if through sieves the rain is pouring.

No one is sleeping in Mazyr.
All watch through doors and windows, seeing
How heaven's gifts to me fall clear
Without accounting or decreeing.

And, all around, thirsts disappear
Which have held sway throughout the summer,
And rain walks, like a guest most dear,
A joyful guest to this world coming.

Dust vanishes from the tall trees,
Vanishes from the cobbled roadways,
Down to the Prypiać all dust flees,
Down the sleevelike alleys floating.

When the rain was over quite,
And it was over close to dawning,
The sun in rays of golden bright
Rose above the hills that morning.

Then, in all loveliness, Mazyr,
Spread wide, to all eyes was discovered;
Then everyone knew well, quite clear,
Nothing could be that was more lovely.

Nil Hilevič

*   *   *

Night.
Utter quiet.
Not a soul in the street.
I stand in the quiet, hear the beat
As the blind apple is torn from the branches.
Striking against the numb scar of a stump,
Dully and soft in the furrow it thumps.
I walk the mown hayfield, shivering rather,
And, long, long, until I slumber at last,
I shall listen as sounds of white ripening pass.

And, at first dawn,
A girl, laughing ever,
With a bow,
Slightly gap-toothed,
Face freckled all over,
Still dazed with sleep, will gather them up in a satchel,
And will take, splendid and lovely, a batch of
Apples, fresh, newly washed by the dew,
Rub one with her hand (an apple, waxed into brightness,
Until it squeaks), and munching the sweetness, delighting,
She will come, bearing the blind harvest home,
To the house, bearing my sleeplessness home.

Vasil Vitka

HEATHERS

What is it: fairy tale or dream,
Or forest voice that speaks?
Or the bows' harmonious boom,
From impetus oblique.

It struck – at once the rain ran gay,
Following the cloud near,
Like a boy, barefoot, makes his way
In a world bright and clear,

And with no choice of path, takes
A beeline to the wood,
Where mushrooms and fungi break
Clear through the mossy sward.

Where sun sparks from wild strawberries,
Where dream the bumblebees,
Where from wild quinces fragrances
The day swoons utterly.

Where the beads of thick dewdrops throng,
Warm periwinkles near,
The heathers give to us a song
For recollections dear.

Nil Hilevič

*　　*　　*

A wonder came – I slept my fill:
At dawn the snow fell thick and still,
Early-early.

And over all the yards it lies,
Covering sheds and wood-supplies,
Purely-purely.

We have a tablecloth for best,
That gleams like this to greet a guest,
Whitely-whitely.

The snow witched pettiness away,
Nor word nor shout nor laughter stay –
Quietly-quietly.

Silent, in quietude apart
I stand, with lightness in my heart,
Brightly-brightly.

Maksim Tank

SCALDING THE PORK

We built a fire out in the barn,
And how it poured with smoke,
And there was nothing else for us
But swallow it and choke.
While we worked to scald the pork,
Searing it in haste,
So that behind the tang of lard
We sensed the fragrant taste.

And bundles of burning straw
We stuffed in well beneath the hams,
Under the collar, covered in bristles,
Under the tusks more we crammed.
And then with our knives we scraped it,
And then with water we scoured,
Then into the house; like a drunken god
We hung up the pork, all the crowd.

The winds in our tracks behind us
Drove many a winter frost,
And the pup and the mewling cat knew
Every small thing that passed.
And then the frying-pan sizzled,
And freshness was roasting its fill,
And out of the pot, to the table
Mother brought of potatoes a hill.

After we'd had several glasses,
I remember the chatter would run
On various cosmic questions,
On various village ones.
We were like monks, all greasy,
After such a task was done . . .

In a far foreign land now
This to my memory comes,
When with some friends I shared a
Titbit of home-smoked lard,
Which mother packed up for me
Before I could depart.

1961
New York.

Siarhiej Hrachoŭski

MAMA

When first soft down above my lips was scattered,
And a girl's name came into my dreams,
Then, my own dear Mama, on no matter
Did I ever talk to you, it seems.

For somehow I felt a shame-faced silence
Among the boys – dashing crowd and tall –
To call you 'Mama', as I did in childhood,
And so I gave you then no name at all.

And in the evenings, I'd go, without saying
A word, to roam by other people's gates,
And I saw in our window the light playing
On the lamp-wick, till dawn, I was so late.

You did not sleep through the long nights of autumn,
Although with weariness your head drooped so,
Into the gloom you stared out from the cottage
With the eyes of a widow used to woe.

You spun fine linen, and you dug clay meekly,
At harvest could not feel your aching feet,
Ever about your son tenderly speaking:
'A lad must grow, so let my dear son sleep.'

And, once more, alone she went for firewood,
And in her hair the grey is growing thick:
'If only he'd say "Mama" as in childhood,
Or some kind word to call me he would pick!'

The years went by. And we ourselves grew greyer,
And, not to me alone unjust this dearth
Maybe, but there is none to whom to say now
'Mama', that holy word, in all the earth.

Pilip Piestrak

WONDER-MIGHT

There is among our folk a plant of wonder,
It walks, a fairy-tale, in all men's sight,
Maybe sometime when hardship you are under,
And thus people call it: 'Wonder-might'.

We sat there by the fence. And Grandma with us
Brought out her old strange tales of long ago,
How, in the time of Lords, so hard was living,
How her son, Apanas, was beaten so,

How the lords pounded on his breast, how living
Was like a fisherman without a bite . . .
'I had thought that he would not survive it,
But then we found help in wonder-might . . .

It put my son back on his feet, I know that . . .'
Grandma goes on to talk of other things,
Of how the earth so wondrously bestows on
This little plant its flowing sap to drink.

And there over the fence its yellow blossom
Is nodding down to us, high overhead,
And of this fact entirely is unconscious
That it to human ills is such a friend.

'If your heart grows heavy, or if illness
Saps your strength and drains your forces quite,'
Grandma got up, 'Do not worry, children,
For the road I'll give you wonder-might!'

Alaksiej Pysin

THE KNOT

By what strange knot it is I'm bound
For ever, I cannot tell you,
To old pines, past the village grounds,
To apple, pear and elm-tree.

To the smooth plank-bridge,
Boulder-stones,
Grass, rye in forest clearing,
To partisans' high gravemounds lone,
Monuments to Guards' heroes.

But I know that on earth can be
No sword forged, no such wonder,
To cut my knot away from me
That would not my heart sunder.

Maksim Tank

AT THE PLANTING OF TREES

My rustling forest!
Maybe to none am I so much indebted,
As to you,
For a house made of trunks speaking,
For a cradle made of boards creaking,
For fishing-rod, whip-stocks, bast-fibre,
For torches you lit for me over my books,
For songs, with which you called me to you with desire,
For warmth in the winter-time snowstorm,
For sand to heap over bomb-trenches,
For all wounds that with fire-shots drench us.
O my dark forest.
With what to repay you, my friend, am I able.
Maybe, till they grow up big and strong, I the feeble
Saplings I should embrace with my arms, hold them growing,
Help them to stand against rain and winds blowing,
My native forest.

VI

'In matters of love . . .'

Maksim Tank

WHY ARE YOU BRAIDING YOUR LONG TRESSES?

Why are you braiding your long tresses,
Circling around in fiery dance,
Why do you try your coral necklace
Before the lifeless looking-glass?

It holds its peace. It cannot, truly,
Even the hundredth part proclaim
Of your fair form, so filled with beauty,
Of your bright eyes, like stars aflame.

Better, my fair one, you should summon
Me, even for the shortest while,
And then I should not feel so glumly,
And I will aid you in your trials:

To try on ear-rings, ribbons weaving,
Drape with a shawl your shoulders' stance,
And patent-leather boots, all gleaming,
Put on, *Lavonicha* to dance.

Yet all this time you cannot pardon
That first time when to help I'd planned,
The string of corals, unregarding,
Careless I broke with unskilled hand.

* * *

I have known folk who knew about everything,
And I envied them;

I have known folk who never would be at fault,
And I envied them;

I have known folk, who had their own
Place always for night-lodging,
And I envied them;

I have known folk who wrote enormously
Long letters to their beloved,
And I envied them . . .

Now I know rather more,
Am at fault rather less,
Have my own lodging,
Write letters, enormously
Long (and unanswered) to my beloved,
And I do not envy me.

Siarhiej Dziarhaj

THE NIGHTINGALE

Home from a party we were returning,
The world was so wondrous, it struck us so sweetly!
The moon over the forest, all jagged, had turned then
It seemed, for a moment, to a drum long beaten.

Look at it with care, you will see all the denting
Which the musician with his palm was making;
Now, at any time, it will ring out, start sending
Over this quiet-songed earth striking, shaking.

Feelings, wishes, emotions upon such a journey,
And words – I had lost them all as I travelled,
But in matters of love you can have no attorney!
Although maybe it might do no damage to have one!

And the evening. . . . The evening was wondrously lovely.
It seems I have found the word needful to it,
But the nightingale suddenly butted and shoved in,
Unreasonable bird, and the whole thing was ruined.

I stopped. I was quiet, as if struck into dumbness. . . .
Have you thus heard a nightingale sing, have you listened?
You have heard it! That means that you realize under
That canticle words of a testament glisten.
I called him unreasonable, but things were other.
Thus I lived then, simply coming and going:
Could not solve youthful problems: 'I went out to gather
Nuts, but I came back with no nuts to show you.'

But the bird around love was wheeling and turning,
That at that time I did not notice nor find out
How that little grey bird, the frail nightingale burned
All the bridges and all the small bridges behind me,

Siarhiej Hrachoŭski

* * *

Could I live without you?
And did not know
That somewhere on earth's vast expanses,
Beyond the deaf forests,
Beyond hundreds of hills, baulks of grass,
In no far constellation
But here on our planet,
In a green quiet alley
Your life you passed.

Could I live without you?
And maybe we might have met never,
Half a year apart
We might have passed by,
And diverged as the paths
In the fields diverge ever,
And would not have known
Whose the blame was, nor why.

Maybe it was needed
To fall into hell first,
To lose near ones, know anguish,
Suffer frost, suffer heat,
That fierce storms might not fell us,
That with you
Beneath the Pole Star
I might meet.

Recognize you,
And at once forget all that has wronged me,
To see beams of light sparkle
In your pupils again,
To be born anew,
And believe there'll come strongly,
Succour and happiness,
One for us twain.

To grow better, grow softer,
To surrender for ever
To your unbribable
Purity, steadfast and stern.
The mystery of your nature
To discover,
To temper the soul in a flame high, eterne.

Time is flying, is flying,
And a snowstorm drifts the brows over,
And the years on the forehead
Have scored through and through.
And I look upon you,
Still, today, wondering ever,
How I lived without you
When I lived without you.

Anatol Vialuhin

EVENING

On the road, dust is resting.
On the river, mist presses.
That is not
Lonely weeping,
Corncrake in the marsh
Creaking.

On the bench a near star shimmers,
A cigarette in the darkness glimmers.
From afar,
Unexpected,
Footsteps are,
By the fence there.

'Where are you going, Natalla dear?'
'To the kitchen garden, Michał dear.'
'Why?'
'For an onion.'
'To kiss you
I'm coming . . .'

And embracing
At the gate there,
They walk beneath the watchful moon
In the dew,
For berries seeking,
Where is corncrake's
Sad creaking.

Pimien Pancanka

THE WHITE APPLE-TREES

I

In spring the bright sap from the birch-bark is breaking,
Rivers sweep to the sea all their armour, unlingering,
In spring on the paws of the spruces are shaking
New bright green fingers.
And tenderly stroking their saplings, each spruce
Gives them amber beads of their resinous juice.

The cuckoos tell fortunes, the lapwings are mourning,
Nightingales deafeningly call;
And from the blossoming apples are born now
Maidens in our land. They all
Yesterday with their dumb dolls were at play,
But are adorned with white corals today.

O the white apple-trees, O the white apples.
The bashful maidens, lads gawky and shy,
The mad exciting perfume of the petals,
And the spring drunkenness on hot lips lies!
Mist does not cool them and firs do not scratch them,
Only their mothers are anxious and watchful.

Bashfully, proudly, they must bring later
Their light burden to this unlight world of ours,
To bring forth and tend their sons and their daughters,
Always remembering the apples in flower.
And for others who find their heart's desire never,
They will see apple-blossom – and tears will well ever.

II

For years wives have looked out, shading their eyes,
Watching for husbands and sons.
The stars have been falling, like glow-worms, they fly
Into deeps of drear dreams, and are gone.
And they did the mowing, the plough they were plying,
And for them their dear ones meanwhile were dying.

And their black tresses grew white as the blossom,
The orchard path covered with grasses . . .
And tomorrow, when men reach out into the cosmos,
Their sorrow will be no more easy.

We shall go forth to welcome the spacemen's return,
And mothers will gulp down hot tears that burn.

All night, till the morning star, they will watch, yearn,
With cold eyes the universe plying,
Thinking – will that star today flare and burn,
Or a rocket with their dear sons flying,
Always for them to pine and to worry,
Their longing multiplies cares by the hundred.

Out there are no milestones, out there are no roads,
No lay-by to rest on your roaming.
The universe grew stale, and fevers corrode
It without the great grace of a woman.
But today I call to the sky: send those clouds running,
For Mars's first citizens are born among us.

We shall see women unearthly in beauty,
– They are our joy and our sorrow –
We shall people the planets, and sow the far blueness
Of stars with love's power tomorrow.
And somewhere in the Cosmos, alluringly laden
With flowers, as at home, there will bloom apple-maidens.

Nil Hilevič

SONG WALKED IN THE WOOD

The pines' shoulders swayed, misted
In smoke for a shroud,
To meet me, from the distance,
Song walked in the wood.

Then, at the evening hour,
In the silence it rang,
With the unwasted power
Of a soul, pure and young.

It was understood clearly
That no shame here could be
For her shy, surprised, dearest
First mystery.

There is no need for fearing
Someone hears or will tell.
Every tree that stands near her
Remembers her well.

See, she is coming,
See, she goes past,
Her blue-white blouse gleaming,
Two plaits down her back tossed.

In her hands are her slippers,
She has bared her feet,
To feel, little by little,
The path lose its heat.

She strides on, through the ride like
A tunnel, alone,
A lovely young maiden
She seemed, and passed on.

But – and night was approaching –
It was quite clear, indeed,
To the village and homeward
Song did not wish to speed!

VII

'My singing, my native language'

Maksim Lužanin

RIGHT TO A POEM

When, wearied out by seeking,
You write, you tear to shreds,
Do not grieve too profoundly,
This is no poem yet.

When with a tender line, a
Maiden to tears you fret,
Be quite clear, friend, about it,
This is no poem yet.

When they praise you, the maestro,
Lift not too high your head:
Think: still the word re-echoes –
This is not poem yet.

First go, secure your spirit,
Set your gaze on this lode:
Steadfastness of your people
On the first of man's roads.

First go, let your hands labour,
Grow calloused as their pride,
With such your folk transformed life,
Won bread and salt beside.

Become a guarding warrior,
And a guild-master proved,
Fertile stars for your reaping,
So the joy of farm roofs.

Roots will grow then, deep under,
Where no shell-burst can fret.
All things so light will seem then,
What you bear, what you deem them,
You will breathe without let.

And then to you will come your
Right to a poem yet.

Piatruś Broŭka

MY NATIVE SONG

Life without you is restricted, mournful, uncoloured and hazy,
O my own well-loved native song, to what heights have you raised me.

You have taught me to know morsels of ryebread, to love them,
You gave me the stars, at night unfolded the heavens above me.

He who learned you in childhood will never from home be turning,
Each of your words is like grain in the ear well-forming.

Song lives through centuries. It gathers its strength for growing,
The word that gives us wings, as if it were lightning blowing.

Winds sharpen down the word, so it may soar, insistent,
So that we yet may hear each other though far far distant . . .

Words come from different sources. Sources both sad and merry.
As honey from different flowers the bees will collect and carry.

Song, you walk at our side, from birth to our death are near us,
My native song, of all things in the world you are dearest.

I know that I'll lodge one day 'neath a gravemound, that time is nearing.
Yet through the roots of oaks, still my native song I shall hear then.

Arkadź Kulašoŭ

*　*　*

I'm dying of this useless idle drifting
Not one month only, two, nor three. Accursed
I seem. I'd sooner hang myself than live so,
Simply for things unnecessary or worse.

All urges disappeared. Well my heart knows it,
That doctors cannot lend them back to me.
I'm losing hope and into madness going.
I do not hope for better times to be.

Such a time comes itself, as health comes, quickly.
And from its freshets and life-giving streams
It will bring sixteen-lined-ness, an elixir,
In sixteen drops, of wonders beyond dreams.

Sixteen paths on a sheet of paper, tracing
Further the things I love with love profound,
Sixteen firm ever-advancing paces,
Sixteen hands to embrace the world around.

TO POETRY

I am your captive and you are my cell
Condemned by love to live out a life sentence.
To shorten my captivity, to end its
Term, you make haste, but vainly you compel.

In vain, wishing another to imprison
You cut by half the guard upon my doors,
This wardership is senseless, without reason,
And all this careful watchfulness of yours.
Though there's no guard, to flee I am not able,
I shall not cease this rattling of my chains,
Each day take exercise by the time-table,
Suffer in 'solitary', know hunger's pains.

Language you cannot take from me, prevented,
You cannot change my fate to your own plan,
It is not you who chose me – I who am
Your captive, I chose you as life-sentence.

POETRY

I knew you as a bolt of lightning,
Through the storm-clouds cleaving,
I knew you to be liberation,
From hell and unfreedom,

A springtime flower
Piercing a gravestone asunder,
The track of a scout
On a road rocky and dusty.

I knew you to be a sweet kiss,
To be joy and true friendship,
To be a crust of dry bread
And the juice that grapes send us.

But you have proved to be more:
To be the blood in my veins beating,
To be the sun with
Its light all space illuminating;

Without which, as without
A mother or country,
One cannot be born
Nor live in earth's bounty.

* * *

I love this roaming; to its fairness
There is nothing near comparing;
Tauridian beauty is unable
To equal it, not landscapes fabled.

Roaming thus through field and village,
Through the oak-groves, boundless tillage,
All my broad native land among,
In my Byelorussian tongue.

In my native tongue, within it
All the rainbow colours shimmer,
With sweet woodland resins scented,
It chimes with living songs unending.

How much in it lies undiscovered;
Shadows in it and azure colours,
And, needful both to folk and poet,
Precious metals, brightly glowing.

Alaksiej Zarycki

TREASURES

Language,
My singing, my own native language,
You are lord of unknown treasures,
For in every word there are banded,
Of meaning, sound, colour, full measures.

Some of your words are filled with the plashing
Of Dniapro's waves plashing.
And others beckon
Like forest echoes,
Buried in deep woodland hollows.
And there are words like gold honey, thick-textured,
That among fragrant grasses has mellowed.

Quietly there sound in this language of mine
Words like a spring splashing,
Words gently caressing,
Words like dew,
In it we find
Thunder crashing,
Stormy pressing.
And the loud roar of battle and strife
Echoing speaks in it too.

Sometimes there is, unexpected, revealed a new
Star, word reborn and commanding.
How many treasures are there undetected concealed in you,
Language of mine,
Singing language.

Maksim Tank

* * *

Not for this cause alone I took this language,
That rivers and primaeval woods spoke in it,

Grain-ears and grasses rustled in the meadows,
Birds in their nests called in it to each other,

And in it you may be the thing you wish to,
A singing violin,
                    a crane,
                              a poet.
But for this reason I took up this language,
Because there were too many sad songs in it,

Because I wanted to bring more abundance
Into it of human joy and sunshine,

So it was harder for me than for others
In this language to become a poet.

NOTES

p. 249: *Year of the quiet sun*
During the International Geophysical Year of 1957–58, the sun was at the most turbulent phase of its eleven-year cycle. To complete the solar data obtained in the IGY, 1963–4 were proclaimed as International Years of the Quiet Sun, so that systematic research could be carried out at the time when the sun was at the most tranquil phase of its cycle.

p. 249: *The discovery*
line 13. 'Jack O Green.' In the original, *listota*, which semantically, should mean no more than 'foliage'. However, not only is this a somewhat unusual form (*liscie* or *liscio* would be the forms expected in prose), it evokes in the mind a strong echo of *istota* 'a (sentient) being'. Hence, in the context of this poem, it seemed important to stress, in some manner, the *listota/istota* equation, and the Nottinghamshire 'leafy-man', Jack O'Green, seemed a suitable and valent symbol.

p. 251: *Much in life forgotten lies*
stanza 2. 'sound-guide'. The word used is *provad*, a noun derived from the verb *pravidzić* – 'to lead', 'to guide', to conduct'. With suitable qualifiers, *provad* can mean anything from a gas main to a lightning conductor. Here, from the context, I have inferred the sense of 'sound-guide', but this can be no more than a personal interpretation.

stanza 3. 'A dense south haze at noontime.' Literally, a *paudzionnaja* haze. Here, it is the adjective *paŭdzionnaja* which causes the confusion. This adjective is derived from the noun *paŭdzien*, which, according to context, can mean either 'south' or 'noon'. Thus the adjective will mean either 'southern' or 'pertaining to noon'. Since the context here will suit both meanings, both are included in the rendering.

p. 252: *Noon*
Paŭdzień again, but this time the sense is clear.

p. 253: *Gnomica*
line 21. 'like poppy-seed'. Since poppy-seed is not a regular part of the culinary stores of an English household, it should, perhaps, be pointed out that the seeds of the poppy are so extremely small that to grind (or rather crush) them for making poppy-seed cakes in the Byelorussian style, requires a very fine mill indeed! (Even a pepper-mill will not work properly – a modicum of the seeds still escaping uncrushed). As poppy-seed plays an important part in Byelorussian cooking, particularly in the delicacies for the traditional Christmas Eve 'ancestor' feast (see p. 231), the grinding of poppy-seed is an important feature of Byelorussian domestic activity, and 'poppy-seed' is a usual idiom for something small to the point of inconvenience (e.g. for illegibly-small fine-print on official forms!)

p. 256: *I bid you welcome*
line 4. 'Like September heath-smoke', literally, simply, 'like smoke of September' (*vierasnia dym*). However, in view of the fact that September (*vierasień*) derives its name from 'heather' (*vieras*), and that the genitive forms *vierasnia* ('of September') and *vierasa* ('of heather'), resemble each other so closely, particularly to the ear, I

have ventured to introduce the 'heather' idea ('heath-smoke') to convey some of the overtones of the original.

p. 256: *On Mars*
stanza 3. 'astronomer–curator' – this is a gloss. The original has *stranom-amatar* ('astronomer–devotee'). However, the second element of this compound seems introduced solely to supply a rhyme for *ekvatar* ('equator'), a function which 'curator' performs adequately in English, while still being reasonably within the context of the poem.

stanza 4. 'Tornadoes' – the original has *śmiarcy*. This is not, strictly speaking, a modern Byelorussian form; it is, however, the word used by Kupała to render into Byelorussian the word *smortsi* in the old East-Slavonic epic, the *Lay of Igor's Campaign*. (In rendering this by 'tornadoes', I follow S. A. Zenkovsky, *Mediaeval Russia's Epics, Chronicles and Tales*, New York, 1953.)

p. 256: *Bound to this house . . .*
stanza 2. 'Seven Fronts'. This rather neatly gives the date of this memory. In 1941–42, when the Soviet counter-offensive against the Nazis began, there were no less than ten 'fronts' – the Karelian, Volkhov, North-Western, Kalinin, Western, South-Western, Voronezh, Don, Stalingrad and Trans-Caucasian Fronts. The number and designation of the Fronts varied throughout the following years, but was as low as seven only in the offensive of 1945, when, starting from a line already so far west as to lie across Poland and Hungary, the Red Army thrust forward along seven fronts as follows (working north to south):
the Third Byelorussian Front (advancing on Königsberg and Danzig);
the Second Byelorussian Front (advancing on Berlin along a route north of Warsaw);
the First Byelorussian Front (advancing on Berlin via Łódz);
the First Ukrainian Front (advancing on Berlin via Wrocław);
the Fourth Ukrainian Front (advancing on Praha via Moravska-Ostrava);
the Second Ukrainian Front (advancing on Praha via Bratislava);
and the Third Ukrainian Front (advancing on Vienna).
(Incidentally, the hero of the Kirenka poem *The letter* (see pp. 220–221) would have been in either the Fourth or Second Ukrainian Fronts.)

p. 258: *Identity disc*
Founded, apparently, on a real incident. There seems to be no particular historical significance in the number 7,000,345.

stanza 3. The names, apparently, are not those of any past or present German generals, but have been chosen for their symbolic meaning: Kriegswulf = War-wolf; von Spadel is apparently a 'German' name-form, derived from the Spanish *spada*, a sword.

p. 261: *The oranges*
Dziamiansk seems to be unidentifiable from Soviet gazetteers. The incident, however, seems to relate to Pančanka's experience on the South-Western Front or in Persia.

p. 263: *Hiroshima*
stanza 1. The often-used poetic image of the 'Shadows on the wall' (cf. Edith

Sitwell: 'The Canticle of the Rose') is, in truth, a poetic image rather than a factual phenomenon. ('The scientists noticed that the flash of the bomb had discoloured concrete to a light reddish tint, had scaled off the surface of granite, and had scorched certain other types of building materials, and that consequently the bomb had, in some places, left prints of the shadows cast by its light. . . . A few vague human silhouettes were found, and these gave rise to stories that eventually included fancy and precise detail . . .', John Hersey, *Hiroshima*, 1946). This, however, does not invalidate the significance of the image *as a poetic image* (see note to the *Sonnet: Where the Egyptian sands* . . . p. 94). Nor, since this poem was written in 1957, is it perhaps fair to point out, except in so far as it places the poem in its historical context, that far from lasting 'for aeons eternal', the shadows are, in fact, fading rapidly (see report in the *Guardian*, March 8, 1967).

stanza 4. 'A single minute.' It is the East European practice to commemorate the dead by a one-minute silence, rather than the two-minute silence customary in England.

p. 265: *The cranes' key-shaped flights*
Mon ami is a translator's gloss. The original has simply 'Jean, the wounds . . .'. The additional words are added to make it immediately clear that it is the French masculine name which is used here, not the Scottish feminine!

p. 267: *Partisan forest*
This poem was first published (in *Polymia*, No. 10, 1956) under the title of *Lasnoje vozera* ('Forest lake'), and as *Forest Lake* this version was first published (in *Manifold*, No. 11, 1964).

p. 267: *The Partisan School*
stanza 1. Junkers. The Junkers divebombers, were, in fact, operational by day only. The word used here, *sutki*, refers to a space of twenty-four hours round the clock. In spite of the limitations on the Junkers aircraft, it seemed better to render forty *sutki* here by 'forty days and nights' as giving a better impression of unremitting attack.

stanza 2. 'tree-shop'. *hajmah*. Apparently a neologism coined from *haj* – a grove and *manazyn* a shop, on the style of many similar Soviet abbreviations, of which the Moscow GUM (*Gosudarstvennyi Universal'nyi Magazin* – State Universal Stores) is perhaps the best-known example.

'Land. Tent. Flag. Slavery and Thirst.' (*Radzima, Vieža, Sciah Palon, Smaha*). The author states that such words occur in the *Slova ab pałku*. By this he must mean the *Slova ab pałku Iharavym* (The lay of Igor's campaign), that short epic of a twelfth-century expedition which is part of the common heritage of the East-Slavonic literatures.

However, of the five words stated, *Sciah* (or, rather, *sciag*) occurs three times (*paragraphs 27, 44, 49*), *vieža* occurs once (*paragraph 54*) but with the meaning of 'tent' and not, as in modern Byelorussian, of 'tower' (hence the rendering of *vieža* in this poem), *smaha* (or rather *smaga*) (*paragraph 30*); but although captivity and the native land are vital themes to the *Lay*, the old equivalents of the forms *palon* and *radzima* do not occur at all. The *Slova ab pałku Iharavym* has been rendered into modern Byelorussian by Janka Kupała, but in the standard edition of his version (Janka Kupała; *Zbor Tvorаŭ* Minsk, 1962, pp. 267–97), these forms do not occur either. However, it should be noted that Vialuhin does not say specifically 'these words' (*hety słovy*) but 'such words', (*takija słovy*) and the emphasis is on the evocative content of the concepts, not on the philological considerations involved.

p. 271: *The air*
line 16. Although the story of Beethoven being deafened by the guns bombarding Vienna in 1809 is so well known, it should, perhaps, be observed that, although this bombardment undoubtedly had a most adverse effect on the composer's hearing, the story of his deafness is far more complicated. As early as 1794 signs of ear infection were already becoming apparent, and by 1802, the onset of deafness was so apparent to Beethoven that, after a period of despondency in which he seriously contemplated suicide, he reached the state of self-conquest and heroic resignation to fate that led him, in 1802, to write the 'Heiligen Testament' for his brothers (an account of his tragedy to be opened and read after his death). Nevertheless, even in 1812, three years after the bombardment, close friends still detected no serious trouble, and thought of the composer as absentminded, rather than deaf. It was only in 1818 that the affliction became so acute that all 'conversation' had to be conducted by the medium of a slate and pencil, and the story of Beethoven's deafness could no longer be concealed. Nevertheless, in view of the deleterious effect the bombardment had on already afflicted ears, the more 'popular' version of the story has undoubtedly considerable validity as a poetic symbol.

On the other hand, the idea that Homer was war-blinded seems to be an innovation of Makal. The legend of Homer's blindness is ancient indeed. Scholars tend to explain it as reflection of traditions of a time when all able-bodied men were potential warriors, the lame could aid the fighting men as smiths (cf. Hephaistos-Vulcan), but the blind could find no role in society save that of prophet-priest (cf. Tiresias) or bard. However, granted any historical basis for the legend of Homer's blindness (and, indeed, the hypothesis of a historical Homer), the idea which Makal introduces is not basically improbable, since the visual imagery of the *Iliad* and *Odyssey* seem hardly reconcilable with the concept of a poet blind from birth, while, on the other hand, apart from the possibility of ophthalmia (which did, of course, break out with sporadic violence from time to time in Greece during the classical era), the most likely was that a man could lose his sight would be in war – either from direct battle-wounds, or by the deliberate blinding of a captive.

p. 272: *They have bombed the house of a writer*
It seems difficult to ascertain the precise historical background of this poem. The first stanza would suggest that it is set in the Second World War – on the other hand, the introduction of Halan in the second stanza suggests a somewhat later setting, Yaroslav Aleksandrovič Halan (1902–49) was a writer and polemicist active in West Ukraine in the period immediately following the Second World War, specializing particularly in the promotion of anti-religious propaganda. He was popularly supposed to be an agent of the NKVD, and to have denounced to them several writers who were opposed to the Stalinist policies then obtaining, and, presumably on account of this, was assassinated in October, 1949. Details of his death are difficult to discover, but the 1954 edition of the large Soviet Encyclopedia (compiled during the last years of the Stalin personality cult) attributes his

death to the 'Nationalists' which could mean anything from the anti-Communist resistance to those elements who simply wanted a regime of National Communism, in friendship with, but separate from, Russia, such as has since been established in Poland and Yugoslavia.

At the time of Halan's death, during the great rebuilding period after the war the need for a new popular hero was felt, and hence the name of Halan was commemorated in a prize for journalism. It is probably in this more symbolic sense that Hilevič uses the name. Pushkin, of course, was shot in a duel engineered by the Tsarist secret police, as a convenient means of eliminating him; in view of the suspicion of Halan's being connected with the NKVD there is a certain irony in coupling his name with that of Pushkin – I suspect, however that Hilevič could think of no other modern example which would fit his verse, and introduced Halan as the only convenient name available.

stanza 3. Federico Garcia Lorca (1898–1936), the Spanish poet and playwright, notable for his poems on death. When the Spanish Civil War broke out, he was working on perhaps the best-known of his plays *La Casa de Bernada Alba.* Although invited to visit Mexico, he decided to remain in Granada, where he was staying with friends. As far as can be ascertained, when the friends were out of the house, an armed group burst into the house, carried him off and murdered him on the outskirts of Granada (August 19, 1936). Since this appears to have been a sporadic attack rather than any act of deliberate war policy, it would seem that here, too, Hilevič is using a name as a convenient symbol, rather than as a deliberate evocation of a historic situation.

p. 278: *The goods' waggon chugging and shaking*
The background to this poem is the 'Virgin Lands' scheme of the mid-fifties, which transformed the hinterland of the Asiatic Soviet Republics from a backward near-desert to a flourishing industrial society.

The transporting of the young 'empire-builders' in goods' waggons seems to be due, either to an absolute shortage of rolling-stock, or to the poor condition of the railway tracks into Siberia (a condition which would not inhibit the use of passenger coaches, provided that they proceeded at a dead-slow pace, but which would 'tie up' the said coaches away from normal service for a considerable time) or to the psychological motivation that the atmosphere of pioneering adventure with which these young people were imbued would be better fanned by riding out to the 'frontier of civilization' in a goods' truck than in a comfortable passenger coach – or perhaps a combination of all three motives!

stanza 2. 'pails brimming over'. An interesting point of folklore. The Volga, being grammatically feminine, is personified as a woman carrying water from the well. Such water would normally be carried in two buckets, attached to a wooden yoke worn over the shoulders, thus leaving the hands free, and relieving the back muscles of strain. For a woman to cross one's path on the way to the well, with her pails is a sign of bad luck, and will bring an empty outcome to any venture on which one is engaged. Should a woman cross one's path with full pails, however, this will bring an abundant outcome to the venture. For an ironic use of this motif, see Shevčenko's mystery play: *The Great Vault* (in *Song Out of Darkness*, London, 1961).

stanza 3. The offering of a spread embroidered towel, together with the giving of bread and salt, are part of the traditional Slavonic welcome to a guest.

p. 279: *On the Taiga road*
The *taiga* is the scrub forest land of the Siberian steppes.

stanza 6. bread and salt. (See note to the previous poem.)

p. 281: *A footpath near New York*
stanza 1. Oyster Bay, Long Island, is the locale of the summer villa of the Soviet 'colony' in New York.

stanza 7. The *Ušačy* administrative region (which contains the small village of Rysilkaviča, where Broŭka was born and grew up, has as its administrative centre the small town of Ušačy, situated on the river Ušačy (a left tributary) of the Western Dvina.

p. 285: *The round table*
Čukotka is an area in the extreme north-east of the USSR, which includes the Čukotka peninsular, the most easterly part of the USSR and, indeed, of the whole Eurasian land-mass (at the point of nearest approach it is only 85 km. across the Bering Straits from Alaska). On-Nioman (Nadniamonne) is, of course, a region of Byelorussia, the most Westerly Republic of the USSR. Thus Čukotka to On-Nioman is a kind of East-to-West 'Land's End to John O'Groats' or 'Bonavista to Vancouver' of the whole USSR. Here it seems to be used to symbolize the vast distances from which UN delegates are drawn, possibly even to typify the whole world.

p. 286: *The first of a dynasty*
The petroleum workers of this poem would work, not in Połack itself, but at the giant new plant of Nova-Połack, some 20 miles away.

p. 289: *Bobbins*
The bobbins of this poem are for *hand*-spinning, and hence the young people have no use for them. With the industrialization of the Byelorussian textile industry, implies the poet, the only place for such bobbins is a museum of folk-crafts.

p. 290: *A little small house*
This translation first appeared in *Manifold*, No. 28, 1969.

p. 291: *The cradle*
The epigraph is, perhaps, the most famous single saying of Konstantin Edvardovič Tsiolkovskii (1857–35), the 'father of Soviet astronautics'. It is occasionally misquoted in English as 'Earth is the cradle of the mind . . .' etc., which makes little enough sense in English and cannot be wrested in any manner from the Russian original (see, for example, the flyleaf of J. N. Wilford, *We reach the moon*, New York–London–Toronto, July, 1969). Oddly, indeed, the now-equally-famous dictum of Neil Armstrong, with which the Tsiolkovskii saying is now so often coupled, has similarly acquired a conjugate, and likewise less sensible misquote, as 'a small step for man', rather than 'for a man'.

For a brief account of Tsiolkovskii's endeavours and career, see his own autobiography, translated, for example in: A. C. Clarke (Ed). *The Coming of the Space Age*, London, 1967.

An English translation of Tsiolkovskii's novel, *Beyond the Planet Earth* was published in Moscow, in 1958, and a collection of *Selected Papers* (relating to problems of space flight and rocketry) in 1969.

p. 295: *In the night pasture*
In view of the scarcity of good grazing land in Byelorussia, there arose a kind of limited transhumance, by which horses were driven out at night far into the clearings of the woods or the 'hards' among the marshes, where they might graze all night on the lush grass. Their owners would camp near by, and the whole countryside would be dotted with the light from their camp fires.

This translation first appeared in *Manifold*, No. 15, 1965.

p. 296: *A green cloud in the marketplace*
This translation first appeared in *Manifold*, No. 26, 1968.

p. 298: *Rain in Mazyr*
Mazyr (Russian Mozyr) is a town in the Palessian lowlands of South Byelorussia on the right (higher) bank of the Prypłać. First mentioned in the Chronicles in 1153, its traditional products are timber and cereals. It was considerably damaged in the Second World War, but has been extensively rebuilt.

p. 303: *Scalding the pork*
Although pork is unique among animal meats in that it is prepared and cooked in the rind, nevertheless, the bristles and the outer epidermis must first be removed. Accordingly, the pork is first rapidly scalded or seared with boiling water (after which the less tough bristles and epidermis may be scraped off), then singed either with burning straw, as in Byelorussia or with charcoal as is the current practice in England. This disposes of the remaining bristles, which, with the remainder of the epidermis may be scraped away. After washing, the meat is then ready either for use, salting or smoking.

stanza 5. Smoked lard (with the rind still attached) is a famous Byelorussian delicacy. It has a pleasant 'nutty' taste, and is not in the least 'fatty' or 'sickly', since the smoking off-sets the original richness.

p. 305: *Wonder-might*
'Wonder-might' is the literal translation of the Byelorussian *Dzivasil*, the name for the herb 'elicumpane'. It is, perhaps, worthy of note that this same herb, in English traditions, from being a normal herbal remedy of the seventeenth century and earlier, has become associated with restorations of a more miraculous nature. In particular, in the Mummers' or 'Folk' Play, the Doctor, preparatory to restoring the slain man to life, proclaims:

> I have a little bottle by my side;
> The fame of it spreads far and wide.
> The stuff therein is elicumpane;
> It will bring the dead to life again.
> A drop to his head, a drop to his heart.
> Rise up, bold fellow, and take thy part.
> See E. K. Chambers, *The English Folk Play*, Oxford, 1933)

p. 308: *Why are you braiding your long tresses?*
stanza 4. 'Lavonicha.' The folk-dance (see note to *Potatoes*, p. 188), not the poem of Bahdanovič.

p. 310: *The Nightingale*
stanza 6. 'I went out to gather/Nuts . . .' A Byelorussian proverb, approximating in significance to 'all cry and little wool' or 'Don't count your chickens before they are hatched'.

p. 313: *Evening*
The corncrake (*dziarhač*) is, of course, the same bird as the land-rail (drač) or Lužanin's poem. Having two names for this bird available in English, corresponding to the two Byelorussian variants, I have used 'corncrake' here, where the sound seems more important, and 'landrail' in the Lužanin poem (p. 206) where the lack of flight seemed more significant.

p. 314: *White apple-trees*
stanza 2. 'The cuckoos tell fortunes.' See note to *Alesia*, p. 123; 'the lapwings are mourning', see note to *Niccolo Paganinini*, p. 195.

p. 319: *I'm dying of this useless idle drifting*
stanza 4. Kulašoŭ does, in fact, seem to have an addiction to poems of 16 lines. Including the present one, he has no less than nine 16-liners out of a total of eleven poems in this section.

p. 320: *I love this roaming*
line 3. 'Tauridian beauty.' Tank may, here, simply be referring to the Crimea under its classical name. However, poets used to a Byelorussian landscape have not, in the past, been greatly impressed by the Crimea; the general effect of Adam Mickiewicz's *Crimean Sonnets* is one more of desolation than of beauty, while the same note is struck even more explicitly by Pušča:

> I stand not on the banks of sluggish Lethe,
> But on the Black Sea's cragged and rocky shoreline . . .
> And out to sea the restless waves are splashing . . .
> And the wind harries the white sea-gulls . . .

Of course, the difference may be simply one of mood – Pušča, in particular, had been absent from Byelorussia some twenty years when he wrote the above lines; it is possible, however, that in the present poem, Tank was thinking not of the Crimea itself, but is using the word in a derived sense to mean a park or pleasure gardens. In this case, the meaning used here in a general sense, would derive from the particular case of the Tauridian Gardens (*Tavridicheskii sad*) laid out to surround the Tauridian Palace in St Petersburg, which was built for Potemkin, the general and favourite of Catherine II, to commemorate and reward his victories in the Crimea. These gardens quickly became one of the most popular parks in the (then) capital. Since, however, the precise sense of 'Tauridian' is not explicit in Tank's original, it seemed better to preserve the ambiguity in the English.

NOTES ON AUTHORS

ANATOL ASTREJKA was born in 1911 in the village of Piasočnaja (Minsk province) into a poor peasant family. He was educated at a two-year teachers' training course, and then in the Faculty of Literature at the Minsk Pedagogic Institute.

His first poems were published in 1928 in periodicals and his first collection appeared in 1940. During the war, he worked on the partisan newspaper *National Avenger*.

His books include *Glory to Life* (1940), *Good Day* (1948) *The Fir Tree* (1950), *My Life* (1952), *Song of Friendship* (1956), *Father Nioman* (1961) and *A Heart Wide-open* (1965).

He is represented in this collection by two wartime poems, pp. 144, 173.

MIKOŁA AŬRAMCYK was born in 1920 in the village of Plosy (Mahileŭ province) into a peasant family. During the war, he was taken prisoner and deported to the Ruhr as a forced labourer, where he worked in the coal-mines. After the war, he worked for some time in the Donbas region (Ukraine). In 1949 he graduated from the Philological Faculty of Minsk University.

His books include *The Leading Edge* (1949), *Friendship* (1950), *On Paths of Friendship* (1952), and *The Cranes' Key-shaped Flights* (1960).

He is represented in this collection by five poems, pp. 162, 163, 190, 216, 266.

MAKSIM BAHDANOVIČ was born in 1891, in Minsk, the son of a schoolmaster, who later became a noted Byelorussian ethnographer and folklorist.

He was brought up in Russia (Nizhnyi Novgorod and then Yaroslavl') and commenced writing poetry, in both Byelorussian and Russian, in 1907. He was the first of the *Naša Niva* writers to insist on publishing under his own name instead of using one or more pseudonyms. In addition to original poetry, Bahdanovič produced a considerable number of translations into Byelorussian and also Russian, from Latin, French, German, Finnish, Ukrainian, etc. In particular, he translated into Russian many of the most nationalistic poems of the Ukrainian poet Taras Shevčhenko, at a time when it would seem inconceivable for a Russian poet to have translated them.

Bahdanovič published a single volume of poems, *The Garland* (1913). In 1916 he graduated from the Juridical Lyceum at Yaroslavl, and returned to Byelorussia. Shortly afterwards, he became seriously ill with tuberculosis. He was obliged to leave Byelorussia once again, and go to the Black Sea health resort of Yalta. He died there in May, 1917.

He is represented in this collection by seventeen items, pp. 72–82.

PAŬLUK BAHRYM was born in 1813, in the village of Krošyn (now in Brest province). He was educated in the village school, and worked on a farm. In 1828, he began to write poetry. Shortly afterwards, serf-riots occurred in Krošyn – for his participation in these, and for the sentiments expressed in his poetry, he was conscripted into the army as a convict-soldier for a term of twenty-five years, and was not heard of thereafter as a poet. He died *c.* 1891.

His one surviving poem appears on p. 27.

FRANCIŠAK BAHUŠEVIČ was born in 1840, of minor-gentry parents, on a farmstead not far from Vilna. He graduated from the Vilna *gymnasium* in 1861 and entered the Faculty of Physics and Mathematics of St Petersburg University. Shortly after his enrolment, he was expelled for taking part in student disorders. He worked for some time as a school teacher in Donicki; he took part and was wounded in the 1863 rising. After suppression of the rising, he went to Nizhyn in Ukraine, where he studied at the Juridical College, qualifying in 1868. He worked for many years as a Court Investigator in Ukraine, finally returning to Vilna at the end of the 1880s, where he became an advocate in the district court.

Bahuševič began writing poetry apparently in 1878. His two collections of poetry. *Byelorussian Flute* (Kraków, 1891) and *Byelorussian Bow* (Poznań, 1894) had to be produced abroad (in the Austrian and Prussian zones of Poland) and were issued under the pseudonyms of Maciej Buračok and Symon Reŭka spad Barysava, owing to the strict censorship conditions within the Russian Empire. The fate of the manuscript of his final collection of poems *Byelorussian violin* on which he was working at the time of his death, and of his collection of short stories, *Byelorussian Tales*, publication of which was forbidden by the censor, is unknown.

Bahuševič, often termed the 'father of modern Byelorussian literature' is represented in this collection by four poems (pp. 28–34).

RYHOR BARADULIN was born in 1935 in the Ušačy district of Northern Byelorussia. He is a graduate of Minsk University. His first poems appeared in print in 1954. Collections of his work include *New Moon over the Steppes* (1959) and *Virgin Soil* (1964). One of the most original and experimental of the post-war generation of poets.

He is represented here by four poems, pp. 273, 278, 289, 291.

ŹMITROK BIADULA (real name Samuił Plaunik) was born in 1886 in the small town of Pasadziec (Vilna Province, now Minsk Province), of Jewish parents. He was educated at the local *Yeshiva*, but left it before completing the course. He began writing poems in Hebrew at the age of 13, later he was introduced by his cousin, Mera Gordon, to the possibilities of Byelorussian as a literary language. He began contributing to *Naša Niva* in 1910, and joined its Editorial staff in 1912. He was one of the founders of the *Uzvyšša* (Excelsior) literary movement of the twenties.

His poems are to be found in two collections *Under our Native Sky* (1922) and *Poems* (1927). In his later years, he turned almost entirely to prose; in this field he published a number of novels and stories and also an autobiography.

He died in 1941, in the general evacuation eastwards from Byelorussia, during the Nazi invasion.

He is represented in this collection by two items, p. 85.

PIATRUŠ BROŬKA was born in 1905 in the village of Pucilkavіca, (Usačy region, Vicebsk province). He was educated at Minsk University, graduating from the Department of Literature and Linguistics in 1931. He has been writing poetry since 1926 and has published some fourteen books of poetry, including *Years Like a Storm* (1930), *Our Country's Spring* (1937), *To Meet the Sun* (1943), *On Sunny Days* (1950), *By Firm Steps* (1954) and *Far From Home* (1960). He is a member of the Academy of Sciences of the Byelorussian SSR, and Chairman of the Union of Writers of the Byelorussian SSR. At present, he is working as Editor-in-Chief of the new Byelorussian Soviet Encyclopedia, the first volume of which is expected to appear in 1970.

He is represented in this collection by seven times, pp. 164–169, 240, 255, 281, and 318.

KANSTANCYJA BUJŁA (real name Kanstancyja Kalečyc) was born in 1898 in Vilna, and was educated privately at home. She began to publish in 1910 (at the age of 12), and is one of the few surviving writers from the *Naša Niva* movement. Since 1923, she has been living in Moscow. Collections of her poems include *Flowers from the Gravemounds* (1914), *Dawn* (1950), *On Reclaimed Land* (1961), and *May* (1965).

She is represented in this collection by two poems, pp. 83, 237.

HIENADŹ BURAŬKIN was born in 1936 in Połack province. He was educated at Minsk University, graduating in 1959. His first book, *May Azure*, was published in 1960, and this was followed, shortly afterwards, by two further collections *From Love and Hate of the Earth* and *Breathing*. He is a journalist, and is at present the principal Byelorussian correspondent of *Pravda*.

He is represented in this collection by four poems, pp. 252, 286, 293.

CIOTKA (Alaiza Paškievič) was born in 1876, in Vilna. She was educated at the Vilna *gymnasium* and then in St Petersburg, returning to Vilna in 1904. Owing to her political activities, she was obliged to leave Byelorussia, and she moved to Austrian Galicia, where she was able to continue her university studies and to publish two collections of poetry, *A Cross for Freedom* (1906) and *Byelorussian Violin* (1906). She was also the author of a number of prose works and political manifestoes. She died in 1916.

She is represented in this collection by two poems, pp. 37–38.

ŬLADZIMIR DUBOŬKA was born in 1900, in the village of Aharodniki (Vicebsk province). He was educated at a teachers' training college, and, after graduation, taught for a time in a village school. Following demobilization from the Red Army, in 1922, he continued his literary studies in the Russian Federated Republic.

He began to publish his poems in 1922, and was a leading figure in the literary movements of the twenties. During the years of Stalinism, he was exiled to the Urals and a number of his works became unobtainable, but since the 'thaw' and his return to Byelorussia the true value of his work has been fully appreciated once more. His works include *There, Where the Cypresses Are* (1925), *Credo* (1926), *Nalla* (1927) and *Palessian Rhapsody* (1961). He is also a noted prose writer and has translated the works of a number of western European writers into Byelorussian, notably Byron.

He is represented in this collection by three poems, pp. 114, 294, 298.

ALEŚ DUDAR (real name, Alaksandr Dajlidovič) was born in 1904, in the village of Navasiolki (Homiel province). He was educated at Minsk University. He began publishing poetry in 1921; his books include *On Sunny Paths* (1925), *More Golden, More Steely* (1926) and *The Tower* (1928). He translated into Byelorussian the works of Schiller, Goethe, Pushkin and Blok and several Russian writers of the Soviet period. He died in 1946.

He is represented in this collection by one poem, p. 116.

SIARHIEJ DZIARHAJ was born in 1904 in Minsk. After completing a course of general studies, he began working, in 1927, as a proof-corrector for the newspaper

Zviazda. During the war, he was a member of the underground movement in Homiel.

He began writing poetry in 1935; his books include *With the Eyes of the Future* (1953), *Flint on Flint* (1958) and a long narrative poem on the life of Pushkin. He is considered to be one of the best Byelorussian translators of poetry and has translated from Russian, Ukrainian Polish and German.

He is represented in this collection by three poems, pp. 253, 263, 310.

LARYSA HIENIJUŠ was born in 1910. During the war, she was taken to Czechoslovakia as a forced labourer, where she was active in the organization of a clandestine Byelorussian newspaper *Ranica* (The Dawn). In 1948, she was arrested in the Czech capital and exiled to Siberia on a charge of collaboration with the Nazis. Following the thaw of 1956, this sentence was apparently reversed, and she is now living in Byelorussia, in the village of Zelva, and publishing her poems in the leading Byelorussian literary magazines.

She is represented in this collection by one poem, p. 295.

NIL HILEVIČ was born in 1931, in the village of Slabada. He graduated in 1956 from Minsk University, where he is now a tutor in the Faculty of Philology. He is a noted translator of Bulgarian poetry into Byelorussian. Books of his original poetry include *Song of the Road* (1957), *The Dawn of Spring Runs Over the Earth* (1959), *Disquiet* (1961), and *The Highway* (1965).

He is represented in this collection by four poems, pp. 272, 300, 302, 316.

PIATRO HŁEBKA was born in 1905, in the village of Vialikaja Usa (Minsk province) He graduated from Minsk University in 1930, and then worked on the editorial staff of a number of Byelorussian newspapers and journals. He has been writing poetry since 1925; his first collection of poems *Briar Rose* appeared in 1927, and has been followed, over the course of years, by twelve other poetic and dramatic works, as well as several volumes of selected works. In addition to his literary activities, Hłebka is director of the Institute of Art, Ethnography and Folklore of the Academy of Sciences of the Byelorussian SSR.

He is represented in this collection by four poems, pp. 148, 170, 172, 241.

SIARHIEJ HRACHOŬSKI was born in 1913, in the Pinsk district. He worked for a time as a forester, before studying at Minsk Pedagogic Institute, whence he graduated in 1935. Since then he has worked as a school-teacher, a journalist, and in radio. His works include *Birthday* (1958), *Waiting* (1960) and two books of poems for children.

He is represented in this collection by four poems, pp. 248, 279, 304, 311.

MICHAŚ KAŁAČYNSKI was born in 1917, in the town of Krupki (Minsk) province. He studied at the Minsk Institute of Journalism and, during the war, worked on an Army newspaper. He has been writing poetry since 1932, and his books include *The Sun in the Blue* (1949), *To Meet Life* (1951), *On the Great Expedition* (1952), *Pines and Dunes* (1960) and *Cluster of Rowan* (1965), as well as several volumes of poems for children.

He is represented in this collection by two poems, pp. 205, 219.

KASTUŚ KIRENKA was born in 1918, in the village of Hajšyn (Mahileŭ province). He graduated from the Homiel Pedagogic Institute in 1940, and served during the war as a war correspondent, during the defence of Moscow and on the Polish and Byelorussian fronts. His poems written during this period were published in 1945 in the collection *Dawn is Coming*. His other books include *My Republic* (1949), *Beacons* (1952), *Love and Friendship* (1955), and *The Living Go Forward* (1964). He has received numerous awards for poetry, including the Janka Kupała Prize.

He is represented in this collection by five items, pp. 176, 215, 220–222, 264.

JAKUB KOŁAS (real name Kanstancin Mickievič) was born in 1882 in the village of Akinčycy, into a yeoman-peasant family. He trained as a school-teacher in the Teacher's Training College in Niasviež and began his teaching career in 1902. He was active in the uprising of 1906, and was sentenced to three years' imprisonment (1908–11).

He began to write poetry at 12 years of age. His work was first published in 1906 (in *Naša Niva*) and his first collection, *Mourning Songs* appeared in 1910. His two major poems *The New Land* and *Symon the Musician* were begun during his years of imprisonment, but not completed until 1923 and 1925 respectively. His poetic output was considerable during the 1920s and again during the 1940s and early 1950s. His collected works, totalling seven volumes were published in 1952. In 1926, Kołas was given the title of 'People's poet of the Byelorussian SSR', a laureateship which he shared with Kupała. From 1929, until his death in 1956, he held the position of Vice-President of the Academy of Sciences of the Byelorussian SSR.

His work is represented in this collection by fifteen items, pp. 61–71, 97–98, 100–106, 145.

KANDRAT KRAPIVA (real name Kandrat Atrachovič) was born in 1896, in the village of Nizok (Minsk province). After completing his education in the local school, he was himself a school-teacher for some time, then, during the Revolutionary war, he joined the Red Army where he began his literary career. Later, he completed his education, graduating in 1930 from the Faculty of Literature and Language of Minsk University.

Krapiva's particular forte is satirical fables. He also writes prose fiction and political articles in a similar vein, and is an accomplished translator, notably of Shakespeare. His books of poetry include: *The Nettle* (1925), *Fables* (1927) and *Laughter and Anger* (1946). In 1956, he succeeded Kołas as Vice-President of the Academy of Sciences of the Byelorussian SSR. In 1962, he published his Byelorussian–Russian Dictionary, which constituted a major working tool for the production of this current book.

He is represented here by five poems, pp. 110–113, 223.

ARKADŹ KULAŠOŬ was born in 1914 in the town of Samaciejevičy (Mahileŭ province). He was educated at the Minsk Pedagogic Institute. He began writing poetry at 12 years of age, and his first book, *The Blossoming of the Earth* appeared in 1930, when he was 16. Seven further collections of his poems were published before the war, including *Song and Sun* (1932), *We Live on the Frontier* (1938), *In the Green Oakgrove* (1940) and *The Good Man* (1941). His major wartime work, *The Flag of the Brigade* (1942) was awarded a Stalin Prize for literature; postwar works include *Simple People* (1949), *Only Forward* (1950) and the verse chronicle *Dread Forest Primaeval* (1956).

He is represented in this collection by eighteen items, pp. 139–141, 152–157, 210, 225, 242–244, 256–257, 284 and 319.

JANKA KUPAŁA (real name Janka Łucevič) was born in 1882, on the farmstead of Viazynka, Vilna province. He studied under a tutor and in the state school; after himself teaching for a time, he attended a series of General Educational Courses in St Petersburg (1909–13). His first poem appeared in print in 1904. He was active in the *Naša Niva* movement (1905–14) during which years appeared his books *The Flute* (1908), *The Minstrel* (1910), *On Paths of Life* (1913) and also his dramas *Paŭlinka* and *The Ravaged Nest*. A great burst of poetic activity immediately after the Revolution gave *Heritage* (1922) and *The Unknown* (1925). In 1925, he was given the title of People's Poet of the Byelorussian SSR. However, under the period of Stalinism, he was arrested as a 'National Democrat' and released only after an unsuccessful suicide attempt. During the 1930s, he was concerned mainly with translation work, but began a new burst of poetic activity on the outbreak of war, which was cut short by his death, in Moscow, in 1942.

Kupała is generally accepted to be the 'National poet' of Byelorussia.

He is represented in this collection by twenty-one poems, pp. 39, 43–60, 99, 107, 115, 117–120, 146.

JEŬDAKIJA ŁOŚ was born in 1929 in the village of Staryna, Vicebsk province. She was educated at the Minsk Pedagogics Institute and in Moscow. She has published two books of poems, *March* (1958) and *Beauty* (1965) and also a collection of verse for children.

She is represented here by one poem, p. 254.

JANKA ŁUČYNA (real name, Janka Niesluchoŭski) was born in 1851, in Minsk, and was educated at the Technological Institute of St Petersburg, whence he qualified as an engineer. He spent several years working on the construction of the Caucasus Railway, then returned to Minsk. He wrote poetry in Byelorussian, Polish and Russian; a collection of his poems in Byelorussian, *A Bundle of Sticks*, was published in 1903, some six years after his death.

Łučyna is represented in this collection by two poems, pp. 34–35.

MAKSIM LUŽANIN (real name, Alaksandr Karataj) was born in 1909 in the village of Prucy (Minsk province). He was educated in the Pedagogic Faculty of Minsk University. From 1934 to 1941 he worked in Moscow. He began to write poetry in 1925; his first book *Steps* appeared in 1928. Other books include *In October, July and May* (1931), *The Broad Field of War* (1945), *In the Language of the Heart* (1955) and *Expanses* (1958). He is also a translator of poetry, especially from Polish, and is a script-writer for the cinema.

He is represented here by two poems, pp. 206, 317.

PIATRUŚ MAKAL was born in 1932, in the Biełastok area. He was educated at the Hrodna Pedagogic Institute and then in Moscow. He began writing poetry in 1949. His books include: *First track* (1955), *Headwind* (1958) and *Eternal Fire* (1960).

He is represented here by three poems, pp. 229, 271, 285.

PIMIEN PANČANKA was born in 1917, in Tallin (Estonia). After taking a teachers' training course in Babrujsk, he became a teacher, while continuing his studies externally at the Minsk Institute of Education. During the war, he fought on a number of fronts, and was attached for a time as a journalist to the Soviet divisions in Iran. He began to publish his poetry in 1933; his books include *The Road of*

War (1941), *Burning Winds* (1947), *Oath of Allegiance* (1949), *The Wide World* (1959), *New York Sketches* (1960) and *Lightning Flash* for which he was awarded a gold medal in 1969.

He is represented here by fifteen poems, pp. 158–161, 175, 179, 187–189, 261–262, 277, 283 and 314.

PILIP PIESTRAK was born in 1903, in the village of Sakaŭcy (Brest province). He was brought up in Russia, on the Volga, and returned to Byelorussia in 1921. He worked in the forestry and timber industries. He was active in organizing the Communist Party in Western Byelorussia, for which he was imprisoned for eleven years (1927–37), during which time he began to write poetry. A collection of poems from his prison years was published in 1940, following the unification of Byelorussia; this was followed in 1946 by the collection *For my Native Land*.

He is represented here by two poems, pp. 127, 305.

JAZEP PUŠČA (real name, Jazep Plaščynśki) was born in 1902 in the village of Karališčavičy (Minsk province). He was educated at the universities of Minsk and Leningrad, and became the headmaster of a school in Vladimir province, Russia. He began writing and publishing poetry in 1922. Books from the twenties include *Vita* (1926), *Days of Spring* (1927), *Songs on the Ruins* (1929) and *Tears of Blood* (1930). In 1930, under the Stalinist purges, he was arrested as a 'National Democrat' and exiled to the Urals. Nothing was heard of him in the literary world for many years, and it was generally assumed that he had died, but in 1956, a new sonnet of his was published in the October issue of the literary review *Polymia*, an event which is taken by some critics to mark the beginning of the 'thaw' in Byelorussia. After that, Pušča once more became active in poetry, publishing *Verses and Poems* in 1960.

He is represented here by one late poem, p. 238.

ALAKSIEJ PYSIN was born in 1920, in the village of Vysoki Barok (Mahileŭ province). He is a graduate of the Minsk Institute of Journalism. He served during the war on the western and Baltic fronts; after demobilization he began a career as a journalist and poet. His books of poetry include *Our Day* (1951) and *Blue Morning* (1959), and *Your Hands* for which he was awarded a Janka Kupała gold medal in 1969.

He is represented here by six poems, pp. 227, 251, 269–270 and 306.

ALAKSIEJ RUSIECKI (real name Alaksiej Burdzialoŭ) was born in 1912 in the town of Studzianiec (Mahileŭ province). He was educated at the Moscow Zoo-Veterinary Institute and is a bacteriologist. He began to publish poetry in 1935. His books include *Tomorrow's Light* (1951) and *The Light of Your Eyes* (1959).

He is represented here by four poems, pp. 192, 249–250, 287.

JANKA SIPAKOŬ was born in 1936 in the village of Zubrevičy (Orša district), and was educated at Minsk University. He now works for the newspaper *Vožyk*. He has published three books of poetry, *Sunny Rain* (1961), *Lyrical Migration* (1964) and *Day* (1968).

He is represented here by one poem, p. 296.

MAKSIM TANK (real name Jaŭhen Skurko) was born in 1912 in the village of Pilkauscyna (Minsk province). He attended primary school in Moscow (during the

First World War) and then a private *gymnasium* in Vilna, whence he was expelled in 1927 for participation in student protests. In 1933, he was imprisoned for political activities in Western Byelorussia, during which time he wrote a considerable amount of poetry. After the Unification of Byelorussia, in 1939, Tank embarked on a literary career which has gone from strength to strength. He is now considered to be the leading poet in Byelorussia today. His numerous books include: *Cranberry Blossom* (1937), *Lake Narač* (1937), *Fiery Horizon* (1945), *That They Might Know* (1948), *Among the Woods of the Nioman* (1951), *On Stone, Iron and Gold* (1951), *On the Road* (1954), *Tales and Legends* (1960) and *My Daily Bread* (1961) for which he was awarded the Janka Kupała gold medal in 1969.

He is represented here by twenty-four poems, pp. 130–132, 186, 208, 213, 228, 230, 246–247, 258–259, 276, 292, 303, 307, 308–309, 320–321 and 323.

VALANCIN TAŬŁAJ was born in 1914 in Baranoviči, and studied at the Vilna *gymnasium*, where he joined the illegal Young Communists' organization. He was expelled in 1929 for political activities, and imprisoned in 1932 for his membership of the Communist party. He was released on the Unification of Byelorussia in 1939. He died in 1947, in which year the first collection of his poems, *Selections* was published (three other editions have since appeared).

He is represented here by four poems, pp. 132–134, 143, 174.

ANATOL VIALUHIN was born in 1923, in the Siennieck district (Vicebsk province). He was educated at the Minsk Pedagogic Institute. He served in the war as an airman and was seriously wounded after which he was evacuated to the Urals. He has been publishing poetry since 1938; since 1945 he has been on the Editorial staff of the literary newspaper *Literatura i mastastva*. In recent years, he has written a number of film scripts. His books of poems include *Salute to Minsk* (1947), *Avenues of Approach* (1952) and *Open Wide* (1960).

He is represented in this collection by seven poems, pp. 180, 191, 217, 267–268, 297 and 313.

ANATOL VIARCINSKI was born in 1930 in the village of Dziameškava (Lepel district). He was educated at Minsk University and now works as a journalist. His books of poetry include *Song of Bread* (1964) and *Three Silences* (1968).

He is represented here by two poems, pp. 275, 290.

VASIL VITKA (real name Cimoch Kryśko) was born in 1911 in the village of Jeŭlicy, near Słuck. He was educated at the Słuck Trade School, and worked in the Babrujsk Timber Plant, where he began his writing career by contributing to the factory newspaper. He began to write poems during the war; his books include *Tempering* (1944), *Rose and Bayonet* (1958) and *A Poet's Fortune* (1951), a narrative on the life of Janka Kupała.

He is represented here by six poems, pp. 142, 178, 211, 214, 260 and 301.

ALAKSIEJ ZARYCKI was born in 1911, in Chocimsk (Mahileŭ province). After leaving secondary school, he worked for a time as an electrician, then completed his studies at the Moscow Institute of Foreign Languages. He has translated numerous works from Russian, Ukrainian, Lithuanian, German and other languages. He began to publish poetry in 1927; his books include: *Epic Fragments*

(1932), *Echo of the Dniapro* (1946), *The Eagle Well-spring* (1947), *Our Son* (1950) and *Conversation with the Heart* (1961).

He is represented in this collection by five poems, pp. 183–185, 245 and 322.

ALEŚ ZVONAK (real name Piatro Zvonak) was born in 1907, in Minsk. He worked for a time on a local newspaper, before studying at Minsk University and then at the Leningrad Academy of Art. He has been writing poetry since 1925; his books include *Storms on the Boundary* (1929), *In the Line of Fire* (1932) and *For You Alone* (1957).

He is represented here by one poem, p. 288.

INDEX OF AUTHORS

Listing poems with their dates of composition/publication

Anatol Astrejka
- Nioman (1941)
- My hut (1943)

Mikoła Aŭramčyk
- The Pigeons (1942)
- The three (1942)
- The soldier's tear (1945)
- Byelorussian pine (1947)
- The crane's key-shaped flights (1960)

Maksim Bahdanovič
- Greeting to thee . . . (1912)
- Soft warm evening . . . (1910)
- In winter (1911)
- Romance (1912)
- The chronicler (1912)
- The weaver-women of Słuck (1912)
- Snowstorm (1912)
- My native country . . . (1909)
- Swifter, brothers . . . (1910)
- To a singer (1910)
- Sonnet (Where the Egyptian sands . . .) (1911)
- From the songs of a Byelorussian peasant (1909)
- Emigrants' song (1914)
- When Basil died (1915)
- Lavonicha (1916)
- The Madonnas (extract) (1912)
- Biełaruś, thy folk long have been yearning (1915)

Paŭluk Bahrym
- Play then, play . . . (1828)

Franciša Bahuševič
- My pipe (1891)
- How they search for truth (1891)
- My home (1891)
- Do not shun me (1894)

Ryhor Baradulin
- The ward of the Sappers (1960)
- The goods-waggon chugging and shaking (1956)
- Bobbins (1956)
- The cradle (1960)

Źmitrok Biadula
- On the soul's anvil . . . (1909)
- A winter tale (1910)

Piatruś Broŭka
- Biełaruś (extracts) (1943)
- Nadzia-Nadziekja (1943)
- Such an hour, also . . . (1954)
- A drop of blood (1965)
- I want no more (1965)
- A footpath near New York (1959)
- My native song (1964)

Kanstancyja Bujła
- I love (1913)
- Though I pass to the shades (1964)

Hienadź Buraŭkin
- Noon (1965)
- Dance at the recruiting centre (1963)
- The first of a dynasty (1962)
- The starling sings (1961)

Ciotka
- The faith of a Byelorussian (1905)
- The musician (1906)

Ŭladzimir Duboŭka
- O Biełarus, my briar-rose cherished (1926)
- The young captains (1960)
- Rain in Mazyr (1959)

Aleś Dudar
- The Tower (1927)

Siarhiej Dziarhaj
- Gnomica (1957)
- Hiroshima (1957)
- The Nightingale (1956)

Larysa Hienijuš
- In the night pasture (1955)

Nil Hilevič
- They have bombed the house of a writer (1964)
- Night (1960)
- A wonder came (1960)
- Song walked in the wood (1960)

Piatro Hlebka
- The partisans (1942)
- Native bread (1943)
- Death of a soldier (1944)
- The wave (1965)

Siarhiej Hrachoŭski

Goodness (1962)
On the Taiga Road (1956)
Mama (1957)
Could I live without you? (1963)

Michaś Kałačynski

Burgenwald (1945)
The apple (1948)

Kastuś Kirenka

The field (1943)
The ships (1947)
My Republic (extract) (1948)
The letter (1948)
Petition (1965)

Jakub Kołas

Our native land (1906)
Do not fret . . . (190)
Native pictures (1908)
Stand back, move aside! (1908)
The peasant (1909)
O spring (1910)
Three wishes (1911)
The New Land (extracts) (1911–23)
I. The Forest Warden's Homestead
II. Sunday Morning
XVI. Evenings
XXX. The Death of Michał
To work (1917)
Symon the Musician (extract) (1918)
Resonance (1923)
The voice of the land (1941)

Kandrat Krapiva

The nettle (1922)
Grandpa and Grandma (1925)
The ram with a diploma (1926)
The Owl, the Ass and the Sun (1927)
The Child, the Hedgehog and the Snake (1950)

Arkadź Kulašoŭ

My Biesiadz (1940)
Moscow Street (1940)
Gliding, the cloud came (1940)
The flag of the brigade (extract) (1942)
By a grave of brothers (1942)
The ear of grain (1946)
You dear, and I (1950)
Quiet happiness (1961)
Elegy (1961)
From happiness the heart leaps like a child (1962)
Time affirms that life is changing ever (1962)
To live each year . . . (1962)
By mills and factories wormwood is not needed (1963)
On Mars (1961)
I am bound to this house (1963)
On the third day I met storms . . . (1962)
I'm dying of this useless idle drifting (1962)
To poetry (1960)

Janka Kupała

The peasant (1905)
My prayer (1906)
Prelude to storm (1907)
To the enemies of things Byelorussian (1907)
Not for you . . . (1907)
From the songs of my country (1907)
And, say, who goes there (1907)
To the reapers (1908)
The spring will yet dawn (1908)
When woodlands gleamed . . . (1911)
The gravemound (1910)
Song to the sun (1910)
Come forth . . . (1912)
My song (1913)
Young Biełaruś (1913)
Heritage (1919)
To the eaglets (1923)
For all (1926)
Thou passest, Village, from bright story (1929)
Alesia (1935)
To Byelorussian partisans (1942)

Jeŭdakija Łoś

I bid you welcome . . . (1961)

Janka Łučyna

To our native land (c. 1890)
What Janka thought, carting wood to the town (c. 1890)

Maksim Lužanin

The landrail (1946)
Right to a poem (1954)

Piatruś Makal

The apple-tree (1952)
The air (1963)
The round table (1963)

Pimien Pančanka

My country (1942)
The gardens forever will bloom (1942)

Blitz babies (1942)
Thou, my dear Biełaruś (1942)
The sniper's eye (1943)
The hero (1943)
You hear honking cries (1944)
The caravan (1945)
Potatoes (1945)
The unburied coffins (1960)
The oranges (1965)
The Estonian's cap (1954)
The boy from the farm (1959)
The white apple-trees (1958)

Pilip Piestrak

Poetry (1935)
Wonder-might (1954)

Jazep Pušča

Greatly am I indebted still (1961)

Alaksiej Pysin

A boy had planted a young tree (1950)
Much in life forgotten lies (1956)
The oak (1957)
My friend is in hospital (1956)
The flag (1956)
The knot (1958)

Alaksiej Rusiecki

May (1945)
Year of the quiet sun (1964)
The discovery (1965)
Muse in a white coat (1964)

Janka Sipakoŭ

A green cloud in the market-place (1965)

Maksim Tank

The visit (1936)
The song of the snipe (1936)
The lyre-player (1938)
That they might know (1945)
It would be well (1946)
Good morning (1947)
Mother's hands (1951)
Good night and sweet dreams (1953)
I am glad to be a man (1954)
Happiness (1960)
The sun-clock (1961)
Identity disc (1954)
The goblet (1959)
The trees have forgotten (1961)
The panes of an old mansion (1961)
Toast to friendship (1956)
My daily bread (1961)
Scalding the pork (1961)
At the planting of trees (1961)
Why are you braiding your long tresses? (1956)
I have known folk . . . (1962)
Poetry (1955)
I love this roaming (1956)
Nor for this cause alone . . . (1962)

Valancin Taŭlaj

Last words (1929)
Verses from Łukiški (1935)
On my poems (1941)
To my little sister (1943)

Anatol Vialuhin

Ballad of the Ural Tank (1944)
The Bull-finches (1945)
Mountain road (1947)
Partisan forest (1955)
The partisan school (1964)
The ripe forest (1959)
Evening (1955)

Anatol Viarcinski

Every fourth one (1966)
A little small house (1968)

Vasil Vitka

Niccolo Paganini (1940)
Father (1944)
At home (1946)
Miracle (1947)
Rose and bayonet (1956)
Heathers (1959)

Alaksiej Zarycki

The heart (1945)
Homeland swallow (1945)
The eagle well-spring (1945)
In fire was I (1956)
Treasures (1963)

Aleś Zvonak

The geologist (1956)

ALPHABETICAL INDEX OF POEMS

(Initial definite and indefinite articles being ignored)

Title (or first line, in the case of untitled works)

The air page 271
Alesia 118
And, say, who goes there? 48
The apple 219
The apple-tree 229
At home 211
At the planting of trees 307
Ballad of the Ural tank 180
Biełaruś (extracts) 164
Biełaruś, thy folk long have been yearning 82
Blitz babies 159
Bobbins 289
Bound to this house by card of registration 256
The boy from the farm 283
A boy had planted a young tree 227
The bull-finches 191
Burgenland 205
By a grave of brothers 154
Byelorussian pine 216
By mills and factories, wormwood is not needed 244
The caravan 187
The Child, the Hedgehog and the Snake 223
The chronicler 74
Come forth 57
Could I live without you 311
The cradle 291
The cranes' key-shaped flights 265
Dance at the recruiting centre 274
Death of a soldier 171
The discovery 249
Do not fret 61
Do not shun me 33
A drop of blood 255
The eagle well-spring 184
The ear of grain 210
Elegy 242
Emigrants' song 79
The Estonian's cap 277
Evening 313
Every fourth one 275
The faith of a Byelorussian 37
Father 178
The field 176
The first of a dynasty 286
The flag 269
The flag of the brigade (extract) 152
A footpath near New York 281
For all 115
From happiness the heart leaps like a child 242
From the songs of a Byelorussian peasant 78
From the songs of my country 46
The gardens forever will bloom 159
The geologist 288
Gliding the cloud came . . . 140
Gnomica 253
The goblet 258
Good morning 213
Goodness 248
Goodnight and sweet dreams 230
The good-waggon chugging and shaking 278
Grandpa and grandma 110
The gravemound 50
Greatly am I indebted still 238
A green cloud in the market-place 296
Greetings to thee . . . 72
Happiness 246
The heart 183
Heathers 301
Heritage 99
The hero 175
Hiroshima 263
Homeland swallow 184
How they search for truth 30
I am glad to be a man 246
I bid you welcome 254
Identity disc 258
I have known folk 308
I love 83
I love this roaming 320
I'm dying of this useless idle drifting 319
In fire was I 245
In the night pasture 295
In winter 73
It would be well 208
I want no more 255
The knot 306
The landrail 206
Last words 133
Lavonicha 80
The letter 220
A little small house 290

The lyre player page 131
The Madonnas (extract) 81
Mama 304
May 192
Miracle 214
Moscow Street 139
Mother's hands 228
Mountain road 217
Much in life forgotten lies 251
Muse in a white coat 287
The Musician 37
My Biesiadź 139
My country 158
My daily bread 292
My friend is in hospital 269
My home 32
My hut 173
My native song 318
My native country 76
My pipe 28
My prayer 43
My Republic (extract) 222
My song 58
Nadzia-Nadziejka 167
Native bread 170
Native pictures 62
The Nettle 110
The New Land (extracts) 67–71, 100–106
Niccolo Paganini 142
Night 302
The Nightingale 310
Nioman 144
Noon 252
Not for this cause alone 323
Not for you 45
The oak 269
O Biełaruś, my briar-rose cherished 114
On Mars 256
On my poems 143
On the soul's anvil 85
On the Taiga road 279
On the third day I met storms 284
The oranges 261
O spring 65
Our native land 61
The Owl, the Ass and the Sun 112
The panes of an old mansion 259
Partisan forest 267
The partisans 148
The Partisan school 267
The peasant (A peasant I) 64
The peasant (I am a peasant) 39
Petition 264
Pigeons 162
Play then, play 27
Poetry (I knew you as a bolt of lightning) 320
Poetry (You beg at the door) 127
Potatoes 188
Prelude to storm 43
Quiet happiness 242
The Ram with a Diploma 110
Rain in Mazyr 298
Resonance 100
Right to a poem 317
The ripe forest 297
Romance 73
Rose and bayonet 260
The round table 285
Scalding the pork 303
The ships 215
The sniper's eye 175
Snowstorm 75
Soft warm evening 72
The soldier's tear 191
The song of the snipe 129
Song to the sun 56
Song walked in the wood 316
Sonnet (Where the Egyptian sands) 77
The spring will yet dawn 49
Stand back, move aside! 63
The starling sings 293
Such an hour also has come to me, truly 240
The sun-clock 246
Swifter, brothers 76
Symon the Musician 97
That they might know 186
They have bombed the house of a writer 272
Though I pass to the shades 237
Thou, my dear Biełaruś 160
Thou passest, village, from bright story 117
The three 163
Three wishes 66
Time affirms that life is changing ever 243
To a singer 77
Toast to friendship 276
To Byelorussian partisans 146
To live each year 243
To my little sister 174
To our native land 35
To poetry 319
To the eaglets 107
To the enemies of things Byelorussian 44
To the reapers 48
The tower 116
To work 97
Treasures 322
The trees have forgotten 258
The unburied coffins 261
Verses from Łukiški 133
The visit 130

The voice of the land page 145
The ward of the sappers 273
The wave 241
The weaver-women of Słuck 75
What Janka thought, carting wood to the town . . . 35
When Basil died 79
When woodlands gleamed 49
The white apple trees 314
Why are you braiding your long tresses? 308
A winter tale 85
A wonder came 302
Wonder-might 305
Year of the quiet sun 249
You, dear, and I 225
You hear honking cries . . . 179
Young Biełaruś 59
The young captains 294